WITNESS
TO ILLNESS

WITNESS TO ILLNESS

Strategies for Caregiving and Coping

KAREN E. HOROWITZ

AND

DOUGLAS M. LANES, M.D.

ADDISON-WESLEY PUBLISHING COMPANY

Reading, Massachusetts   Menlo Park, California   New York
Don Mills, Ontario   Wokingham, England   Amsterdam   Bonn
Sydney   Singapore   Tokyo   Madrid   San Juan
Paris   Seoul   Milan   Mexico City   Taipei

Grateful acknowledgment is made for permission to print: essay by Lee Rubenstein; journal excerpts by Richard Andrew Lamasney; journal entry by Dale Tyler Robertson.

The names, occupations, and other identifying characteristics of all the people in the case studies have been changed to protect their privacy.

Library of Congress Cataloging-in-Publication Data

Horowitz, Karen E.
   Witness to illness : strategies for caregiving and coping / Karen E.
Horowitz and Douglas M. Lanes.
     p.   cm.
   Includes bibliographical references and index.
   ISBN 0-201-56796-2
   1. Critically ill—Family relationships. 2. Caregivers.
3. Adjustment (Psychology) 4. Medicine, Preventive   I. Lanes,
Douglas M. II. Title.
R726.5.H68 1992   92-21647
362.1'0425—dc20   CIP

Cover design by Ruth Kolbert
Text design by Anna George
Set in 11½-point Goudy Old Style by CopyRight, Inc.

1 2 3 4 5 6 7 8 9-MA-95949392
First printing, November 1992

To my husband, David Bruce
and in memory of
my mother,
Sarah

K. E. H.

To my patients and their families,
to my family and for my friends,
this work is offered in the hope
that it may aid Nature's
three great physicians:
Time, Patience,
and
Humility

D. M. L.

Contents

Preface

This book is the product of a long evolution, but the concept was born in the summer of 1987 when my intimate friend of twenty years, Rebeccah, discovered she had Hodgkin's disease. From the time she told me she felt a lump in her armpit, I followed the process of her illness closely. While her doctors were searching for a diagnosis, she called to tell me about her bone marrow test, a procedure she knew I had experienced several years earlier. Expecting a horror story, I was surprised to find I was laughing by the end of our conversation.

A newlywed at the time, Rebeccah was accompanied by her husband, Michael, who wanted to give her support. He stood next to Rebeccah in the examination room and held her hands. As he watched the huge needle approach her back, he leaned over Rebeccah and whispered, "Concentrate. Give me your pain. I can take it. Give me your pain."

The needle was inserted, and Rebeccah apparently complied with his request: Michael fainted. Leaving Rebeccah's side, the doctor rushed to Michael's slumped body. Rebeccah, mistakenly thinking the needle was still inserted in her back, screamed, "What about me?"

Both of us thought this was hilarious, but I also told her that Michael's caregiving strategy was more chivalrous than wise. "It's never a good idea to take on another's pain," I told her. "Someone should write a book about witnessing illness." I got off the phone, and with a rush of clarity, I realized this was going to be my job.

I had already learned some costly lessons while I watched members of my family suffer through illness. In my late teens, I had witnessed

the cancer deaths of both my maternal grandmother and my mother.
I was only eighteen when the large and serious responsibilities of being a witness fragmented my life as a college student in Philadelphia.
In the late sixties, while my friends were politically active, protesting
and marching against the Vietnam War, I was visiting the hospital,
ordering nursing care, and dealing with the doctors. I watched my
grandmother, and then my mother, deteriorate before my eyes. My
grandmother died of colon cancer when I was nineteen. Nine months
later, my mother died of the same illness.

The experience of caregiving and loss changed and sobered me.
My mother and I were extremely close. She had a passion for reading
and the arts, and we were lifelong companions, venturing together
to the theatre, concerts, museums, and films. My mother was gracious,
loving, gregarious, generous, and sensitive. She never failed to encourage
and support my education and independence of spirit, and she was
a loyal family member and a friend to many people. Witnessing her
progressing illness and her death was painful and traumatic for me.
It continues to be the most devastating ordeal of my life.

With hindsight, I wish I could have been a better caregiver. Given
the tenor of the times and my personal evolution, I understand my
shortcomings. I could not have known then what I know now. My
father and I did our best during the illnesses, but we lacked experience
and guidance. We knew little about caregiving; we relied on the advice of the doctors and nursing staff, and on our own common sense.
We didn't know how to be advocates, nor did we know we should
be playing that role. In retrospect, I think we were too passive and
compliant. We made two costly errors.

When my mother first complained of stomach and intestinal problems, her doctor could find nothing wrong. He had insisted she was
neurotic, until a later visit when he finally felt her tumor. By then,
it was too late. When the surgery was performed, the medical prognosis
was "terminal."

My mother had a bad doctor. I am still too angry to say that more
kindly. He didn't take her complaints seriously. Unfortunately, we had
trusted the doctor, didn't challenge his authority, and didn't think
about getting a second opinion. Though my mother might have suc-
cumbed to cancer in any event, I will never know whether my father
or I could have prolonged her life if we had sought a second opinion
earlier. This mistake haunts me with regret.

In addition to naively trusting only one doctor's opinion, I made another error in caring for my mother, though it, too, was understandable. My mother was horrified by the ravages of cancer. Having just watched her own mother suffer the indignities of death by colon cancer, my mother had threatened to commit suicide if she ever learned she had the disease. Thus, to prevent her from taking her life, my father and I agreed not to be forthright about her diagnosis and prognosis. One day, when she asked me if she were dying, I gently lied. I told her she was not.

I can see now that my doing this may have prevented my mother from finishing her life gracefully and completing any of her business or personal affairs. We were not able to say our good-byes. My father has since assured me she knew how ill she was, but I still regret not speaking honestly, and not letting my mother take control of her life and death. I am left with an uncomfortable closure with my mother, and no second chance to change what had occurred.

Six years after the death of my mother, my husband, David, was diagnosed with testicular cancer. At that time, David was an architecture student. Vibrant and strong, he had been a gymnast most of his life. The diagnosis shocked everyone. This time, I was determined not to be passive. I vowed to help save David's life by any means I could. Yet, even though I was better prepared—at least to the extent that I had already experienced caregiving— I would still find that witnessing illness was difficult. I had much more to learn.

Despite my motivation to be a dedicated, active witness, repeated mistakes were made in the course of David's treatment, twice nearly killing him. While David fought the cancer and coped with his physical and emotional traumas, his family and I fought with fatigue and helplessness. Though we were, in varying degrees, medically conversant (David's father is a dentist, his mother a nurse), we all struggled to communicate with some of his doctors.

During David's illness, I learned how to become a witness—acting as an advocate, researcher, empathic partner, "lay healer," and activist. Yet, at the same time, I struggled with feelings of anxiety, fear, guilt, powerlessness, anger, and fatigue. I became depressed, and normal activities were a strain. I did not expect or understand all these feelings. David's illness affected not only his family and me, but also his friends, even those who knew him slightly and heard his story. Yet, no one I encountered acknowledged the impact that illness has on those surrounding the patient. There were still no books, no support groups, no identity for those of us who watched and suffered in our own private ways.

Difficult life lessons can have purpose. If there is one overriding reason I can pinpoint as my motivation for writing this book, it is to persuade readers of the necessity to be well-informed health-care consumers, to choose their doctors and medical treatment carefully, and to participate in the entire course of a patient's illness. Witnesses can help patients to receive optimal care. Lives can depend on it. I also want to encourage honest and sensitive communications between witnesses and the patients to help prevent witnesses from suffering needless guilt. There will always be difficult conflicts, but I hope, after reading this book, witnesses will be better informed to make sensible choices.

Witnessing illness, for most of us, is a job we take on suddenly with little qualification or preparation. As I continue to do research and listen to more witness stories, I am struck by the similarity of issues and problems facing those who are close to people with serious illnesses. Their concerns are common, transcending the specific details of diagnosis or prognosis. I am also convinced that seeing someone you love suffer is one of the worst of all human experiences. Like my friend Michael, we wish to take the pain away magically and "make it all better." Unable to do that, witnesses quietly suffer, often without recognizing the stress and strain of their helplessness. Sometimes we feel as sick as the patient, though in different ways.

Although I am experienced in the role of witnessing, I am not a medically trained professional. In thinking about writing this book, it also struck me to ask my close friend Doug for help. Since he is a psychiatrist, I thought his medical and psychological viewpoints would add valuable perspectives to the book. I knew that he had counseled other physicians, medical personnel, and family members as they coped with the physical and psychological consequences of witnessing illness. He had also helped me during David's illness and recovery.

Stylistically, it has been a challenge for us to present our two voices. We have come to learn we have different styles of thinking. Thus, the nature of our partnership was complex: sometimes frustrating and yet enjoyable.

At first, I acted as a journalist, interviewing Doug and recording our conversations. That soon proved to be a cumbersome process, which evolved into regular meetings where we would discuss ideas and concepts, share stories and medical studies, swap books and articles. While Doug worked full-time in his medical practice, I worked full-time putting together the book: writing and organizing most of the text. However, by the end of the process of writing the book, we had discussed and sometimes argued over every line—and our friendship survived.

This book is intended to focus attention on the witness. I want to illuminate the challenging and underacknowledged role of the witness to illness, to recognize that a patient's pain affects family and friends, to lend support to caregivers, and to provide an identity for those undertaking this responsibility. The role of witness has value and meaning, both for the patient and the witness.

Karen E. Horowitz

In the summer of 1987, when Karen told me of her idea to write a book about witnessing illness, I was enthusiastic. I am interested in the study of human behavior, I am intrigued by the problems of trying to understand motivation, and I am a student of the healing arts. This project interested me, because it offered the hope of improving the working relationship between doctors, witnesses, and patients. I could work together with an old friend, an attractive opportunity in itself, and, as a bonus, take aim at the problems of preventive medicine for the witness to illness. I already knew from both published reports and my own experience as a psychiatrist that witnessing places risk on the health of an individual, and such a book might help many people reduce the chance of stress-related illnesses marring their witness experience.

.   .   .

Barbara, a 40-year-old bookkeeper, said, "My mother was driving my father to the emergency room to get his chest pain checked out. On the way through the door, she had this crushing pain beneath her breastbone.

"So, this morning, I had to visit the both of them in the hospital. My father is in the ICU, and my mother is in the telemetry unit. Feels like surgery is in the cards for at least one of them."

I asked her how she was holding up.

"Well, my sister who lives a couple of hours away is coming down, but she's never much use to us. I always thought I'd like a brother who would share things and do things with me, but the fact is that I bear the burden of being the one who's there to do and go-fer. And I'm tired."

•   •   •

Every day, I hear witness stories from my patients and from my colleagues. In my training at Hahnemann Medical College in Philadelphia, I learned about Consultation and Liaison Psychiatry under the tutelage of Robert J. Nathan, M.D. I made teaching rounds with the Professor of Medicine and the Dialysis and Transplant Team, and I helped medical students learn how to communicate with sick people and how to understand the workings of the relationships of their patients to their families. I taught medical students to learn how to become empathic partners with their patients. I also assisted witnesses. After I had completed my own period of training, I taught at Jefferson Medical College, where this experience with the role of empathic partnership continued.

This project also allowed me to explore some ideas that were inspired by a part of my training with Anna Freud at the Hampstead Child Therapy Course and Clinic, where she conducted a nursery school, taught the art of psychoanalysis, and developed powerful tools for the understanding and treatment of mental distress and illness.

One of Anna Freud's ideas struck me as being related to the evolution of a caregiver's experience. In her book *Normality and Pathology in Childhood: Assessments of Development,* she described the concept of "developmental lines." Normally, an individual evolves from dependency upon others for all physical and emotional needs to the "state of emotional self-reliance and adult object relationships." The term *object relations* refers to the emotional bonds between one person and another, by which usually is meant the mature capacity for loving and reacting appropriately to others.

It occurred to me that the idea that Karen was suggesting—the witness phenomenon and the importance of empathic partnership—lent itself to a developmental line of its own. The pathway would begin with the witness identifying a special relationship with—and dependency on—the person who might eventually become a patient. Then, there is the state of anxiety with the initial discovery that something is wrong. This, then, leads to a state of interdependency where the witness gives care to the patient. This phase of interdependency would subsequently open to a phase of completion, where the patient either recovers or does not. Both possibilities demand that the witness further evolve: toward a richer relationship, having survived one of life's challenges together, or toward independence and separation demanded by death.

The opportunity to see Karen's unique view expanded by a concept learned in a favorite setting from a treasured learning experience has proved gratifying as we've struggled through the rigors of the writing process (especially in making complex issues clear). The product is a tool that I hope will assist witnesses to understand themselves better and to communicate better with the patient.

I have another motivation. My father's illness and death during the course of writing this book have deeply affected my own views of the witness phenomenon. I agree with Karen that the loss of a parent and the witnessing of the illness must be ranked high on the list of life experiences that are most emotionally distressing.

In witnessing the ravages of heart disease on my father, I have felt angry and powerless that some of the medical testing and treatments were much more harmful than helpful. I have unresolved feelings of being critical about my medical brethren for their lack of skill and luck in their efforts on my father's behalf.

This is especially true in the realm of preventive medicine. My father's massive first heart attack was precipitated by an allergic reaction to dye used for a kidney X-ray test. Such reactions happen. They are uncommon, and arguably, they are usually preventable.

Once my family and I got through the stages of denial, we accepted the reality that this medical event shaped the future of my parents' marriage, their retirement, and their relationship to me. We looked for a villain, someone to blame and to be a receptacle for the powerlessness and anger we were feeling. My folks wondered if they should sue the doctors. However, I felt caught in the middle. Not only had I helped to choose the physicians who were responsible, I didn't like the idea of suing other doctors. There were also the facts that not all allergic reactions are preventable, and it was not the doctors' fault that my father had been more than fifty pounds overweight for most of his adult life.

Finally deciding against any lawsuit, we settled into a routine of hoping that medical treatments and the power of doctors would allow for a recovery of the lost vitality. We had crossed into a phase of coping with the illness and trying to accept the limitations. During much of this phase of my witness experience, I became a distant witness, since my mother and father had moved far away. The telephone played a larger role in our relationship. Visits were less frequent, and I participated even less directly in the decisions about which doctor to use and what medicines to take. This phase dragged on over the space of several years.

Then came the phase of exacerbation. My father's energy continued its inexorable decline, and I found myself on the airplane responding to a sense of urgency that death might be near. Up until that point, the threat of mortality and the immediacy of death, loss, and grieving had been only fleeting concerns. Now these concerns became my constant companions, as were the sights and smells of disease and decay in the intimacies of the hospital.

I continued to use my medical training and experience as a tool to help my mother and father. It was also a defense against the powerlessness which constantly nagged at me. Though I feared that I might not see my father again, I finally had to face the time to choose between staying on at the bedside or returning to my wife and daughter. I left for home. He died shortly after I left.

I wish I could have had more time with my father. When my daughter and I joke about our time spent in "father-daughter bonding," which we enjoy, I often feel sadness and regret about the lost and missed opportunities with my father. A large part of my inheritance consists of my father's extensive collection of fishing tackle and a shared fondness for that pastime. When I sort through the equipment, I never know which piece of plastic or metal, which knife or fishing reel, will set off the tightness in my throat or the tears. I am fortunate that we enjoyed a loving relationship. There was no complicating abuse or neglect; I suffered no unbearable, traumatic blows at his hands. He cared, provided, and helped me learn about respect, compassion, honesty, and integrity.

Witnessing an illness is hard even when the relationship doesn't have much unfinished business. There's a fierce unwillingness to let go of the person you love: someone you want more of and more from. Nonetheless, for all of us, death is inevitable, and survivors must grieve for the loss and go on with living.

Even though, as a doctor and witness, I was more of an insider than the average person, I had to confront the same feelings of pain and powerlessness. There were also the universal questions: How did I do? Did I learn anything? Where do I go from here?

At some time in all our lives, we experience the process of witnessing an illness in someone we love or care about: to be a witness is one of the most common and certain of life experiences. By exploring common issues, problems, and situations that witnesses encounter, I hope we will assist, educate, and enable witnesses—and physicians as well—to become more effective and empathic witnesses. In doing so, both witness and patient will benefit. I hope this book will offer companionship, solace, and guidance, and I hope that the role of the witness will be recognized as a powerful one for healing and easing pain.

Douglas M. Lanes, M.D.

Acknowledgments

Many people have contributed their time, energy, and support to this book.

I thank our agent, Carol Mann, for her interest in our subject and her persistence in finding the perfect publisher for us. I'm grateful to Martha Moutray for our meeting and her pitching the project to Addison-Wesley. Nancy Miller has been a gentle, patient, and thoughtful editor and friend.

My readers have generously and graciously given their time and suggestions, and I am lucky to have received their valuable revisions. Marlene Benjamin, Tim Lyons, Shelley Evans, Alexandra Johnson, Jenny Esencourt, and Ally Hines have read the manuscript in its various drafts. My loving husband read every draft, and he should get a medal for his indefatigable tolerance and diligence.

There have been other contributors of support, spiritual sustenance, articles, tips, anecdotes, and empathy: Dave Seibert, Dr. Alan Greenwald, David Greenwald, Paulette Douglas, Woody Freiman, Brad Shapiro, Barb Sherf, Gladys Williams, Amy Klainer, Dr. Gail Brown, Leslie Reidel, Janice Brody, Mark Mondol, Urs Gauchat, Juliet Gauchat, Richard Lamasney, Dale Robertson, Lee Rubenstein, Susan Oristaglio, Virginia Gamage, Bill Hamilton, Michael Ward, Maurice Melchiano, Kim Crawford Harvey, Brenda Starr, Tim Habick, Ellen Cook, Trudy Gelman, Pat Macaulay, Red Blanket Woman, and The Wind.

My family, my friends, my neighbors, my colleagues, and my students have also boosted and enheartened me, along with the many exceptional people who have shared their stories and wished to remain anonymous.

I thank Doug for his invigorating and challenging collaboration, the continued pleasures of his friendship, and his luncheon treats.

And for Bruce, thanks, love, and appreciation for his stimulating, exquisitely handsome, creative spirit.

Karen E. Horowitz
Marblehead, Massachusetts

This lengthy and rewarding project has received invaluable aid from many, many encouraging friends and patients. I must especially thank my co-author for her persistence and patience and for her capacity to focus the writing. My wife and daughter have been loyal and inspirational. Special thanks to my mother and Bruce. To my office staff, a host of colleagues, and to Pam—thank you all very much for your input and encouragement without which I am sure that I would have lost interest and hope that the project would ever reach completion. Our agent, Carol Mann, found us a fit at Addison-Wesley, and I am grateful to both.

But more than any other, thanks, Karen—for sharing with me your vision of a book about those of us who witness illness and try to understand the whys, the hows, and the why nots.

Douglas M. Lanes, M.D.
Bedford, New Hampshire

WITNESS
TO ILLNESS

Introduction

The therapist Erving Polster defined embarrassment as a radiance that doesn't know what to do with itself. We need a book that will teach the sick man's family and friends, the people who love him, what to do with that radiance. If they know how to use it, their radiance might do him more good than radiation.

– Anatole Broyard
Intoxicated By My Illness

Currently there are approximately 20 to 25 million Americans suffering from chronic illness; another 25 million are acutely ill. This book is for the rest of us: the 200 million who are watching.

Witnesses to illness can choose to help patients (and themselves) by becoming advocates, empathic partners, or lay healers. Most people are naturally drawn to help, but often do not know how. This book offers strategies to encourage and teach witnesses an active approach to caring, and methods by which they may contribute to the survival, well-being, and health of patients—as well as to themselves.

Given the technical complexities of the medical bureaucracy and the healing process, patients have a difficult time doing the work of healing on their own. The process of recovery can, and should, be a team effort. While doctors and nurses attend to the patient's medical needs, the witness can—in addition to participating in the patient's medical treatment—monitor the patient's emotions and remind the patient of the joy of living by providing recreation, relaxation, and laughter.

The witness may have the power to coach a patient back to wellness. Current research suggests that the immune system and emotions are interrelated: that positive thinking, love, and caring do promote the healing activity of the immune system. Thus, to the extent that stress, anger, hostility, or depression aggravates the diseased condition, helping to alleviate such symptoms may encourage healing and wellness, and improve the quality of a patient's life.

Witnessing involves facing a number of issues. The most common and difficult of these will be discussed here in their general contours. But because general points are more powerfully made when illustrated by particular examples, we have brought in individual voices and experiences to complement and complete the "objective" landscape of witnessing. The witness will also find practical suggestions to:

- help identify and cope with their complex feelings;
- promote better communication with medical personnel;
- develop strategies for researching illnesses and treatment plans;
- care for the patient, using love, common sense, and healing techniques;
- adjust to the changing needs of the patient over time;
- define their own roles and needs;
- explore the future role of witnessing, considering activism as an option.

Since the process of witnessing an illness can be a devastating emotional marathon, we will also advise the witnesses how to care for themselves successfully. Witnesses may have to conquer the common feelings of helplessness and hopelessness which so often lead to depression, anxiety, physical weakness, or accidental injury.

No two situations or personalities are ever identical. Each witness must choose from many alternatives to regain well-being and/or psychological equilibrium. Some chapters of this book may be more useful or appropriate to some circumstances than others. However, whether dealing with someone who has AIDS, cancer, or a long-term chronic ailment, witnesses share a common ground of issues and experiences. Whatever the type or length of illness, there is no single correct way to be a witness. Thus, this book tries to honor and respect many paths. Religious and spiritual issues, as well as traditional and alternative medical solutions, are discussed. But the suggestions and strategies here are not intended to supplant individual judgment. Rather, they are meant to aid thinking and inspire solutions.

There are trials, traumas, and rewards in witnessing illness. This book is meant to help witnesses aid the patient and find their way through the rigors of this difficult process, encouraging them to attend to mind, body, and spirit in the face of this assaultive change. We also aim to empower the witness with an identity as a caregiver, incorporating a sense of integration with other witnesses. We hope that this book will enable witnesses to understand their limits and realize their potential, for the witness can be a powerful agent for relief and healing.

1

THE NEW GENERATION OF CAREGIVERS:
The Emerging Role of the Witness

To be a friend to one person, to inspire one heart to clarity, that is a special gift. Too often we may think the gift is something else, something we must get from outside. The gift is in each of us to give.
— Dhyani Ywahoo
Voices of Our Ancestors: Cherokee
Teachings from the Wisdom Fire

THE CHANGING EQUATION OF MEDICAL CARE

In the recent past, physicians have been not only healers, but also power brokers—the people in control. They told patients what to do, and patients mostly complied. Only twenty years ago, opinion in the medical profession was fairly evenly divided on the issue of truth-telling: some believed in telling patients the truth, others thought it better to withhold the truth to encourage hope. Sometimes patients were told their diagnoses, sometimes not; often, only the closest family members understood what was going on. Sometimes, patients were told their lives were about to end, but frequently, patients had to die without the chance to say their good-byes.

Times have changed. The practice and the philosophy of medicine have evolved. Along with technological and scientific advances, the power, control, and responsibility of patient care have been rebalanced with the expectation of a doctor-patient therapeutic alliance. Doctors are expected to tell their patients about diagnosis, treatment, and prognosis in terms the patient can understand. In addition, the doctrine of informed consent requires that doctors tell patients more about their conditions: the risks and benefits of testing, treatment, possible alternative courses of action, as well as the likelihood of complications or adverse outcomes. The burdens of truth and responsibility are thus shared among the doctors, nurses, patients, and the families or additional caregivers.

Certainly, some shifts have been most welcome. Because societal attitudes have also changed, we are—for the most part—more health-conscious and forthright about our bodies and the subject of death and dying. More health information and education are desired and available so patients and their families can be well-informed consumers to make appropriate therapeutic choices. However, there has also been a shift in the economy of time. Those who work with computers or fax machines or cook with microwave ovens have begun subjectively to experience time differently. Things need to be done faster. There is less patience, yet the body still maintains its own timetable for healing.

In a less fortunate development, three medical crises are thrusting additional psychological and financial pressures on patients and their families. The first problem is the most basic: the spiraling cost of, and lack of access to, high-quality health care. According to the U.S. Pepper Commission Report, there are 38 million adults and children who are without health insurance: one out of seven, or 15 percent of our population, lack coverage. An additional uncalculated number are underinsured. Nine million Americans now require long-term care; seven million of them live at home or in their communities. **Three-quarters of all home care is provided without financial compensation to family members or friends.** For the two million living in nursing homes, 56 percent of the cost is paid by patients and their families. With the current fiscal crisis in federal, state, and local governments, this problem is not likely to be solved soon. Probably, the patient, family, and government will continue to share these fiscal burdens.

The second health-care crisis is the current nursing shortage. This development forces family or friends of the patient to take a more active role in caring and nurturing, both within the hospital and in outpatient care. In many major hospitals, nurses have just enough time to perform the most basic of nursing care tasks in addition to their administrative duties. They manage technology for seriously ill patients

8

during short hospital stays. There is no time for leisurely back rubs anymore. Talking to patients is becoming a luxury. One nurse recently confided she had only one minute to tend to a man who was overwhelmed after he learned he had cancer. "It was a shame," she said. "Nurturing the ill is what we like to do. That's our art."

The third problem—the change in patient release time from hospitals—has evolved from the heavy financial burdens of the hospitals coupled with the demands of the insurance industry. Though technology has improved and experience has taught medical practitioners that patients can be released earlier, patients often leave hospitals with what appears to be alarming speed. Some "major" surgical procedures are now routinely considered "outpatient."

· · ·

Susan, 40, is a real estate agent who underwent gynecological surgery: she had a D&C and had an ovarian cyst removed.

To her surprise, she was discharged from the hospital the afternoon of her surgery. Given this quick discharge, she did not have a miraculous recovery. She and her boyfriend were totally unprepared for the amount of care that she needed until she came out of her postoperative pain. Her boyfriend took three days off from work to tend to her needs. Fortunately, he was able to work from home.

· · ·

Only fifteen years ago, this same operation usually required about a week's stay in the hospital. But statistics, and dollars and cents, have become a most weighty determining factor in the length of a patient's hospital stay. With the exception of extremely ill patients (labeled by Medicare as "outliers"), the decisions for patient release dates are strongly influenced by medical care statistics that serve the financial interests of the government and the insurance companies. Hospitals must comply. They are now places for emergencies. They are no longer a place where people are warehoused. Doing so is too costly.

Though hospital social workers often assist in finding alternatives to replace the hospital's previous role in extended care, more and more, families and friends—the nonprofessional witnesses of illness—are

9

becoming the primary caregivers of patients. This is an economic and social relocation, if not revolution, in health care. When patients are released from the hospital still in need of close care, they are often forced to hire or share the cost of expensive caregivers like visiting nurses or to make do creatively on their own with the help of friends, family or volunteers. With physical and emotional care of patients increasingly deinstitutionalized, the family and community consequently bear more burdens. This situation presents problems. Outside the hospital setting, the patient and family must cope not only with physical pain, but also with emotional conflict, anger, powerlessness, grief, and depression—often without any outside resources.

Physical recuperative caregiving aside, there is yet another subtle shift in healing psychology that affects the patient and witness. New discoveries in mind and body research have put an additional pressure on patients. Many medical professionals—like Bernie Siegel, in his book, *Love, Medicine & Miracles*—believe that mentally fit and "exceptional" patients have a better chance of recovery. They contend that a patient's psychological well-being—positive or negative, relaxed or stressed—is an essential part of the healing equation, along with an astute and caring physician and a correct treatment plan. Dr. Herbert Benson, an author and researcher of behavioral medicine, is one of many who theorize that a relaxed state of mind bolsters the immunological system. Similarly, sociologists contend that patients with a supportive community or network of friends stand a better chance of survival. Therefore, pressured by the medical community, current self-help literature, friends, or family, the witness to illness is tacitly—or sometimes explicitly—given another responsibility: to promote the psychological health of the patient.

Fortunately, the recent escalation in lay caregiving is gaining recognition, and progress has been made. Social service agencies, homecare agencies, and visiting nurse teams are supplying advice and help. In New York's Booth Memorial Medical Center, the director of nursing education developed "Nursing 101" for families. Boston's Joslin Clinic has been educating diabetes patients and their families for years. There are also more support groups for patients of specific illnesses like cancer, heart disease, and AIDS.

However, there is still much more work to be done concerning the effect of the patient's needs and changes on their friends and families and patient care. The caregiving burden is not likely to improve soon. Most experts agree that our health-care system is strained and in disorder. We spend tremendous sums for health care, yet the health status of people in the United States seems worse than in Canada and Japan. With the AIDS problem alone, the Hudson Institute has predicted a worst-case scenario of 14.5 million Americans infected with AIDS by the year 2002. As the population lives longer, many in their middle years will be caring for both their own parents and their children. There may also be the future health complications of air, water, and food pollutants. If the medical establishment lacks in caregiving now, it is painfully obvious we will all have to learn to care for each other in the future.

The nascent trend—that patients now work with their doctors, sharing the responsibility of decision-making whenever possible—seems the most sensible and well advised of possible alternatives. Yet even a sensible plan carries difficulties, for patients can sometimes feel burdened with responsibility beyond the fundamental task of attending to their immediate health needs. And this, at times, can be too much.

THE EMERGING ROLES
OF THE PATIENT AND WITNESS

The ordeal of illness has changed for patients, with an active recovery becoming the acceptable ideal. Their job description—in the midst of illness with its inherent stresses and pains—now includes researching their illnesses, making decisions and plans about the appropriate treatment, *and* managing their emotions along with an active fighting spirit.

Yet, how can patients research their illnesses or become their own advocates if they are in pain? Or medicated? Or newly sliced from surgery, or otherwise handicapped or impaired by their illness? How much pressure can patients withstand on their own? Even without the pain of illness, the process of decision-making can be utterly bewildering. Rebeccah provides a good illustration of one patient and her decision-making dilemmas regarding treatment—and why witnesses can be helpful in providing support.

• • •

Two years after her initial diagnosis of Hodgkin's disease and now a mother of a two-month-old baby girl, Rebeccah was told by her gynecologist that she had enlarged lymph nodes. After blood tests, a CAT scan, and other diagnostic tests, her doctors were convinced that—given her medical history—Rebeccah had a recurrence of Hodgkin's. However, the only way to prove it was by a laparotomy— surgery in the abdomen to remove and biopsy lymph nodes.

Still recovering from a cesarean section and cautioned by a surgeon about having too much surgery, Rebeccah was not convinced about the procedure. Though pressured by her doctors to proceed with the diagnostic workup for tissue diagnosis, Rebeccah looked for alternatives and other opinions.

But as she did more research, she became more and more per-plexed. One doctor suggested a bone marrow transplant, another radiation. Yet another told her radiation might not be effective and might ruin her chances for chemotherapy, the treatment strongly ad-vocated by her most conservative doctor. There were two chemotherapy regimens suggested: one standard and guaranteed to make her ill; the other experimental, which might not make her ill.

To add to her frustration, the physicians were not able to answer all her questions: How many lymph nodes would a surgeon need to biopsy? Could her lymph nodes be swollen from the pregnancy and c-section, and not from Hodgkin's?

She found alternative therapies—like dietary changes, vitamin therapies, and visualization techniques—unconvincing; she was un-sure any would work without additional traditional medical treatments. There were no statistics or hard evidence. While the alternatives were less invasive, she would need to make decisions based on intuition or faith.

Though it was important for Rebeccah to make the choices and assume control of her treatment, the experience quite naturally filled her with anxiety. Her fears, the apparent need for haste, the confusing range of alternatives—all nearly paralyzed her ability to make a deci-sion. She asked for help, turning to her husband and trusted friends to listen to the information she gathered and to provide feedback.

With her husband and friends providing support, she finally decided to take one step at a time, get a final diagnosis by surgery and proceed from there. After her decision, she canceled surgery once because she felt the surgeon was not the right one for her. Her surgeon of choice did find evidence of Hodgkin's, and her surgery was luckily trouble-free. She had chemotherapy shortly thereafter (without experiencing nausea), and she went to an acupuncturist to maximize her energy, an alternative therapy Rebeccah felt helped her.

•   •   •

The point here is that, in many cases, patients need a think tank—a network of family and friends—to help analyze alternatives, make calls, provide assurance, solace, and sympathy. Patients need assistance not only in the beginning of their illnesses, but in all stages of their recovery. As the role of the patient has shifted from a passive to active one with more responsibilities and complex choices, so too has the role of the witness emerged as a necessity.

Spouses, lovers, mothers, fathers, sons and daughters, siblings, family members, friends, and colleagues all enter the drama of patients and their illnesses. As witnesses to illness, they become advocates, researchers, caregivers, coaches, collaborators, healers, troubleshooters, listeners, counselors, dieticians, entertainers, financial advisors, administrative assistants, secretaries, tax accountants, comedians, and more.

DEFINING THE ROLE OF WITNESSING

Just what, exactly, is a witness to illness? Witnesses are, in the first place, observers, not themselves in the dramatic spotlight as is the one who is ill. Just outside the circle of attention, witnesses tend to be in the shadows of illness, sometimes as caregivers, or sometimes just as those who watch or hear about the person who is ill. Many witnesses become a new type of health-care provider, a nonprofessional recruited by necessity to care for a patient. There have always been witnesses to illness. Before the 1950s, families cared for their ill at home more than in institutions. However, the role—it bears repeating—has intensified as a result of cost-shifting from health-care institutions and the government back to the family and community.

Though witnessing may entail "simply" watching, the action of *being* a witness is far more complicated. Being a witness has the peculiar property of being separate from the action, yet at the same time fully engaged. Witnesses are held by the invisible cords of their relationship with the patient. There is sympathy and empathy, resentment and compassion. There is even the pain of *not* suffering in a like fashion. Often, the patient's pain or distress is indirectly felt, transformed, vividly imagined, or distorted (by thinking it is much worse than it really is). Witnesses often are afraid for the patient and themselves as they, too, face change, while wishing for a return to normalcy.

Precisely because illness extends beyond the patient to touch a wide range of people, family and friends, relatives and colleagues are included in the group of people we call witnesses. Generally, there are three types of witnesses:

- **Primary witnesses**: the most intimately related person(s), the caregiver(s) with the greatest responsibility;
- **Secondary witnesses**: friends and/or family members who do not have daily contact, but are nonetheless concerned and available, or close enough, to provide some kind of caring or support;
- **Distant or tertiary witnesses**: concerned and related to the patient, but too far away either in terms of miles or emotional distance to give the patient full attention or presence; though the least directly involved, and perhaps the easiest witness relationship (at least on the surface), this distant witness may suffer if circumstances do not allow action to mitigate feelings of guilt, disloyalty, shame or doubt, if they arise.

Most people will experience all three types of witnessing at some point in their lives; some will switch categories even when dealing with one patient (for example, a distant witness to a parent may relocate, and then become a primary witness out of necessity or choice). All three types of witnesses can be powerful in their own way. For example, consider this story of distant witnessing.

•   •   •

Charles, a fastidious and witty history professor in his mid-40s, sat silently at his Alcoholics Anonymous meeting.

He was distracted for most of the evening, watching Sam, a fellow dedicated AA member, sitting in front of him and physically struggling to remain alert and upright. It was obvious to Charles that Sam was dying of AIDS.

Charles had noticed him before. They had nodded to each other at the meetings, but tonight was different. Kaposi's sarcoma, as well as his severe weight loss, had disfigured Sam. Occasionally, he coughed violently and spat mucus into his coffee cup. Though Charles admired his dedication in getting to the meeting despite his physical difficulties, he also couldn't help feeling repulsed at the sight of Sam. This disturbed Charles, and he launched a critical self-review of his humanity. What if that happened to me? How would I want someone to react to me?

Charles walked over to Sam, took his coffee cup, threw it away, and offered his hand in support until the end of the meeting.

With one touch, a slender but magnanimous connection was made: a bonding that reverberated for more than that one moment. For Charles, it became a breakthrough, a personal anecdote, and then a small story for others to read.

Charles never saw Sam again.

•   •   •

Occasional rewards aside, being a primary witness to illness can be, and usually is, a full-time and overwhelming job. This is complicated by the fact that the witness may already have a full-time job and other pressing family responsibilities. This produces not only stress, but raises difficult moral dilemmas as well as problems of priority-setting. The factors of time, proximity, economics, nonpatient responsibilities, and personal physical and emotional strength all contribute to the type of witness one can be.

It is possible for witnesses to participate at different levels of awareness and activity. These may range from a position of noninvolvement to that of an extremely sensitive and industrious spectator. Thus, all witnesses can further be divided into two categories: active and passive.

- **Active witness**: one who is involved and participates in all or most aspects of a patient's illness and care; sometimes a part of a team of witnesses, active witnesses do not necessarily need to be present (they can be secondary or distant witnesses), but are engaged in the patient's progress to recovery.
- **Passive witness**: one who is concerned and related to the patient, but is unable to participate in the patient's caregiving for a variety

of reasons (financial, geographic distance, job or child care responsibilities, time, physical or emotional abilities, etc.).

Active witnessing has its compensations. As having children rekindles the child within, witnessing an illness connects us to our appreciation and love of life. At the same time, for those who are witnessing chronic illness, this revelation can often wear thin, since there is precious little time for the joy of life, as they watch the people they love being stripped of their energy or intoxicated with disorienting, yet lifesaving, medications. Sometimes, the only satisfaction from active witnessing is abstract, derived from personal integrity, accepting moral and ethical responsibilities.

Some witnesses leave the patient. For some, the emotional pain and depression is too severe. Some feel they are sinking with the ship and must bail out or die. Some witnesses observe enormous changes in the patient, and find they cannot cope. Sometimes the body is severely disfigured, handicapped, aged, or burned. Medication transforms a spouse into a different personality: suddenly there is someone new in the same body. Family or friendship roles are reversed or permanently altered. A mother with Alzheimer's no longer recognizes her daughter, and the daughter must place her mother in a home with supervised care. A teammate is confined to a wheelchair after a car accident, and a friend faces the trauma of his anxiety by choosing to forget about what is going on. Or there are times when the patient's condition can risk individual safety or can adversely affect children, and the patient needs to be placed in an institution with professional caregiving.

Witnessing illness can be life-changing. The experience may force introspection, rethinking goals and re-examining relationships. Though it is not often planned for, or even thought about, being a witness is part of the deal ("in sickness and in health") when the intimacies of a relationship are sought after and accepted. In a relationship, there is always the threat of loss, and one of the pathways to loss is illness.

While exploring the options and complexities of witnessing, it is important not to make judgments about those who must choose to be active or passive. Just as we all are likely at some time in our lives to be primary, secondary, and distant witnesses, we will probably all be active and passive witnesses as well. Our styles of behavior change with maturity, experience, financial ability, time, age, or philosophy. We may never know what motivates another's action, and thus, we can never say what course of action is right for other people. For all of us, our personal boundaries are highly individual. It would be easier, perhaps, to assess the role of witness if there were some standard or sensible code of ethics or behavior. But the possible configurations are beyond calculations, and the decisions required seem too numerous to capture in rules. Sometimes active witnessing will appear to be the best action; then there will be times when a passive strategy will be better. Sometimes both strategies are employed. Of course, there are also the gray areas: by helping, we can sometimes hurt; thus, sometimes the best "action" is passive—retreating in order to help.

Thus, the role of a witness is complex and difficult. During a psychiatric consultation, Doug heard complaints from a middle-aged witness that were not atypical.

. . .

"My father got sick 2 1/2 years ago, and I got the job of taking care of him." Speaking urgently from the edge of her seat, she said, "My parents were with us all the time. They were with my husband and me on every vacation. None of my brothers will take care of them. They will visit twice a year and still get their fair share of the inheritance. Now, my mother is sick with cancer.

"My doctor said I'm a nervous wreck. I have all sorts of aches and pains and problems with my kids and my marriage. I'm unhappy and depressed. I just don't know what to do.

"It's not fair," she lamented. "Life is unfair."

. . .

This woman is expressing the normal ambivalence over the complexities of being a caregiver. She feels compelled to care for her mother, yet she mourns the loss of her own independence. Having assessed her own needs, her mother's likely needs, and the network available, she assigned herself the role of primary witness, though not happily. She derives pleasure from nurturing, but she also feels freighted by

17

her sacrifice to refocus her life through the course of her mother's illness and the inevitable painful prospect of loss.

Witnesses may have to parent their parents, provide financial help for previously independent spouses or family members, or alter their life-styles to accommodate a sick child. Previously independent, witnesses may suddenly become emotionally, financially, or physically dependent on others for help. They might become as confined as the patient. These needs and new demands require adjustment. With the prevalence of fractured and long-distance family units, more economic, physical, and emotional complications may arise to make the task of caring for an ill person an enormous job, necessitating much exploration, understanding, and some fresh, creative solutions.

THE WITNESS AS "HEALER"

Witnesses may feel like outsiders in the healing process; however, healing is much more than the science of alleviating physical symptoms. Healing is an art. All people are potentially healers. And most healings are alike in the deepest of ways, containing elements of love, sharing, communion, and faith. Healings do not have to be invasive or involve drugs. Nor is there necessarily a need for anatomical and pharmaceutical expertise. The act of healing can be as basic as listening and sitting at the bedside of the patient or as complex as facilitating a guided visualization.

The traditional definition of *healing* is to make whole; to restore health, make sound, well, or healthy again. For most people, healing means cure or recovery, the absolute reversal or elimination of disease. More recently, healing has encompassed a wider meaning: the process on the way to health, or an improvement of the quality of life despite ill health. Thus, healing can refer to the relief of physical or psychological symptoms: a range including the mending of a wound to the restoration of emotional equilibrium. The writers Ted Kaptchuk and Michael Croucher have said, "Healing may have more to do with a person's purpose and destiny than with blood pressure and soreness."

Healing, then, can be seen as an internal and external process, involving complex interactions between and among the following: the patient's mind, body, and spirit; the patient's body and its reaction to medicine; patients and their professional and nonprofessional healers; patients and their social environments; and the mysterious combination of elements that remain undiscovered. Healing also has multiple perspectives, different for the patient, the family, the health practitioner, and the researcher. Physicians may evaluate healing by an objective or provable change in the body, controlling the disease or alleviating symptoms. On the other hand, patients may subjectively evaluate healing as feeling better. While curing may be the ultimate goal, healing can sometimes be a helpful substitute.

While specialists deal mostly with diseases, malfunctioning organs, or deep problems of the psyche, witnesses are, then, most concerned with the patient's illness. Arthur Kleinman, a psychiatrist and medical anthropologist, defines the subtle distinction between disease and illness in a way useful for witnesses. He defines *disease* as a malfunction in biological or psychological process, and *illness* as a [condition of] secondary psychosocial and cultural responses to disease: that is, how the patient, the family, and social network react to the disease. He says that, ideally, clinical care should treat both disease and illness, but our present Western medical system mostly concentrates on curing, controlling or managing the problems of the physical body.

Because of the proven efficacy of modern medicine, it makes sense to rely on the wisdom and practices of health-care professionals. The problem is that treatment can feel alienating, especially in hospitals, and physicians can sometimes fail to treat the patient's underlying source of the problem—the psychosomatic yet very real distress that accompanies disease, causing a patient's continuing discomfort. Because of the high cost of health care and the resulting time management practices, professionals may neglect the humanity of healing: the importance of attention and social support, the respect of the patient's feelings and spiritual beliefs, the strength of a *team effort* that includes non-professional witnesses and multiple healing strategies, and the healing tool of love. This is why witnesses are so crucial in the healing process.

• • •

Sarah, a Unitarian minister, describes a little about her work as part of a healing team, being the only one within a 50-mile radius whose spiritual doors were open to a gay community dealing with the AIDS crisis.

Sarah was invited to witness, becoming a welcomed newcomer to an intimate group of friends. "They needed someone who had a spiritual connection or road map. They felt I had the 'bat phone' to God. They were asking the same questions all do when facing serious illness or death: Why me? Why now? And they added the questions: Why us as a culture? What meanings does AIDS have to our culture?"

Together, they started a healing group for those who were sick and for those who were still well. They experimented with meditation and breathing exercises. They felt that new healing practices might help living with the disease. For Sarah, her role presented her with an extraordinary opportunity to help those who were seriously ill to work on mending their past. Because they had nothing to lose, many opened their hearts, gaining a spiritual depth and centeredness. "We focused on dying not being the traditional death sentence. Dying is a wake-up call: a time to come into full spiritual power and radiance.

"The community became very close. The group helped each other along and got to know each other's hearts—all the while continuing to celebrate in the face of death.

"It was not all 'doom and gloom' even in the worst of times.

"One Catholic priest who was in his final days had a group of friends sitting vigil with him. The group respectfully put a Gregorian chant on the stereo.

"The priest groused, 'Don't you think that music is a little morbid?'

"They switched to Tammy Wynette.

"We learned to view their final times as sweet and precious and learned to give great send-offs. This focus burns, it becomes so intense. Though it's horrible to see someone die, caregiving for the dying can become addictive. So much bullshit drops away. Greatness emerges."

•   •   •

Witnesses are, in fact, an integral part of the healing network—a fact too often overlooked—working on the psychological and social aspects of illness with the patient. For a witness, taking time out from

normal daily activities to focus attention solely on the patient is healing. Caring increases the patient's morale and feelings of self-worth
and esteem, helping to decrease suffering that comes not just from the
disease itself, but from fears of:

- medical treatment—the pain, the mistakes, the unknown;
- the strange people and equipment of the medical environment;
- change of feelings, energy, career, relationships, social routine, food,
  life-style, life expectations, and goals;
- failure, abandonment, isolation, disorganization, disorientation,
  death.

Patients may also fear the pain they cause to friends or family members.

•   •   •

*When Doug flew down to Florida after he heard his father had
suffered another massive heart attack, his father's first words to him
were, "I really appreciate your being here for your mother." He
was concerned and afraid first for his wife—not himself.*

•   •   •

Additionally, these fears may be amplified by guilt, anxiety, shame,
or depression. To the extent that fear magnifies the illness, witnesses
can help heal the patient by relieving or alleviating the suffering just
by empathic partnership: their concentrated listening, presence, and
support.

Because of a shared past of images, conversations, and events with
patients, witnesses already have a relationship that has its idiosyncratic
sense of allegiance, trust, strength, commitment, and responsibility.
Often deeply motivated to help patients, witnesses can be intuitive
and imaginative in creating ways to distract, amuse, encourage, coddle,
or comfort a patient. They are apt to know what the patient likes to
read, eat, or hear, more so than any distant or busy medical professional. Witnesses might know what to say to make patients laugh or
feel better—or know what not to do. Even distant witnesses can be
effective.

• • •

Jamie, a breast cancer patient in her 40s, preferred to go alone to her daily radiation treatments. In a way, as she explained it, this was a personal challenge, empowering herself by taking care of herself.

However, she said she did not feel alone. She knew there were friends and family members thinking of her all the time; they were calling and writing her notes. It was important to her that they trusted her ability and maturity to make reasonable decisions and take the right actions about her medical care. That in itself, she insisted, contributed to her healing and recovery.

• • •

Witnesses can function as facilitators, helping patients to heal themselves. Witnesses can influence healing through love, determination, sensitivity, intuition, and one of the most important contributions—companionship. Social relationships contribute to the health of *all* people. Why this is true is hard to pinpoint, but scientists speculate that relationships—or the mere presence of another person—provide practical help, emotional sustenance, information, motivation to facilitate health-promoting behaviors, and a sense of meaning or coherence. **One recent study found that the lack of social relationships constitutes a more serious health risk factor for mortality than cigarette smoking**.

By understanding the nature of healing and some of what that encompasses, witnesses will understand that their role in healing is quite substantial. Any help the patient receives from witnesses—from the simple touch to a more active coaching, as in biofeedback—is a contribution worthy of effort. For the person who is sick, anything that provides solace is important and helpful. If patients can cope better, finding meaning for their illness and resolving social personal problems, this is healing.

NOTE OF CAUTION: **This is not to say witnesses can cure diseases or psychological problems without professional guidance**. On the contrary, the patient should seek a professional diagnosis and take care of all physical ailments first, using whatever system of medicine the patient desires. However, it would be wise for the patient and the witness to consider a multifaceted approach for the overall strategy to wellness. After physical concerns are cared for by professionals, patients can subsequently deal with mental, emotional, life-style, or spiritual problems that prevent or even slightly hinder the healing process.

WHAT WITNESSES NEED TO LEARN

As primary active witnesses, most of us have not been trained in care-giving. At the outset, we are unprepared and under stress. Witnesses quickly need to learn how to provide the best care and, also important, how to be present without making matters worse for the patient or themselves.

Throughout the book, the following skills most needed during the experience of witnessing an illness will be discussed:

- understanding complex emotions;
- coping with worry, anxiety, and change;
- finding information resources for the patient;
- becoming a patient advocate with medical personnel;
- improving communications with patients and physicians;
- facilitating communications with the patient's family, friends, and colleagues;
- sharpening listening skills, learning to elicit information from the patient;
- increasing patience and tolerance during emotional and physical crises;
- reducing stress and fatigue;
- comprehending the wisdom of taking care of oneself as well as another;
- coaching and supporting the patient through impasses and traumas;
- learning healing techniques for the patient and oneself;
- improvising healthy distractions;
- being an empathic partner to a patient;
- developing creative problem-solving techniques;
- building networks for support;
- planning realistically;

- honoring personal feelings, finding meaning in the experience and self-esteem;
- improving the system: activism for the future.

RISKING INVOLVEMENT

Witnessing another's illness will involve, affect, and change most people who go through this profound and intense experience. At times, perspective is lost, buffaloed by guilt, loss, panic, sadness, discontinuity, or powerlessness. Distant, passive witnesses may want to help, but not know how. Endless unanswerable questions may arise: What's wrong with me? Why can't I help the patient? Why am I feeling so guilty? Why can't I seem to do anything? Why is this happening to me?

Witnesses may also be asking themselves why they should become involved in the healing process. In their book *How Can I Help?*, Ram Dass and Paul Gorman explore the battle of the heart and the mind in this process of self-exploration. They say that people help for many reasons: the need for self-esteem, approval, status, power; the desire to feel useful; to find intimacy or to pay back debt. They say, in "caring for one another, we sometimes glimpse an essential quality of our being....We're reminded of who we really are and what we have to offer one another." On the other hand, people resist caregiving, because of natural feelings: nervousness; self-protectiveness; defensiveness; caution; and the reluctance to sacrifice, feel vulnerable, learn new roles, to grow, or contend with the unpredictable. Thus, during this internal debate about what can be given to patients, caregivers also must be prepared to face their own questions of identity, their doubts, fears, and needs in relation to another in need.

Though these questions will seem most pertinent at the beginning of a patient's illness, often the debate is ongoing. Answers will fluctuate according to the patient's needs at different stages of healing, and will differ if the caregivers are the primary, secondary, or distant witness or if caregiving is continuous or episodic. However, periodically setting aside time for contemplation and consulting with other friends or family members who have made similar complex decisions might help prepare in deciding how to act. Sometimes, surprisingly simple acts of healing do not take much effort.

. . .

*After Jamie had a lumpectomy and had undergone radiation
treatments for her breast cancer, she discovered enlarged lymph nodes
in her neck as she went for her first, six-month checkup.*

*The doctors were concerned, asking her to return in six weeks
instead of three months. Jamie became frightened, and, instead of
relating the news to her friends, she kept the news to herself for
five agonizing days.*

*When she finally did share her concerns with me, Jamie said
she knew it would be easier to bear if she had a partner or husband. They would be able to commiserate every night.*

*Knowing this was an impossible problem to remedy immediately,
I offered a suggestion instead: Jamie could call me every night during the crisis or more than once a day, if necessary.*

*Jamie asked, "You mean you want to hear about this every
night?"*

I said, "Sure, it will be easy."

*Jamie didn't actually call every night, but she did call often.
It was no problem, and I got to unload some of my problems as well.*

. . .

Caring for another also can be personally healing, preventing the
"illness" of guilt or depression in ourselves that is generated by
helplessness or inactivity.

. . .

*Harriet, a young mother in her 30s, knew her aunt was gravely
ill and dying. Though living in another state and a "distant" witness,
this niece thought it would be wonderful to send a letter and pic-
tures of her two little daughters. However, she kept putting off writing
or calling.*

*Increasingly, she faced the common double-edged demon of guilt:
guilt urged her to help her aunt ("I should send that letter, I ought
to do something more than what I am doing now"), and guilt stopped
her from acting ("I'm embarrassed that I haven't called; I can't face*

that I haven't acted better; I'll do something tomorrow"). She was preoccupied with the rigors of child-raising, but also she admittedly did not want to face the impending death of her aunt. Guilt was not helping in any case.

Unfortunately, her aunt died before she was able to send the letter, and now she feels grief, anger, regret, and the lost chance to perform a last loving act, her way of saying good-bye.

In retrospect, however, she said it was an important lesson. From now on, she will try to feel "complete" with her emotions, treating every interaction with friends and relatives as if they were the last—not filled with high drama, but rather feeling no unfinished business was in limbo. She realized, too, that guilt was not her ally.

. . .

Most of us will feel better when we feel we have done all we can or all that the patient permits us to do. By making time for active caring in our lives, we can improve the quality of life or even prolong life for an ill loved one. Caring is not an exclusively altruistic act. Sometimes when we see our help makes a difference to another, we feel tremendously satisfied. Especially when the service feels easy, we feel the virtue of compassion and beneficence. In traditional healing, when the patient and healer have reached their mutually decided goals, the relationship ends. With the witness and patient, however, the two will both probably be more bonded, having gone through this shared intense experience.

This is not to say the caregiving experience will be without pain or risk. Witnesses may endanger their health, because they don't have time to take care of their own needs. They may suffer from loss or grief. Because emotions are raw and everyone's behavior seems to be at their worst under stress, witnesses might feel abused, misused, or rejected by the patient or by other witnesses. Confounding the situation are difficulties of communication. Patients may not be able to speak. Caregivers and patients might not be listening very well. Or selectively hearing only what they want to hear, witnesses may interpret a communication primarily considering their own feelings—rather than understanding the situation from all perspectives.

.　　.　　.

Susan, a writer who was recuperating from a miscarriage, told her friend Carol she needed to be alone and did not want her to call or visit. Carol agreed to her terms, but felt rejected and hurt.

For quite some time, Carol continued to feel badly about not being able to help her friend by active involvement. It was difficult for her to understand that the way to be helpful was to back off for a while and allow the silence of healing.

.　　.　　.

Witnesses have to make hard decisions—whether to take action or not; be intrusive or not. They need to find out if patients want their involvement, and consider priorities and setting limits, asking questions like:

- Does the patient want help?
- What can patients do on their own?
- What kind of action needs to be taken?
- What amount of energy should go into this?
- Where does the role of being a witness fit in with my other responsibilities?

Witnesses will need to look at the choices—if they are lucky enough to have choices—and think about the consequences of involvement. Perhaps witnesses will need to call on others for help, and forgive themselves if they cannot do it all on their own.

There are times when being a witness will feel very rewarding. The act of witnessing another's illness is one of life's most profound experiences. While helping in varying degrees of activity—from being a distant witness to a primary caregiver—witnesses will find that rarely will their hearts be pulled more urgently by anxiety and guilt and soothed by love and caring. Being a witness is an opportunity to expand understanding and mercy. It is a time to feel connected in our humanity and our frailties when we ask ourselves: how would I feel if that were me? As a reward, the details and small joys of life become sharpened, refocused, and appreciated.

It is true that watching a loved one in pain is hard, sometimes insufferable. Watching the effects of physical change on another's life and spirit can be distressing. Yet to participate in another's recovery and to be of service can also be deeply rewarding. Few experiences teach the lessons of compassion as well. In *Love in the Time of Cholera*, the Nobel Prize-winning author Gabriel García Márquez wrote this exquisite passage about an elderly married couple who were close to ending their time together, but its sentiments could easily be applied to other relationships:

> *It was as if they had leapt over the arduous calvary of conjugal life and gone straight to the heart of love. They were together in silence like an old married couple wary of life, beyond the pitfalls of passion, beyond the brutal mockery of hope and the phantoms of disillusion: beyond love. For they had lived together long enough to know that love was always love, anytime and anyplace, but it was more solid the closer it came to death.*

It is doubtful that any relationship will stop even if death does ultimately separate. That which was shared will always remain.

We are dealing with life at one of its most dramatic of circumstances. The conflicts ensuing from change are likely to be many. In the process of witnessing a patient's progress from health to illness or illness to health, it is inevitable that we confront the issue of mortality along with varying degrees of shock, loss, and disbelief that illnesses naturally bring.

Yet inherent in the many lessons of witnessing illness is the ability to transmute our pain to compassion, that quality that connects us with all living creatures. If we make time for personal contemplation, we can recognize the suffering of all humanity distilled from our own experience of witnessing illness. The negativity, the pain, the stress, the poison of helplessness and hopelessness—once ingested through the filter of our emotions—can transform into a larger understanding, sometimes necessary for growth. Our awareness somehow expands us. Our hearts communicate silently with all those we see in the same life experience. That is a great gift.

Most times, witnesses will have no other choice than to accept the responsibility, though they may want to rail against its presence or want to wish it away. Some people do run away, it is true. But most don't, for in acceptance, they will find the energy to do what they must—being resolute in doing the best they can.

2

THE BEGINNING
OF CHANGE

Worry has not helped any man live one hour longer.
– Denys Arcand
Jesus of Montreal

SOMETHING IS WRONG

Your husband finds a lump in his testicle. Your mother has a memory lapse. Your father says his urine looks funny. Your girlfriend finds an unusual growth on her neck. Your child seems uncharacteristically fatigued. Your colleague is coughing too much, and a doctor suggests getting tested for the HIV virus.

For the patient, learning that something is wrong is the first step in a long process of examination—tests, diagnosis, consultations, and possibly treatment. For the witness, learning that something is wrong with a loved one strikes a silent alarm that lingers, sometimes even long after questions are answered. The witness's role as an advocate begins sometime between the discovery that something is wrong and the search for a diagnosis.

Immediately, the relationship between a witness and the person who is ill can get dicey. The main issue is finding out what is wrong. But occasionally family members or friends might not be self-motivated to go to the doctor, denying a problem exists or insisting on waiting to see if the situation clears up. For witnesses, this can be a sensitive time to negotiate. Should a witness insist, push or nag someone to get a diagnosis, or relinquish control? Does the family member or friend want nurturing and prodding to prove that witnesses care or time to digest fears and own them? The answers here depend on the situation, and the relationship and its level of intimacy. No matter what position is taken, it is possible to end up in the middle of an argument. Even when witnessing a low-grade or an aggravating chronic condition, illness can strain the relationship.

Patients know better about how they feel than anyone prodding from the outside. If a patient has an intuitive feeling that something is wrong, this should not be ignored—even when the first doctor cannot find the problem. In some instances, it may take several medical opinions to make the diagnosis.

Often, however, those who are not feeling right will delay or resist visiting the doctor to check whatever feels peculiar. Though the ill person may balk, witnesses should be prepared to take a stand and encourage a swift diagnosis. As a witness, if aware of the problem at this stage, urge an immediate medical consultation, then a second opinion with another physician or specialist if the initial doctor does not take the problem seriously. Time will never be wasted by checking out a potential problem. In fact, speed may be of vital importance. Though this is disheartening to report, even when witnesses, patients, and physicians do the best they can, patients may not get the right medical treatment they need—at the right time.

. . .

One morning, just as Rebeccah was finishing up her treatment with chemotherapy, her arm swelled up to twice its size. She said it felt like she was wearing rubber bands.

She had a 1 o'clock appointment at the hospital. Michael, her husband, insisted she go earlier, despite Rebeccah's protests that her doctor would not be there. She was at the hospital only two hours after she noticed the swelling.

Her doctor told her not to worry about treatment, and he left on vacation. A week later, her arm still swollen, she sought out two more doctors, one a vascular surgeon. The surgeon told her nothing could be done now. For treatment to be successful, she should have been put on blood thinners immediately.

Rebeccah's arm stayed swollen for quite a while, though it finally returned to normal. Her doctor said he was more concerned with her survival than her arm, and that mixing a treatment of blood thinners with her chemotherapy might have endangered her.

.   .   .

The difficulty with several opinions can be that there is no simple, correct assessment of a problem. Still, if a problem persists or a new problem appears during the process of treatment, please encourage the patient to look promptly with another medical professional for the source of the problem. This is one time witnesses can risk the accusation of being a nuisance. The single most important issue at the outset is for a patient to get the right diagnosis, because everything else is based on that. Patients and witnesses must remember that doctors are human and fallible. They can and sometimes do make mistakes. Test results can be incorrectly reported. Medical knowledge is incomplete on many points. Hospitals also suffer from the inefficiencies of large, multifunction institutions. Occasionally, people need to challenge the authority of their doctors. Lives may depend on seeking a second opinion.

Witnesses, sometimes no matter how hard they try, might not be able to persuade someone to seek medical attention. If patients are mature and mentally capable, they are the ones in control. Witnesses must remember that they should defer to the patient's wishes. This is a tricky balancing act, but that does not mean giving up persuasive efforts to get the patient the proper care. Prevention of larger problems and easier treatment with early detection of most illnesses may be arguments to use. In the meantime, witnesses will know that they tried to do the best they could to help.

THE EMOTIONAL MARATHON BEGINS

Though uncertainty shields both the patient and the witness from potentially bad news, the experience of waiting can bring with it a staggering array of emotions: anxiety, shock, anger, annoyance, stress, disbelief, worry, guilt, exasperation, powerlessness, and confusion. In the process of waiting and discovery, witnesses often also confront painful fears of mortality.

Each witness will feel or behave differently. Some will be calm, controlling their emotions before a diagnosis is confirmed. Some will not even be able to describe or pinpoint the stress they are feeling. Others will experience a distressing combination of emotions—especially in a crisis—that nearly paralyze their normal activities, as Doug describes at the beginning of his father's illness:

.　.　.

I was paged in the hospital. "Dr. Lanes, go to the emergency room." I sense something is wrong. Within minutes, I'm looking at my father, whose face is purple. He's not breathing well. He's hitting his chest with his hand. He's scared. He's having a heart attack.

I'm scared, too. He could die. I am a doctor. How could I have prevented this? Where am I to blame? This is bad. I hold his hand, and I think how I will have to take care of my mother, my wife, and my daughter. I think of the rearrangements, the problems, the grief.

I withdraw my hand. I go to speak to a colleague. I need assurance and another perspective to relieve the building sense of panic. I need to be alone with my thoughts, yet I have to deal with my mother. I tell her he's doing okay. He's in good hands. He's not going to die now. The doctors can take care of this.

.　.　.

In Doug's case, the space between realizing something was wrong and finding answers was short, but disconcerting. Often, patients and witnesses must wait longer for answers.

When we hear something is wrong, our response is immediate. The mind reviews the new circumstances. Associated feelings, thoughts, memories, and future possibilities occur: a kaleidoscope of mental activity spins in response to the threat of change that illness introduces.

We are rarely prepared for change. Being in a relationship nurtures us, but we conveniently forget that it may also open us up to the wounds of change, loss, or rejection. Why should we think about problems before they exist? Why deal with problems until they cannot be escaped? But when something is wrong, the possibility of illness and the reminder of our mortality force us to prepare for new developments without the capacity to measure what these will be. Some developments may be positive, but change is a difficult challenge even when seen as an opportunity for growth.

When witnesses are intimately involved with the patients they care for, they commonly float in and out of a state of guilt, fear, and suspense. Though they may experience a range of emotions during this waiting period, the most vexing emotion they may encounter is anxiety. Answers curtail anxiety, and this is a time when there are precious few.

ANXIETY AND THE PROCESS OF WAITING

The process of illness includes a variety of situations that involve waiting, both for the patient and the witness. There is the waiting for the test results, waiting for the patient to get out of surgery, waiting to see how the illness will develop, waiting to see if the treatment is successful. There is frustration with waiting, and sometimes annoyance with the office or hospital staff. This is simply a hard time.

For the witness or caregiver, the source of anxiety is different than it is for the patient. The caregiver does not fear the physical harm of the surgeon's tools or the side effects of medications. Yet, caring for another is tiring in addition to the physical accumulation of stress the body bears. Unanswerable questions feed the psychological and physical effects of anxiety. What could be wrong? What will happen to my spouse, lover, parent, child, friend? What if there is an illness I will have to deal with? How serious is this? Will I know what to do? If something is wrong, can I handle the demands of caregiving? How will it change our relationship? How will this change other relationships in my life? What if there is nothing I can do? What might be the short- and long-term effects of the illness, if there is one? What will I lose? How much will it cost me? Whom can I blame? Why me?

Anxiety is a common denominator for all witnesses. The unknowns and repeated questions fuel the unending spin of anxiety like a continuous loop of words that won't stop. Thus, for witnesses and patients alike, it is worth the time to understand anxiety, to try to control its exasperating and exhausting effects.

Anxiety may be the first emotion we experienced when we emerged from our mother's body. Though this idea is hard to prove (or remember), Freud has suggested that "all moments of anxiety reproduce the painful feelings of the first separation from the mother—the tightening of breath, the congestion of blood, etc." Thus, he guessed that all moments of separation and birth (or perhaps change) bring anxiety. Similarly, Judith Viorst has written in *Necessary Losses*, "Separation from mother is worse than being in her arms when bombs are exploding." This immense feeling of anxiety, she says, derives from the literal truth that without a caretaking presence, we would die.

There are different kinds of anxieties, and some are more elusive to define than others. We are more or less aware of the daily anxieties of our lives—our concern for the future, our need for self-esteem, our pressure from family, job, or peers. Preparation and performance anxiety involve noticeable bodily changes, like muscle tension, trembling, or the sweaty palms that are often present before a performance or before taking a test. Psychiatrists see these types of low-level anxiety as a basic and ever-present feeling, serving to motivate and check our behavior. Anxiety is normal and considered a part of being human and alive.

At times of crisis, however, anxiety moves to the forefront, becoming a dominant feeling, one that "disturbs the mind and keeps it in a state of *painful uneasiness* [emphasis added]." The word *anxiety* is derived from the Latin *angere*, meaning to choke or to trouble. Indeed, the metaphor of being choked is apt and chilling. Anxiety feels like a threat that is impossible to ignore. It is as if our very being were in a fight for psychic breath. This type of anxiety—closer to panic—is worse than depression, and intolerable when extended over long periods of time: hard to live with and considered by mental health professionals near the top of the list of unbearable emotional states.

Anxiety, then, is a term that labels a spectrum of feeling. Its intensity may be out of proportion to the significance of the threat anticipated. Severe anxiety is akin to panic. As the author Joseph Campbell graphically points out, the word *panic* recalls the Arcadian god Pan, the powerful spirit of the forest who drove people crazy if they were not properly respectful of him. If humans trespassed into his territory, Pan would not directly harm them; instead, he made them perceive imaginary threats, filling them with a sudden, horrifying, yet groundless fear. A mere sound or innocent rustling could literally "panic" the trespassers to death as they conjured the worst of their imaginations.

For witnesses, this heightened panicky form of anxiety may be worse than depression, because it can combine realistic and unrealistic worry. The reality is that something, in fact, is not right. But this can be combined with crazy-making, intrusive, repetitive, "what if" scenarios—many of which are, in fact, unrealistic and overly dire or dramatic.

Fear of the shadowy and ill-defined troubles us the most. In anxiety, our creativity, our overactive imaginations, may do us in, as if the mind contained the seed of its own collapse. Left in suspense, we may fear that a person who is unexpectedly late has been delayed by a terrible catastrophe. Or when we are out alone after dark, we may fear attack when we hear footsteps. Some of these fears may be realized. Most prove groundless.

For the witness, though, the threat is more of a probability than it has been in the past. The witness already knows something is wrong. Just *what* is wrong, and how wrong it is, remains unclear. When we review the possibilities, we are attempting to prepare ourselves for change, but the process may trigger anxiety.

Feeling anxious bleeds into other sectors of life. Feeling helplessly suspended is troublesome and preoccupying. Moreover, anxiety is like an extremely infectious flu. If others around us are anxious, we are likely to "catch it."

. . .

A writer and college lecturer said she didn't know what was wrong with her. She felt as if she were in an iron fog that had descended on her, wiping away her physical, libidinal, and all her creative energies.

Totally distracted for weeks, she had failed to connect the fact that she was waiting for results from a thyroid test. When she found out she was fine, she—and her husband—suddenly noticed it was spring and that the tulips were blooming.

. . .

Ironically, in a state of anxiety, we project resolutions even when we know they cannot exist. This state often brings on a condition that the psychologist Joan Borysenko has called *awfulizing*. This is the tendency to escalate a condition into its worst possible conclusion. In other words, our minds may settle on the most "awful" scenario just to stop the buzz of confusion.

DEALING WITH ANXIETY

For witnesses and patients alike, the anxiety of uncertainty can be relieved by some answers. But even when the medical diagnosis is in, we will all continue to live with some level of anxiety. Some anxiety is worthwhile, motivating action. However, understanding our own types of anxiety and moderating anxiety that is not helpful is a worthwhile goal.

The following is a list of suggestions to help master the state of anxiety. Because we are capable of collapsing into panic, it makes sense that we also have mechanisms for control. Most of the discussion in this chapter assumes that the witness is dealing with personal anxiety, but the same concepts may be extended to the patient.

The suggestions are not necessarily meant to be taken in the order of their presentation, nor is this an exhaustive list.

Recognize the physical and psychological symptoms of anxiety. These may include:

- vague feelings of loneliness, helplessness, distress;
- uncomfortable feelings of impending danger, coupled with powerlessness;
- prolonged feelings of tension and exhaustive readiness for the expected danger;
- increased heart rate, flushing, and sweating;
- loss of appetite, nausea or queasiness, cramps or diarrhea;
- disturbed breathing, palpitations, tightness in the throat or chest;
- trembling, weakness, and odd feelings in extremities.

As an attentive witness, watch for signs of excessive, pathological anxiety in the patient as well as yourself. Crisis may place the patients or witnesses in such an anxious state that their physical condition is in jeopardy. If tension, irritability, and unremitting worry persist, or if the witness or the patient experiences panic in everyday life situations, it is time to consult a doctor. Anxiety is a treatable problem.

Maximize the doctor's appointment: use a pre-office-visit plan. To make a visit to the doctor efficient, the witness can help the patient to communicate directly, clearly, and quickly about the physical problem in order to aid the diagnostic process. Dr. David Stutz and Dr. Bernard Feder, authors of *The Savvy Patient*, contend that physicians generate hypotheses early, within minutes or even seconds, during a visit. Therefore, they say it is a good idea to plan ahead and prioritize a list of symptoms or complaints.

While at the doctor's office, patients often get distracted, or forget to mention important points. Many doctors have noticed that right before patients leave the office, they will slip in crucial pieces of information: exit lines like, "Oh, by the way. . ." or "I almost forgot. . ." often precede new pieces of the puzzle. Therefore, the patient—or the witness and the patient—might want to review the following pre-office-visit planner. Most likely, the doctor will routinely probe these issues or ask these questions, but it is a good idea to think about them in advance.

- Are there any physical symptoms, problems or changes in your body that need to be addressed?
- When did you first notice the changes?
- Is there a specific time of day the problem is worse?
- Has any family member had the same problem?
- What are the present life situations that are producing stress— from family, job, life changes?
- Are you experiencing any dietary, appetite, weight, or libidinal changes?
- What are the present medications that you are taking? (If you need a prescription renewal, remember to ask for it now.)
- Are there any questions you would like to ask about exercise or nutritional information?
- Are there any other issues or questions that you want to discuss that are pertinent to you?
- What have you almost forgotten to mention?

This list should be helpful in emergency office visits as well as routine checkups.

Develop a plan of communication with medical practitioners about receiving test results.   Witnesses should suggest to patients that they arrange to receive the news of test results as soon as possible. This may seem like an obvious suggestion, but often patients and witnesses do not plan how and when they want information communicated to them from the laboratory and the physician. The doctor and the patient have the right to confidentiality. Whether a witness is included in this communication is decided by the patient, with few exceptions: if the patient is unconscious, a victim of Alzheimer's disease or otherwise mentally impaired, or a child. However, many patients desire a witness—whether it be a family member or close friend—to join in this process.

Generally speaking, if a test result reveals a problem, most physicians will call promptly. However, many patients and witnesses fail to ask how long the test will take or who will call. Getting in touch with a physician can be difficult, and we have noticed that even normally assertive personalities have second thoughts about calling. Patients or witnesses often fail to anticipate their own anxieties during the waiting period, and they make curious arrangements with their doctors.

·　　·　　·

Jamie, a breast cancer patient waiting to hear whether she was having a relapse, had a good relationship with her doctor. She wanted to keep it that way, so she deliberately held back from calling him. She didn't want to be a nuisance.

She told her doctor he didn't have to call if everything was all right. She would wait to hear the details of the test at the next office visit.

However, her anxiety increased as she waited, and she started to panic. She called me and spilled out her concerns: What if my doctor forgot to look at my test results? What if my test results got lost? What if my doctor is afraid to call me and tell me bad news over the telephone, knowing another week won't make a difference in treatment?

To avoid repeating this nightmare, I told her to supply her doctor with a stamped, self-addressed postcard so he can send her the good news right away. It was a good solution, though now, she has anxiety about other aspects of her life.

.   .   .

Planning ahead to receive the news will eliminate communication confusion as yet another source of anxiety.

- Find out when each test result will be ready.
- Ask the doctor about the best method of communication: telephone, letter, or another appointment.
- Find out the doctor's style of handling good or bad news. Does the doctor wish the whole family be present? Communicate the needs of the patient and the witness.
- If the physician's policy is to call, what time of the day will it be? Make sure home and work telephone numbers are up to date.
- Should the patient or witness call? When is the best time to reach the doctor on the telephone?
- If a doctor is not available, will a nurse or receptionist be able to relate the news?
- Would it be helpful to leave a stamped, self-addressed postcard or envelope to speed the process? (This might be particularly useful in follow-up studies where the illness or doctor-patient relationship is already clear.)

Think realistically about the possible outcome: accept the possibility and the state of uncertainty.   What is the wisdom of thinking about and dealing with the possible outcome while waiting? The way witnesses react to potential problems is related to their nature and to past experiences of waiting. They may be optimists or pessimists, or they might find that talking to others about the problem—or silence—suits them best. Whatever the nature or style of waiting may be, it is nevertheless best to take some time to review realistically what may be ahead.

"Positive thinking" alone can have bad consequences. If the outcome is negative, witnesses will be unprepared, at the very least. Subscribing to what some purveyors of positive thinking believe—

that we create our own reality—might either be disappointing or, worse, damaging. They might believe that the patient—or the witness—did not wish or hope hard enough to create the desired outcome. This irrational type of positive thinking can produce guilt, self-doubt, and blame—at a time when physical and psychological resources need to be rallied. On the other hand, purely "negative" thinking might prematurely waste energy without cause. Therefore, if it is possible, a wiser strategy would be to understand that the outcome may be good, bad, or somewhere in between. (This is similar to a doctor's process of evaluation where test results are reviewed before making a final diagnosis.) Moreover, without further information, neither patients nor witnesses can take any action that is necessary.

If it is possible, witnesses can try to spend a limited amount of time dwelling on the possible outcomes of a diagnosis or illness, especially if this, in itself, is causing too much anxiety. That doesn't mean it should be ignored.

.   .   .

During high anxiety, David and I have a policy of "whine time."
When either one of us declares it, the other listens to unlimited moaning, groaning, complaining, or otherwise whining until it is out of our systems. When it's over—and sometimes concentrated crankiness can be finished within 15 minutes— we hug and try to find some form of lighthearted distraction.

.   .   .

"One day at a time," one of many slogans from Alcoholics Anonymous, is a reminder for the recovering alcoholic to set manageable steps towards an intimidating goal. Though some may argue that "negative" thinking can be emotional preparation, the projected, imagined future reality is never the same as the experience. Knowing someone is going to die and experiencing the reality of the death, for instance, are completely different. Moreover, the effort may already be redundant. Aware of it or not, the unconscious mind is already incubating ways to deal with any outcome, mulling about the issue, and rehearsing how to react. The mind has ingenious methods for performing practice drills, which are essentially brief visualizations intended to strengthen and prepare us for the uncertain future.

. . .

I was waiting for news about a bone biopsy of my friend, and I had a dream my friend was in a wheelchair. I feared I was experiencing a precognitive dream, but soon I found out my friend was fine. While I have had precognitive dreams in the past that came true, in this case, my mind was preparing me to cope with a severe outcome.

. . . '

If the news is better than the unconscious mind has prepared for, so be it: there merely is an extra built-in mechanism for adjustment.

Disciplining thoughts is not easy. To ease anxiety, people may tell witnesses, "No news is good news." If they can actually believe that, witnesses will find it easier to go about their business—more or less. More likely, there will be periodic, intrusive thoughts—worrying, praying, dreaming—that take on a life of their own. Only when powers of concentration and/or denial are great, will witnesses be able to banish the problem from their minds entirely. A preoccupation with outcome can seriously interfere with life as usual; anxiety may sabotage concentration and affect work. Inadvertently, friends—if they know something is wrong—may make the situation worse by raising the subject in conversations: "Have you heard anything new yet?" or "When will you hear?" However difficult the task of controlling thoughts may be, any attempt will help. Even if thinking about the worst case scenario is limited to, say, ten minutes, this will be a victory.

. . .

Jamie, the breast cancer patient we described earlier in the chapter, had a hard time sleeping while she waited for her test results. Her mind flooded her with fears and incessant, unanswered questions, leaving her little peace.

She called to talk about this.

I told her to try to balance her negative thinking, deliberately invoking this thought: I am fine until I hear otherwise. Repeating this to herself put her to sleep.

Reciting to myself she was fine also helped me not to worry about her.

Her tests showed she was fine.

•   •   •

While waiting and anxious, then, rather than rerunning alternative courses of action that can't be carried out until there is further information, consider the wisdom of mental discipline and balanced thinking: conscious mental movement from negative to positive. The true meaning of positive thinking may be realistic thinking, never outlawing hope.

Living gracefully with uncertainty is a challenge. Some people recommend a state of surrender during anxiety, not in the sense of giving up the battle, but accepting fate without worrying about what is beyond our control. Their point is that the worry itself can cause debilitating panic and anxiety. Though this is certainly sage advice, few people are able to accomplish it simply or completely. This surrender may be easier for witnesses who have an unquestioning spiritual or religious faith. But it surely will not work for witnesses who are habitual worriers. They might be forced to reconcile themselves with this temporary lack of news or be persuaded to embrace the mysteries of life and its constant challenges. For them, action might be the best bet: the pressure might be relieved temporarily by redirection—distracting work or entertainment, as we will explain later in the chapter.

People use different styles of thinking or perception for different occasions: for example, optimism, pessimism, logical thinking, intuition, speculation, forgetfulness, denial. All can be useful in some circumstances. The suggestions offered are not meant to limit thinking, but to increase awareness of the limitations of some styles.

Prepare to hear the news.   Hearing the news, the shock of reality, can quickly discompose normal, rational thinking. Most people go into a mild form of shock when the news is not good. In shock, people are capable of understanding what is going on, yet it is common not to hear all the details correctly. Information can become confused or muddled. When one is emotionally vulnerable, it is hard to be articulate and listen well. Frequently, a second briefing is needed to clarify the course and nature of a patient's illness. Even when the patient is prepared to ask questions, mild shock can short-circuit planned actions.

. . .

Linda, 25, an art student, was with her mother before an exploratory operation. Her sister-in-law, who was an experienced witness, gave her questions to ask the doctor after the operation.

Despite the preparation, however, Linda got only the barest of details beyond the news that her mother had a form of colon cancer. She was so upset, she heard little more than that. She remembered only details that were spotty and actually incorrectly heard. It took the family—who were scattered around the country—a couple of days to gather more cogent news.

In her case, preparing to hear the news might have meant having another witness with her, though that would have been hard for her to predict, because she didn't expect the bad news or anticipate how the news would affect her.

. . .

Often, in the doctor's presence when a diagnosis is given, a witness and patient have become mute after getting the news, letting the doctor leave without getting the information needed for taking the next steps. Ideally, doctors account for shock and wait a while before they proceed.

The following list of questions can help to improve communications with witnesses, patients, and doctors at this stage of getting the diagnosis. It will help organize the information when the doctor presents the news of the diagnosis either postoperatively or after a series of tests.

1. What is the diagnosis?
2. What are the medical and lay terms for the problem? Explain the condition.
3. If possible, ask disease-specific questions. For example, if the diagnosis is cancer: What is the cancer cell type? What is the stage of the disease? If the problem is heart disease: Is the problem with

circulation or the heart muscle, its pump or valve? Is the problem primarily with the heart, or secondary? Witnesses and/or patients may have to do some research before they can ask these specific types of questions.

4. If the patient is in surgery: When will the patient be returned to the room? What are the immediate reactions?
5. How will the patient be informed of the diagnosis? Who will tell the patient and when? Ask to be present at the time. (When dealing with a surgeon who has just operated on the patient, request another appointment to ask more questions—or consult with the primary or attending physician.)
6. What is the prognosis? Do not expect to get a precise timetable, but try to get a general picture.
7. What are the next steps? Are there any other doctors or specialists to be notified or called for a consultation? Who? Where?
8. What can be expected in the patient's recovery from surgery, other procedures, and the disease or illness?
9. What is the normal treatment plan? What are the alternative treatment plans?
10. Where are the best places to receive treatment locally and nationally?
11. Are there research specialists in the field? Who and where are they?
12. If the patient is being discharged from the hospital, is there a need for the caregiver to have lay postoperative training (for instance, learning how to change a bandage or learning to look out for warning symptoms)? What kind of supplies, if any, will be needed?
13. Will a visiting nurse be necessary to help perform procedures with the patient?
14. What kind of postoperative care will best help the patient? What kind of diet or exercise regimen is needed?
15. What are the names of the prescribed medications, their schedule, and their side effects?
16. About the caregiver's role: How much care will be needed? Will adjustments be needed in a work schedule, temporarily, or for a longer time?
17. Ask about any financial or insurance questions to be cleared up.

Patients and witnesses might have to budget time with their doctors or seek out other people or resources to get all these questions answered.

Survey your defenses against anxiety. Varieties of martyrdom are defenses against anxiety. "How can I complain? I'm not the one who is sick." Or, "I can't think about coping. I have to focus on my husband."

Most witnesses experience "selfish" thoughts, but have a hard time dealing with them or even admitting them. Because they think the patient is more needy, they feel self-examination is a luxury. When witnesses help others and focus on them, excluding their own feelings, they relieve and diffuse the anxiety of their helplessness. On the other hand, witnesses might find it easier to feel guilt and blame. This is yet another defense from anxiety, protecting themselves against the more serious threats of change or immediate loss. Anxiety defenses are natural and mostly healthy, if not taken to the extreme.

A more problematic defense against anxiety is emotional detachment: "I won't suffer loss if I don't care." Generally speaking, preventing emotional investment is how medical personnel are taught to defend against anxieties of dealing with the ill. The technique is called professionalism. For witnesses, though, doing this may mean prematurely claiming independence from patients, or even leaving during a time when patients need them the most. Wanting to escape a bad situation or to retreat emotionally is quite normal, but witnesses who leave permanently may regret this decision in the future. They might also want to rethink this strategy, given the fact that they, too, someday might be in a situation similar to the patient's.

Postpone major life decisions and increase comfort and security. Because this period of anxiety is usually emotionally intense, witnesses should try not to make any major life decisions at this time, such as changing jobs, challenging existing relationships, moving, or making major investments. Emotions are likely to overwhelm rational thought and behavior; thus decision-making tends to be misguided, imprudent, or ill-considered. Later, in retrospect, the choices may be regretted.

In times of turmoil, it is more often wise to act conservatively, rather than impetuously. When there is unavoidable chaos, it usually does more harm than good to introduce more change. Though sudden changes may, in fact, become necessary, if possible, try to build on and develop what is continuous, stable, and predictable.

In general, any areas where witnesses can increase security or improve comfort deserve attention. This might simply mean allocating more time to tasks to avoid rushing. A schedule also helps. As Annie Dillard has written:

> *A schedule defends from chaos and whim. It is a net for catching days. It is a scaffolding on which a worker can stand and labor with both hands at sections of time. . . . it is a peace and a haven set into the wreck of time; it is a lifeboat. . . .*

Even distant witnesses who are closely concerned at this point of uncertainty may play a part in creating more security and comfort. Making a telephone call to stay in touch or writing periodic postcards is a wonderful expression of support and caring. Small gestures of kindness are especially meaningful in all stages of witnessing illness.

Work on contingency planning. Since anxiety feeds on uncertainty and imagination, witnesses might try to counter worry by concentrating on what is already known and real: working on controllable problems, taking care of ordinary, "junk of life" tasks. With good news or bad, completing these concrete tasks will shift focus, provide productive distraction, and free up time for more important work later. Here are some suggestions:

- Make sure that food that is easy to prepare is available in the house. For instance, consider cooking in advance and freezing individual or family portions; stocking the pantry or freezer with convenience foods; keeping an additional supply of vital or easily forgotten items; storing an emergency ration of entertainment food for visitors who may drop in unexpectedly.
- Shop for items that may be needed for the future: for example, buy birthday, anniversary, wedding, or Christmas gifts or cards a month or two in advance.
- Take care of the car, plants, and animals.
- Review and tackle financial matters: pay bills and make a schedule of the dates these come due; organize health insurance policies.
- Organize the house as clutter can increase anxiety: arrange drawers and closets; mend, maintain clothes, and give away those no longer in use to the homeless or a charity.
- Start networking with friends. Find a medical expert who is a friend, family member, or friend of a friend, for an extra consulta-

tion to get advice or explanations.
- Exercise, rest, and sleep. Structure time for non-witness activities and think about alternate care providers for respites.

This may seem like a daunting list taken all together, but tackled separately, these jobs do not take much time, and they can be accomplished in small stages. Take pride in the items checked off the list, rather than concentrating on those that remain. *Organizing and deciding priorities will help bring a sense of control and order at a time when witnesses are most apt to be forgetful and preoccupied.* In performing everyday tasks, witnesses will find a beneficial outlet for energy as well as frustrations: balancing and counteracting feelings of helplessness and hopelessness, while experiencing a sense of accomplishment.

Follow general guidelines for health, mastering relaxation techniques, and recognizing special needs.
Witnesses will be better able to alleviate their anxiety and enhance their strength and resistance if they take care of themselves. Chapter 6 will address the importance and wisdom of self-nurturance.

Unfortunately, witnesses tend to think of themselves last, but it is important to take time to exercise, eat well, rest or relax regularly, have fun, spend time with friends, alter mood with music, escape in a book or in television, go to a film, get extra sleep, soak in a hot bath, and allow small rewards and indulgences. Take personal time out every day. At the very least, organize time so that personal body rhythms and energy levels are respected.

Worry can compromise the haven of entertainment and self-indulgence, but perhaps it is nevertheless possible to find some moments, even if rare, which can be truly rich and diverting. This is not selfish. It is healthy to make the most of every moment, maintaining a life apart from witnessing. It may even help to have a private project or goal, however small.

Both the patient and witness can also try to learn the healthy tools of yoga, meditation, or other relaxation techniques. Learning to relax may include finding a way to successfully express or release anxieties. This might mean counseling, therapy, having a heart-to-heart talk with friends, or writing in a journal.

CONCLUSION

Uncertainty and fear about the future are recurring themes for the witness. Some unknowns may be resolved when evaluations, tests, surgery, diagnosis, therapy, or a phase of treatment is completed. Some threats remain. Even after what may seem a successful recovery, many patients are described as being in remission rather than cured for the rest of their lives.

As an informed witness, recognizing anxiety and learning how it operates will help limit its more corrosive influences. This awareness can help witnesses through the dark passages that characterize the experience, and conserve energy for caregiving.

For witnesses who are waiting to find out what is wrong, the best approach may be active—to try to manage feelings of anxiety and guilt, which can be debilitating. Whatever actions witnesses may take will depend on their relationship to the patient, personal style, and inventiveness.

The suggestions in this chapter may not be enough to achieve complete relief of anxiety. Anxiety may have a timetable of its own. For some, no amount of reasoning or suggestions for release can erase it, or persuade its retreat. Even the easiest commonsense methods for coping with anxiety may take enormous effort and discipline to incorporate them into a busy and disrupted life, especially over prolonged periods of anxiety and waiting. Achieving a state of emotional equilibrium is a tough goal even when life appears to be normal. Witnesses may have to learn to say no to some responsibilities, and ask others to help in accomplishing certain tasks. In all cases, the mental health and well-being of the witnesses and the patients should be the top priority.

3

THE CHALLENGE
OF COPING

*[Sickness] is no betrayal. God and nature promise mortality, and sickness
is the rehearsal.*

> – Mark Helprin
> *Swan Lake*

*At the moment you are most in awe of all there is about life that you
don't understand, you are closer to understanding it all than at any
other time.*

> – Jane Wagner
> *The Search for Signs of Intelligent
> Life in the Universe*

COPING WITH THE NEWS

Getting the News

Getting the news can be a relief. In and of itself, diagnosis can be a
healing act. It is a movement from the unknown to the known and
recognizable. Most everyone has experienced relief when an illness or
discomfort is finally defined. The psychiatrist E. Fuller Torrey refers
to the phenomenon of relief after naming a problem as the principle
of Rumpelstiltskin. (In Grimm's story, the only way the baby can be
saved by the queen is by *naming* the evil man, Rumpelstiltskin, correctly.) Torrey explains it is a relief that:

- something indeed was wrong (as opposed to the problem of its being in our imagination or our perceived feeling of hypochondria) and either measured by external or internal tests or attributed to understandable psychological factors;
- someone may at least understand the illness enough to name it and maybe know what to do about it;
- the imagination is stopped from running wild, looking for explanations (and fearing the worst);
- energies can now be focused on actions to be taken to deal with the illness.

An exception to this apparent diagnostic relief may be when the news is grave, when patients feel they have been given a death sentence. There is relief from the mystery, but concurrently there may be fear, resignation, and a relinquishing of hope.

If patients think a situation is hopeless, they may give up fighting, and by doing so, inadvertently help accelerate the illness. Similarly, this is a time when witnesses can succumb to helplessness, especially when the shock of the news makes coping appear more difficult as the scope of the problem becomes more clear. The researcher and author Jean Achterberg says, "Helplessness can literally be lethal, or barring that, significantly detrimental to the individual's health and well-being.... Helplessness... is normally associated with severe depression, apathy, and loss of energy."

As the news is digested, however, it may be good for both the patient and the witness to distinguish the difference between feeling helpless and feeling perplexed. Being perplexed means being entangled in thoughts or a situation that is complicated and hard to unravel. However, as Emmy Gut has pointed out, it also implies "a continued curiosity to find ways of solving the problem at hand"; on the other hand, "helplessness implies the unpleasant feeling of reaching a seeming dead end of our functioning."

Rarely at the point of getting the news is the battle over. Rather the process of illness, of caregiving and coping, has just begun. It is crucial for the witness and the patient to be clear that helplessness, although the feeling is understandable, is one step in the process of coping, but one to be moved away from as hope becomes the more desirable feeling and strategy.

Defining Coping

Like anxiety, *coping* is not easily defined. The concept of coping is simple to grasp, but describing it is elusive. In a formal psychological definition, coping encompasses all the conscious and unconscious ways we adjust to stress without altering our goals. But to us, that definition is problematic; in life and in witnessing illness, we may have to cope by changing our goals, especially when relationships change. The dictionary defines coping—striving for or contending successfully; being a match for; meeting or encountering—but that misses an essence of coping we are more familiar with: the feelings and actions of just making do, hanging on in there, managing to find the energy to do what is needed in extraordinary circumstances.

●　　●　　●

I realized something was wrong when David told me he felt a lump in his testicle the size of a pea. He was a college senior and 21. I had known him for only about six months, but our relationship was loving and close.

He had checked his condition with his local western Pennsylvania doctor a couple of months earlier. The doctor told him not to worry, but the lump had enlarged since then.

Three months later, I went with David to the doctor in Philadelphia and within two days, David was in surgery for an orchiectomy—the removal of his testicle. The surgeon told us David had cancer. The surgery, the diagnosis—it was all frightfully fast.

I remember the day of the operation. My hands were numb with December frost, and my stomach ached with anxiety. While I waited during the operation, I tried to block out previous hospital memories—without success. I kept thinking about the day I had heard my mother had cancer.

It had been warmer then, some six years earlier—a spring day full of growth and promise. After my father spoke to the surgeon on the phone, he had told me everything was fine. Then he disappeared for a walk, leaving me with two of my aunts in the waiting room.

When the surgeon came into the waiting room, he told me my mother's tumor was inoperable. When I asked why he couldn't remove the tumor, the surgeon quickly said the case—not my mother—was terminal.

I had not been expecting this.

I looked at my aunts blankly as the surgeon hurried away; they were expressionless and still as a photograph. And in that stillness, I attempted to comprehend the words. Terminal. Mother. My mother would soon be dead.

As soon as I understood, I ran to be alone. One aunt ran after me to comfort me, but I don't remember her words, and no solace came from the attempt. I just felt pain, overwhelming shock, and tears.

I remember seeing our family doctor later that day, but I don't have much recollection of that meeting, and I had no energy left for fighting or asking questions. He wasn't very technical. I never understood why they couldn't remove the tumor. I was angry. This doctor had previously diagnosed my mother as neurotic, her stomach complaints as imaginary.

I cursed that spring day. And life. And God. As I relived that memory on this cold, stormy day, I reran the news. I heard about cancer from yet another surgeon. David had cancer.

The silence of the snow encouraged questions. Why this again? Why this now? Why David? What new lesson did I have to learn that I didn't already know about grieving or cancer? I was overwhelmed emotionally. I didn't want to go through this process again.

Yet, I also suddenly and strangely became positively energized. I was very clear about my goal, and this goal helped me to cope throughout the crisis: I was not going to let David die. I knew with all my being I was going to save David by any means I could: by research, by prayer, by the right medical attention, by cunning, by strategy, by psychic healing, by love. I would not be passive.

That day, I was too much in shock to understand or feel more than a sadness and a will to help save David.

That this goal was wildly filled with wishful thinking that I could make a difference did not matter to me; I am not sure whether it even occurred to me.

•   •   •

The Reverberations of Change

Heart disease. Cancer. Alzheimer's disease. Multiple sclerosis. Cerebral palsy. Cystic fibrosis. Lupus. Epilepsy. Ileitis. Infertility. Liver disease. Kidney disease. Muscular dystrophy. Parkinson's disease. Reye's syndrome. Sickle-cell disease. Kidney failure. Diabetes. Spina bifida. Spinal cord injury. Stroke. AIDS.

Sometimes we already know; sometimes we are able to put the puzzling hints together. Sometimes the news is a shock ("He was fine until the stroke"). Sometimes we cannot, or will not, believe it ("This is not happening to me. Somebody's test got mixed up with hers").

Relationships are always altered and sometimes lost in the natural circumstances of the life cycle: birth, growth, illness, and death. Getting the news that someone is ill confirms the beginning of a process of change.

Change can be a disorganizing, threatening, and disruptive experience. For the patient, the news of the diagnosis names the problem. From that point on, a process of acknowledgment, treatment, grieving, and acceptance begins. Though what happens to patients is more visibly dramatic, their illnesses affect witnesses as well. Patients suffer, but so do witnesses—in their own way. Disease and illness may confine, constrict, and alter the lives and expectations of witnesses. Witnesses may experience confusion and emotional chaos, especially if the news is shocking or if the patient's illness will mean increasing their burden.

Witnesses will cope with the news differently from the patient, with much depending on past life experiences, age, personality, and style of thinking, although there may be a parallel of feelings with the patient. Both will go through shock, disbelief, denial, anxiety, anger, uncertainty, and competing and mixed emotions. Most witnesses are emotionally touched during the process, but some get machine-gunned.

Getting the news about a life-threatening illness of a family member, friend, or colleague is disturbing no matter how old the patient may be. In every stage of life, patients may bring challenges for a witness.

If the sick person is elderly, witnesses may feel some comfort if the patient has lived what is considered a full life. But for the witness who is a spouse, close friend, or child, impending separation—and some caregiving decisions—is more traumatic. The specter arises of patients needing full-time care at home or in a nursing-home facility—both requiring substantial financial sacrifice and life-style change. Witnesses whose parents are ill mourn the possibility of their parents' not seeing them mature and prosper. Depending on the witness's age, he or she may also be losing financial support. In addition, the witness's own support group may be inattentive or less patient with the grieving process, if they feel that the death is somehow timed correctly, the natural outcome of life.

Witnesses of ill patients who are younger—middle-aged adults, young adults, adolescents, or children—might mourn, along with the patient, lost opportunities for fulfilled careers, dreams, or the promise of a long life. A sick child seems like an injustice to everyone, including medical personnel, whose stoic veneers are often lost when watching a child suffer. Helplessness, intolerable pain, and the possibility of premature separations racks the witness in such cases. Typically, parents cope well during a child's illness. P. Chodoff, S. Friedman, and others discovered that parents function by denying their own needs, isolating their feelings (putting them aside in the face of the greater pressing need), and performing caregiving tasks. But statistics also suggest later strain on the parents, especially after a child's death. In a study by D. Kaplan and others, 50 to 70 percent of families whose children died of cancer were found to suffer subsequent marital discord or divorce.

Everyone has a different way of coping after getting the news about a patient's diagnosis. Some people remain stoic and "rational," and continue to take care of business calmly. Others have a more immediate "emotional" reaction: the numbing shock is quickly followed by some public or private emotional outburst. Some people need to be alone immediately to sort through and fully comprehend the news: solitude gives them strength and time to evaluate the situation, work out their feelings, and formulate a personal strategy without interference. Others need companionship, deriving solace, strength, and help through team efforts.

Some people will ignore the situation, staying away from patients as if the illness were contagious. This behavior is possibly caused by the fear of identification: "It could easily have been me." Reminded of their own vulnerability, mortality, and the fragility of life, those who do stay away add an additional loss to the patient and other witnesses—

a loss in empathic resources. Consequently, after the crisis is over, most relationships experiencing this loss never regain their prior level of intimacy.

Sometimes, people act in confused and apparently illogical ways.

. . .

At first, when Michael, an electrical engineer, learned that his mother was dying, he seemed to be unaffected. This puzzled his wife, Susan. Later that night, Michael started picking on his wife, accusing her of petty misdemeanors. Susan, usually a patient woman, quietly simmered and tried to hold her temper. She felt guilty about getting angry at Michael, because she knew he was deeply upset. However, as Michael continued his attacks, Susan finally blew up and launched a full-scale argument. Michael started to cry.

Since Susan had been able to drive him to tears in the past, Michael—probably unknowingly—fought with Susan to get to his grief about his mother. Fighting with his wife allowed him to cry; it may have been his only known path to tears.

. . .

Whether one is alone or with others, emotions will emerge when the shock has worn off. But this can take a long time to happen.

. . .

Both a patient and witness, Stan, a robust and stoic retired businessman, discovered that a previous melanoma had reappeared, and his cancer had spread to his bones. He was tough, humorous, and good-natured throughout his chemotherapy and radiation, despite his pain and uncertain prognosis.

Stan had a German shepherd dog who was his steady walking companion for many years. In a follow-up visit to the veterinarian, he learned that the dog, too, had cancer—a lethal melanoma.

At first, he joked with the vet that the dog was being competitive: when Stan previously had undergone heart surgery, his dog had heartworms. But later that night, Stan's sturdy veneer broke, and he cried bitterly. Stan's dog became the catalyst to express his grief about their mortality.

Months later, as Stan went into the hospital for what was to be his final stay, the dog became so ill he finally had to be put to sleep. This was agonizing for the family, for they were afraid that once Stan heard the dog was gone, he'd check out, too.

The afternoon after the dog was put to sleep, Stan said to his son, "The dog's gone, isn't he?"

His son told him the truth.

"That was the right thing to do," Stan said. "I'm glad you did the right thing."

The family then knew that Stan had accepted the idea of his own death, or certainly its possibility. Stan died a few days later.

•   •   •

Arguments are likely when the news is heard, though this may seem to be a time for cooperation. Yet people can suddenly become tactless, or inconsiderate. The arguments can be messy, unexpected, and undeserved. But for some, fighting may feel like the only available avenue to express fear, anger, and grief, and thus can sometimes serve the useful purpose of releasing tension. For this reason, it may not be a good idea to suppress verbal fights. We do not advocate picking an argument; nor do we advise creating trouble in a relationship when it is not necessary. Yet in our example above, because Susan vocalized how she felt, she stopped her husband from isolating his grief, and instead they became more intimate.

When people are digesting the news, suddenly there are many unknowns. The news may bring about changes that can restructure life-styles or plans. Thus, witnesses might think about questions that may occur with bewildering rapidity. Questions like:

- What does this news mean?
- How does this change my life?
- What action should I take? What action can I take?
- What do I need to do first? What do I need to do in the next 24 hours?

- Can I take this day by day, or do I have to make decisions about the future?
- How do I want to behave? Can I take the time to grieve about this news? Do I need to fall apart for awhile? Am I allowed to feel self-pity? Can I afford to fall apart for a while?
- Do I want to or need to look strong for others? Am I strong enough for the ordeal ahead?
- How have others managed this?
- How have I coped in other similar situations? How is this situation different than those?
- What about money? Do I need more?
- What about my present responsibilities? How will they be altered? Should they be altered?
- How do my goals and dreams get affected? What sacrifices do I need to make? Do I need to change jobs? Do I need to move? Do I have to change my house to accommodate the patient?
- What is the practical strategy? What is the path of the heart?
- Whom do I have to tell?
- Whose help will I need? Whose help do I want to avoid?

Some of the answers reached in the first flush of the news may be overwhelming. Witnesses may not feel they have the strength to do what they must. Shock and grief are great drains of energy, but the mind and the body are naturally regenerative, and slowly, witnesses will be able to translate ideas into action.

While processing the news and searching for answers, witnesses and patients need to protect themselves from the risk of insensitive or inappropriate intervention by carefully selecting who will hear the news. Here is an example of a patient who encountered a close witness who was an alarmist.

· · ·

Melissa was told she had mastitis, a breast infection easily cured by antibiotics. Her doctor was not alarmed and had not acted worried about the problem.

When Melissa's mother found out about the problem, however, she yelled at her daughter and informed her that she didn't have a minor problem, but a major one.

Melissa immediately became frightened and questioned herself: Maybe I should have done more research about the condition? What if this leads to breast cancer? What if I need to have a mastectomy? What if I need radiation or chemotherapy? Will my husband feel the same about me? Why didn't my doctor act more concerned? What if my doctor is wrong?

Melissa became alarmed, despite the fact she had acted properly. She was seeing a physician, she was taking her antibiotics, and she had scheduled a mammography to insure that nothing more serious was going on. She was, in fact, acting rationally.

But after the phone call with her mother and until she could talk to her doctor the next day, she became unglued. She couldn't sleep, she had cold sweats, her imagination went out of control, and she developed a migraine from the stress.

The next day, her physician assured her that she did not have a serious problem and advised her to relax.

Melissa now thinks before telling her mother— who is almost certain to overreact negatively—about her physical problems.

· · ·

Some friends, family, medical personnel, and even strangers can offer insightful and reassuring thoughts. Many will offer needed empathy and provide useful information. However, this is not always the case. Though family members and friends usually have good intentions, they may offer strange, irrational, or just plain irritating solutions. They may offer unsolicited advice, solace, or platitudes that they hope will make witnesses feel better. Luckily, patients and caregivers usually know which people to avoid in emergencies. Here are a few of the many kinds of responses people might offer:

"I told you he would get sick if he didn't stop smoking. Why don't you sue the cigarette industry?"

"Life is tough, and then you die."

"Shit happens."

"It's just a trial. It's a learning experience."

"God gives you only what you can handle."

"It's God's will."

"Suffering is good for you."

"It's not the end of the world."

"It's just a streak of bad fortune."

"You shouldn't be so emotional."

"Life is not brain surgery."

"Everything will be all right."

Everything may indeed turn out to be all right in the end, but no one really knows. The etiquette during crisis situations is primarily guesswork. For example, what does one say to the wife of a spouse who has had a heart attack? People feel considerable awkwardness in situations of stress, and instead of being silent, they offer clichés that are meant to soothe, but often make already brittle witnesses angry. It is hard to keep the news silent. It is also hard not to listen when people say stupid things. However, if possible, witnesses might try to take time to center their thoughts, think about what they need to do, and review questions privately or with people they trust before going more public.

Witnesses should expect a confusion of focus, ricocheting between the patient and themselves. No doubt they will feel concern for the person who is ill—very concerned, so concerned that they may forget their own needs. But witnesses will also be thinking about themselves. Though they may think doing this is wrong or selfish, being self-centered in a time of crisis is natural and necessary. There will likely be thoughts about the reality of the burden: wishing the patient's illness were just a bad dream; or asking "Why me?" in addition to "Why him?" or "Why her?"

We have yet to hear a satisfying answer to "Why me?" God's will, karma, destiny, the need for life lessons are vague and abstract guesses. Joseph Campbell, in his book *The Hero with a Thousand Faces*, writes about the end of Buddha's struggle for enlightenment after years of physical and psychological hardships. As Buddha sits under the Bo Tree of enlightenment, he first learns about his previous lifetimes. He then receives the divine eye of omniscient vision. The last gift of wisdom is understanding the chain of causation. The point of the story is that understanding "why" is the last gift to be gained, its mystery opaque to "ordinary minds."

Yet the impulse to ask "why me" may be practical. Could this circumstance have been prevented? It may reveal a need to be in control, a "powerful need to make sense of the incomprehensible." If witnesses can do that, they might feel less powerless, angry, and helpless. However, there is the danger of answers that create guilt or a fantasy of omnipotence. Suggested causes of illness like those that imply that "bad" karma of the witness or patient or those that imply the patient's lack of positive thinking is preventing their recovery are simply not helpful. Asking "why me" is common; finding answers about the fragility of life and mortality is not. Still, introspection and the quest for spiritual understanding will be useful for those who wish to make the experience of witnessing a meaningful life event.

COPING AND THE CAREGIVER

Ideally, some witnesses will manage to stop asking questions about "why me," and find the strength to make the best of the situation for a simple reason: they must go on. There are the patient's pressing needs to be considered. Some are helped by gaining perspective: they can always find others who have greater problems. There are other philosophical styles used: accepting illness as a part of life; fighting and raging against illness as a battle to be won; living life to the fullest, appreciating small pleasures in nature and the sensual pleasures of the moment, to the end; experiencing life as poignant, sweet, but tragic and unfair; and looking at illness and death as a quest to the next frontier. And finally, some witnesses use humor to help them cope.

．　　●　　．

Dale, the exhausted writer of this journal entry, is describing the first day her mother-in-law came home from a rehabilitation facility. Richard's mother had been recovering from a stroke.

Ma arrived home at 1:55 p.m.

2:05 p.m.—Water and leg rub.

2:10 p.m.—Candy bar, almonds spit out!

2:25 p.m.—Change diaper and bathe.

2:30 p.m.—Cookie and water.

2:50 p.m.—Teeth brushed. Worried about tooth decay.

3:01 p.m.—Change and wash.

3:09 p.m.—Ma wet again—8 minutes, a new record.

3:10 p.m.—Richard to Eaton's for more diapers.

3:35 p.m.—Richard returns, and we change Ma AGAIN.

3:50 p.m.—Richard and Dale have first beer of the day.

4:25 p.m.—Ma sleeps—Ahhh!

4:30 p.m.—Feed Aunt Helen.

4:45 p.m.—Ma needs another leg rub. Food goes up to Ma (20-minute catnap).

4:55 p.m.—Ma eats very little; however, she liked it.

5:00 p.m.—Richard wipes lobster salad from my glasses.

5:10 p.m.—Lights out—we hope.

5:15 p.m.—Richard leaves on errand to airport. HELP!!

6:45 p.m.—Richard returns. All's quiet on the Western Front, we hope.

9:45 p.m.—Leg rub and diaper change. We say goodnight to Ma, hoping to encourage a full night's sleep. We'll see.

4:35 a.m.—Richard gets up and gives Ma a leg rub.

4:55 a.m.—We change her and return to bed.

5:15 a.m.—Ma wants and gets another leg rub.

5:25 a.m.—Ma wants a night-light, and I retrieve one from downstairs.

5:35 a.m.—Light is too bright. Richard exchanges it for another.

5:40 a.m.—Tyrone [the dog] runs off. Wish I was with him.

5:45 a.m.—Ma calls my name and wants another leg rub.

6:30 a.m.—Leg rub. Damn leg!

6:35 a.m.—Another leg rub. God, for some sleep.

7:10 a.m.—Another leg rub. Wish someone would rub mine! Richard tries to explain normal sleep patterns to Ma, then he takes a bath.

7:30 a.m.—Another leg rub. Ridiculous.

The following night—with the doctor's support and encouragement—
Richard and Dale gave their mother a sleeping pill during the night
so they could get some sleep themselves.

• • •

As Susan Sontag so aptly described it, illness is the "night-side of life." However, all who reside near illness have the darkness coloring their landscapes. Life, indeed, seems to be a different color.

There is no such thing as perfect coping. For witnesses to illness—especially for primary witnesses—coping is tough going, and any attempts at getting by are an accomplishment, even a minor miracle. There is no magic formula to relate, no easy path to make life easier. The truth is that caregiving and coping are a complex struggle for most people, presenting enormous psychological and physical challenges. Uncertainty, doubt, frustration, anger, and fatigue are only some of the intense feelings witnesses will encounter.

Coping is an individual process, sometimes a difficult act of will, and its methods vary for individuals. How one copes depends on age, previous experience, personal spiritual or religious beliefs, the nature of the situation, and whether the problem is mainly internal, external, individual, relational, or a combination. In addition, witnesses may be coping with a problem alone or with family members or friends.

Some people seem to have an advantage in coping. Secondary witnesses might not feel as emotionally distraught as primary witnesses.

• • •

When my friend Molly was in the hospital for a bilateral oophorec-
tomy—removal of the ovaries and fallopian tubes—I acted as a secon-
dary witness. I joined her for a few minutes of preoperative time, and
I stayed until the end of visiting hours. Since I had met with Molly's
surgeon previously, we had decided my job was to get the post-op
report from him and to help make decisions should there be an
emergency—or if the surgeon thought a hysterectomy was necessary.

Molly's boyfriend, who could not be there before the operation,
joined me in the waiting room. We spent about three hours together,
talking and waiting for Molly to be released from the recovery room.

When Molly regained consciousness after the operation, her boyfriend hovered closely over her, stroking and nurturing her. He was much more intimate than I could be. This was his job.

When Molly said she was nauseated from the morphine, her boyfriend told her to vomit in his breast pocket, which made her laugh. I took care of asking the night nurse to get some antinausea medicine, while he kept close to her.

As the secondary witness, I had an easier time dealing with the hospital administration and with the whole witnessing event than when I was a primary witness. I was concerned for my friend but, as a primary witness, her lover was clearly more stressed and worried. His caregiving was sweet and considerate, but it was more of an emotional challenge for him than for me.

. . .

If witnesses have never suffered a loss, there is a certain confidence that is the grace of those yet untouched by the tragedies of life: an energy, strength, determination, and a sense of invulnerability. Yet the experience soon changes everyone in ways too complex to generalize. The next case study illustrates how much can change in the process and style of coping. This witness has watched and worked with people with AIDS for ten years.

. . .

At first, Jeremy learned that his lover's initial diagnosis was called GRID, Gay-Related Immune Deficiency. The acronyms HIV and AIDS were not yet part of the vocabulary in the early '80s. It was still early enough to believe something would be found to cure the problem.

Stephen, Jeremy's longtime companion, was a Ph.D. in literature. Jeremy was a psychotherapist. Both had been doing very well—professionally and personally—up until Stephen's diagnosis. They were strong men, successful in their professions, and high achievers. Both had "come out" early, and this action had not affected their careers. Both felt they had never met anything they couldn't deal with. Consequently, they felt if they worked hard enough, they could beat AIDS.

This was not to be so. Stephen would later ask, "Why am I sick now? I have never been more alive, nor more loved."

After the news of the diagnosis, both of them went into action. They read everything. They talked to many doctors, getting multiple opinions. They did public speaking to raise funds for research, and Stephen became one of the first members of the People With AIDS (PWA) support groups started by the AIDS Action Committee. They were totally immersed in the quest for information, medical treatment, and community and societal involvement.

Stephen's energy flagged despite megadoses of vitamin C and every treatment they could find. They continued to focus on using the community in a healthy way, and the PWA group was very tight.

Jeremy and Stephen were also well supported by their network of friends, who would tell them what they would be available to do: laundry, shopping, cooking, taking Stephen to the doctor, companionship, etc. For most of the time, Jeremy would not let them help. "Stephen was mine. I couldn't use their help. I didn't know how to ask. I felt I would take care of it all."

Jeremy worked full-time until the last three weeks before Stephen died, and then he asked for help. "Night and day, there were always food, coffee, and companionship. Stephen was never left alone. Stephen's parents were there, too, and they discovered more about their son and his relationships."

However, even as Stephen was getting weaker and sicker, his level of denial was great. They were able to work on the practical aspects of living—even writing a will—but Stephen became angry whenever Jeremy brought up his deteriorating condition. It was not okay to discuss death and dying, God, a higher power, or possibilities of an afterlife. Up until the very end when Stephen had a hard time breathing, he whispered, "I'm not going to die."

To his continuing regret, Jeremy was not able to say his goodbyes. In Stephen's final hours, Jeremy simply asked Stephen to be there for him when he died.

Stephen's death devastated Jeremy. At 42, this was his first experience with death, though he had counseled his clients about the process of death and dying. "I didn't believe he would actually die. I couldn't have imagined the stunning pain of the loss. I felt amputated. There were days I would crawl on the floor into the space between the wall and my bed—and cry. It was the only place small enough to hold me. I kept on saying nothing will ever be the same."

The next time Jeremy was a witness to AIDS, it was a different experience. He was a secondary witness to a close friend, Tom, who was in his late 20s and a physician.

Jeremy was able to observe the process as a survivor, having been transformed by the death of Stephen. Despite the grief and continued sadness, the experience gave him strength and wisdom.

Tom, in his final stages of AIDS, looked like a man in his 70s— painfully thin, stomach distended, and totally bald and hairless from chemotherapy. Jeremy said he looked like a starved vulture. There were also the indignities of Kaposi's sarcoma, cytomegalovirus, and Raynaud's phenomenon, causing Tom's fingertips to deteriorate. In his final days, Tom was so sick that his lover could look on no longer.

Jeremy stayed. Jeremy explained that Stephen's death had changed and helped him, because he now realized that part of his work was facilitating people making the transition from life to death.

Unlike his experience with Stephen, Jeremy was able to talk with Tom about death.

As Tom outlived a tough weekend, he didn't understand why he was still alive. Jeremy told Tom, "As long as you need to stay alive, I'll stay. I'm grateful for the opportunity. I'm learning from you." Moments later, Jeremy realized something was different in the room. Tom had stopped breathing. Jeremy held Tom's hand until it became cold.

"My life has changed. I'm watching dozens die. Watching them die horribly. Skin rotting off. Skin burning from the inside out. Grotesque and terrible suffering. People dying long before they should. All this death has forced me to engage in a level of life I've avoided— moment to moment. Life can change in a second—and it does."

Every year since the death of Stephen, Jeremy has lost another friend to AIDS.

He is currently in a new relationship, committed to love, growth, his work, his spiritual path, and dealing with life on life's terms. Since he knows that everything ends, he thinks he will no longer be devastated in the same way. "Sad, yes; pole-axed no more."

He says his feelings about control are gone, and that he is more open-hearted. He has also pulled back a bit from his AIDS activism. "Death was everything for a while. Not now. I need life to not be focused on death and dying. My focus is on being alive."

.   .   .

Some witnesses who experience many people in their lives being chronically ill or dying are more resilient than others in their coping abilities. Witnesses who may be particularly resilient are those who: act as distant witnesses; come from functional families; were "desired" children; have a powerful sense of identity and self-esteem; have solid relationships with their parents and other men and women; have strong, consistent role models; are employed or have outside interests; have internal resources from religious, philosophical, or spiritual faith, and have experienced few childhood or adult traumas. However, some lucky witnesses have a natural resilience that remains no matter what problems or challenges life has presented them.

Coping with illness is influenced by past memories and experiences of witnessing illness—even though the incidents may have been very different. It is often thought that past experiences—the lessons learned, the wisdom accumulated—always help in present situations, but that is not necessarily so. They can cause problems, too. Sometimes a witness's behavior from the past is duplicated inappropriately. For example, a witness might have had a parent who died of cancer. When a second family member is diagnosed with cancer, the witness can't seem to shake the fear of the relative's death, despite evidence that this patient's type of cancer is curable. Or the witness is fatigued from childhood or continuing life traumas—a dysfunctional family, career frustrations, deaths in the family, psychological or physical abuse, or just plain bad luck. Pain can be cumulative, and personal resilience can snap like a worn-out rubber band. Tolerance, the strength to withstand stress, and the motivation to take action can decrease.

Additionally, how one copes depends on the severity of the patient's illness and its length. Some illnesses can be terrifying; cancer and AIDS come to mind first, but who would not be terrified of abandonment, of watching a loved one suffer continuing pain or the slow deterioration of mental and physical independence? In fact, chronic illness (as opposed to acute illness, where the course of the disease is shorter) is likely to be more of a challenge for both the caregivers and for those suffering the chronic problems.

.   .   .

"The woman on the phone didn't know what 'iatrogenic' illness meant. What kind of system of health care do we have in this country, anyhow?" Betsy asked her husband with great exasperation. [Iatrogenic illness is unwittingly precipitated, aggravated, or induced by the physician's attitude, examination, comments, or treatment.]

A registered nurse, patient, and wife of a doctor, Betsy already had undergone surgery on her painful left foot about a year earlier. She'd had the surgery done, because 18 months of treatments had not helped the pain she felt was caused initially by a podiatrist's error in treatment. She wanted to walk again without discomfort and get back to the skiing she loved.

Unfortunately, her experience with the uneducated clerk at the physician's office was just the most recent frustration on a long list of unsuccessful efforts at medical therapies. It was almost three years, and her foot still hurt every day. And the pain had increased.

"When I feel discouraged, I get angry," she said in a choked voice.

Her husband, and primary witness, once again felt defensive, impotent, and angry. He knew he had an indefinite future of further second opinions, trials of treatment, and frustration.

.   .   .

Just as the pain and burden of doctor visits wear out the patient, they also grind up the witness who powerlessly watches the suffering, which can become a chronic tribulation of months and years. Tolerance vies with impatience for pre-eminence. Demands for support, the long-term sacrifices, and continuing adjustments to different phases of the illness can consume and corrode energy. Additionally, since our medical system works best for crisis management, continuing support from the professional community can be be harder to find or absent in chronic cases.

COMMON FEELINGS OF THE WITNESS

What we perceive, what we think, what we remember, and what we conclude from our observations arouses emotions. Our emotions, on the other hand, cause us to think and look for information. They color our memories and our conclusions.

– Emmy Gut

Witnesses are likely to wade through a landscape of emotional quicksand. Intense and complex feelings constantly change. John Bradshaw has said that emotions are positive or negative feelings that propel us to act. They can be complex, flat, inappropriate to the situation, and changeable, yet he feels that they monitor our needs and give us energy to get what we want. Emotions facilitate survival.

The emotional level of witnesses can be off-putting, even frightening, for those who observe them.

.   .   .

During the Persian Gulf War, Harriet, a woman in her 20s whose husband was away at war (thus, she was a witness to potential injury or death), felt so "hyper" she couldn't calm down.

Her family was critical of her emotional state.

When she went to a therapist for a consultation, the therapist told her that the family might be scared by her feelings. Her therapist said she could be as hyper as she wanted, "If not now, when?"

.   .   .

Like witnesses to illness, Harriet was experiencing fear—fear of financial insecurity, life-style change, the unknown, and fear about personal survival. She did not know what would happen, and she did not know when or how this crisis would end. The uncertainty—like the "basic human nightmare of being entirely helpless in the hands of malignant persecutors"—can be extremely tormenting.

Stress, fear, helplessness, depression, and shame are only a few of the specific emotions witnesses are likely to experience. These emotions, in turn, affect the life of the witness outside the caregiving role. Tension, depression, and concern can affect the ability to work. They can be felt as a generalized anger that many witnesses feel—anger at the illness, at medicine, at life—or as a specific anger (which witnesses might feel harder to admit) like having to deal with unexpected caregiving chores. Unfortunately, this emotional flood can then be projected onto co-workers or colleagues—as well as the family.

The effects of caregiving can cause witnesses to suffer at the workplace. The drain of time away from work will often cause worry about a weakened or distracted job performance. Witnesses might worry about getting laid off or financial survival. And all the while, this anxiety overlaps their concerns about the patient. Fatigue and disrupted sleep, stemming from a constant state of uncertainty and insecurity, also affect work. Because witnesses might not feel up to their personal standards of excellence or perfection, they may experience shame or frustration—for whatever they do, it seems as if it were not enough. This sense, in turn, can lead to feelings of helplessness.

While some witnesses feel helpless, others feel numb. Some witnesses prefer social isolation. Still others experience an emotional hemorrhaging that is severely debilitating.

Although there are often common emotions that witnesses encounter, few descriptions approach the gut-felt reactions of direct experience; however, writing clinically about emotions and directly experiencing them are quite different indeed. There are no easy witness stories. Emotions are feverish and high-pitched, and situations are often filled with anger and intensity.

•   •   •

This excerpted portion of my witness journal recounts a particularly exhausting and difficult patch of caregiving: nine straight days of watching David undergo his first chemotherapy infusion (an infusion that lasted the entire nine days without letup) in the hospital.

I am including this because I feel that talking generally about coping can appear a bit academic rather than real. The specific details of any caregiving story will reveal a more complex picture. In relating this one short period of time, it is possible to see the multiple problems and challenges that witnessing an illness can bring: life-threatening episodes, fighting for proper medical care, dealing with fear, family tensions, work stress, and personal exhaustion.

The coping mechanisms are also diverse: solitude, anger, research, advocacy, lay healing techniques, introspection, writing, sharing problems, and asking for help.

I am no expert in coping. If you had observed me during the more dramatic episodes of David's bout with cancer, you would most likely have seen me as angry, emotional, introspective, complaining, confused, intense, aggressively questioning, moody, not always polite, and hardly a picture of equanimity.

This is not to say I didn't eventually come to peace of mind. Rather, for me—and no doubt countless others—coping is a process and sometimes a torturous one on the road to decision-making, action, or just plain accomplishing life's daily needs during the crisis.

This excerpt picks up my personal story a year after David's first surgery and subsequent radiation. After David and I moved to Boston, a suspicious result from a blood test revealed David was out of remission. His cancer had spread.

Just prior to the hospitalization, David's brother—who is a physician—reviewed David's hospital records from Philadelphia. He obtained another sample of David's malignant tumor and gave it to a pathologist who was a colleague.

His brother's consultant disagreed with the initial pathologist's report. He said that the first pathologist in Philadelphia misread the slide of the malignant tumor. There were two types of cancer rather than one.

The mistake resulted in improper treatment—unnecessary radiation—and David's cancer grew unchecked for a year.

This caused David to undergo a serious surgical procedure: a periaortic nodal dissection where some 50 lymph nodes were removed from his chest, leaving a two-foot scar.

This chemotherapy episode started a few weeks after that surgery. From his surgery to the beginning of his second hospital stay, I had constant visitors—friends and family—staying in our apartment. I was already exhausted. I was afraid of the effects of chemotherapy. And I felt enormous anger and mistrust towards doctors in general—even though we were in a new medical environment when this hospitalization began.

In other personal case studies throughout the book, I have rewritten my journal from the perspective of hindsight. Here, I have kept the journal much as it was written to maintain the emotional truth as it was then.

Day 1—*David is reacting severely from the chemotherapy. He is vomiting every 15 minutes. A nurse checks the dosage and finds the doctors are giving him twice the concentration he should be getting. We realize the dosage could be lethal, because the drugs are dangerously toxic. When summoned, the doctor mumbles that the mistake is of little consequence since it was caught. He wrote the order "unclearly." David vomits violently again.*

He didn't say he was sorry, and we noticed.

I challenged the doctor, "You'll never make that mistake again ever, will you?" The doctor stared at me, apparently shocked by my anger, and walked out the door.

Later that day, when David's roommate's doctor came in, David got violently ill. He ran to the sink to puke, tied to his I.V. pole, and knocked over a pitcher of water with the tube backlash.

The doctor looked at me with disgust and demanded that I take him to the bathroom; David was disturbing his concentration. There were no toilets in the room, only some 50 yards down the hall. I gave him the finger and called him a jerk. I wished I could have been more creative.

David vomited regularly all day long. I have never seen anyone sicker with nausea.

David resented my advocacy—and me. He didn't like my being so stern with the doctors. He appeared more fatalistic and complacent about the mistakes and the rudeness. Actually, he was just concentrating on holding himself together.

Later that night, a nurse let him sleep in the interns' quarters. His being hooked up to the chemicals was driving him crazy, and his roommate snored.

Day 2—*Already I am falling apart, and I am ashamed of this. I don't know why, but I can barely talk, I can't make a decision about what to eat, I can't touch the dishes, I don't know what to wear, I can't remember telephone numbers, and I can barely manage to dry my hair.*

I needed to go to the hospital, so I called a friend, thinking I was having a nervous breakdown. She assured me that, indeed, things were miserable, and she volunteered to drive me to the hospital. I knew I needed therapy, but I couldn't afford it.

I arrived at the chemotherapy ward—the oldest and worst section of the hospital—during crisis time. It was after lunch, when vomiting escalates. The patients and their visitors had an unmistakable glare—a combination of fear, desperation, and hope. Many of the patients wore masks to protect their low immune systems.

It was Easter Sunday.

When I entered David's room, he was having convulsive, uncontrollable shakes. He was conscious, but he looked as if he were dying. He was white and out of control; his eyes rolled upward.

I ran for a nurse and rushed back to David to encourage deep breathing. I worked on him myself, giving him healing energy while I kept on buzzing the nurses. Nothing I did helped. When the nurses finally showed, they panicked and said they didn't know what to do. I screamed for them to get a doctor.

They told me it would take 20 minutes. The only doctor for the ward had an emergency. I told them this was an emergency. They said the doctor had 50 patients, and everyone seemed to be getting sick. I told them to find someone else. It was a huge hospital.

Meanwhile, David was getting worse. An hour passed. The shape of his face was literally changing as his jaw locked. His shaking was increasing. He could barely talk. I finally ran out to find a doctor, and I found one reading charts. I dragged him to the room.

The doctor left to do research, and finally came back with an antihistamine to counter David's apparent anaphylactic shock. He had been suffering from an allergic reaction to the antinausea medications.

Hours later, I went home. I called David's parents. David's mother wanted to fly to Boston. I told them politely it was not a good idea. David had requested that they not be there, because it was hard to have anyone around watching him vomit like clockwork. His mother was horrified, "You mean, my son doesn't need me?" I hoped she wouldn't come. I was exhausted from anxiety, and I didn't want company.

Day 3— At the hospital, I learn that David's mother is on her way. I am angry and feeling guilty. How could I be angry at her wanting to be with her son?

I understood her need, yet after four weeks of company, I relished my privacy, and my silence. I felt like a different person. I had no more patience left in me. I hardly had enough strength for David. I had no reserves for kindness, hospitality, and warmth. I couldn't support his mother's anguish this time as I did during the last surgery. This was yet another distraction from work. All selfish reasons, I knew: this made me miserable.

I started fighting with David. I brooded and complained. David just sat there being sick. In the midst of the argument, David's mother arrived. He wasn't happy about seeing her, but he didn't have to live with her at home. It was easier for him, though, because she was his mother.

I knew taking it out on David was cruel and ridiculous, but I had no other outlet. I told him to keep checking the dosage amounts, and David would not. His passivity also infuriated me.

Despite his experiences, David argued in favor of trusting doctors. I disagreed. Though I had chosen not to tell him earlier, I finally disclosed that 3 or 4 patients had died with this particular drug therapy, because of improper dosages or complications from the drugs.

David's mother just sat and listened to us argue; we couldn't resolve the other real issue, which was her visit and what to do with my anger.

David finally did suggest—in a moment of privacy—that I be tough and tolerate it since we had no choice or control. Then he told me I should be working. I was writing an article for a Sunday magazine supplement of a local newspaper. My productivity was suffering.

I agreed, yet how could I write when I had to straighten the house, worry about food shopping, transportation, the emotional status of Mom, when I was already worrying about his dying, my debts, and yet a new problem?

While David was on his long trek to the bathroom, his mother dropped a bombshell. She was carrying a message from her husband. She told me that David and I had to drop our plans for a July wedding. That if we got married, his medical insurance would be canceled and no one would be able to take care of his medical bills. ("Previous" illnesses are not covered on new or adjusted medical insurance policies. A marriage would require a new policy; thus, costs from any cancer-related illness for David would not be reimbursed on a new contract.)

Great. . . as if we didn't have enough problems without taking away our hope. This sent me over the edge. Now economics and medical insurance were my new nemeses.

I told her that as far as I was concerned, I couldn't be more married to David or more committed. I didn't mind being unmarried, but didn't she understand it was our one positive goal? She knew.

The discussion continued. She said she felt terribly unwanted and unneeded, because she was told not to come.

This was a real challenge to explain. I told her we loved her. She was indeed a terrific, loving person and probably the best future mother-in-law I could have, but life appeared bleak. I was incapable of behaving well, and I didn't want her, or anyone else, to see me that way.

She said she couldn't sleep at home or function. She was suffering more deeply than when her mother died. Once she was here and saw her son, she felt much better.

I explained I was exhausted.

She asked for tolerance, and understood I needed time to work.

This helped me, but I was still feeling brittle and guilty, wanting to run away and disappear.

Day 4—I took a day off! David's mother goes to the hospital without me.

Day 5—Today, David's mother leaves for the hospital earlier than me. She gets to spend time alone with her son. I get the chance to be alone and work for some sense of normalcy.

When I arrived at the hospital later, David was feeling particularly weak. He was depressed from the chemotherapy, so I tried psychic healing twice. I surrounded him with light, and I fed David my energy—giving him what I called an energy transplant. I held his hand in mine, and I visually transferred all my energy to him. I saw my energy as a golden bolt of light that poured like liquid out of my body and into his.

To my surprise, not only did it work, David actually said he felt it enter his body. The first time, I was distracted—listening to *ambient hospital noises—but David experienced it as a smooth flow of energy.*

The next time David asked for help, I sat next to him on the bed, relaxed quickly into a slow-breathing meditation, took a deep breath, and gave him all I had in one shot—visualizing a strong golden flow of energy coming out from my hand and into his body. David jumped and said it jolted his body too much. He said he preferred the slower buildup.

I was stunned. It was the first confirmation that what I was doing not only worked, but that it worked in degrees. After the second "transfusion," David was able to get out of bed and walk. He had had no energy to do that earlier.

The problem with this method, though, was that it was too exhausting for me. I had nothing left for myself; I felt so depleted I could barely get myself home.

Day 6—Slowly, David's Mom and I work out our routine. We take turns being supportive and upset. When we are in the hospital, we alternate taking breaks and getting our times alone with David. When we are home, we do what we each need to cope: she takes 10 mg. of Valium while I take 5 mg. I'm glad she is with me.

I understood my initial problem with having David's mother live with me. I learned that to be loving I needed to take care of myself first. I had been totally spent, burnt-out, close to dead emotionally. I learned to ask for help, telling others when I needed time to regenerate my energy by whatever method was best at the time— whether it was being alone, going to the movies, watching TV, buying myself a treat, going out to dinner, taking a walk, or working on a personal project. This wasn't an easy lesson for me.

Day 7— I am still doing all the research I can to help.

Last night, I called a local spiritual/psychic healer to see if she had any advice. She told me she would include David in her daily healing meditations and told me I could join in. She said her healing energy was for everyone; distance didn't matter.

She said his being sick could be an active and positive path to health and happiness and a cleansing. At the end of the conversation, she reminded me to join her in prayer.

Her talking about prayer made me think about David's

roommate—another man in his 20s with the same testicular CA problem. Every day, 8 – 10 members of his family would pray around the bed. Every time after the prayers, he was energized and doing so well, I was certain they were onto something with prayer.

I have started to read The Psychic Healing Book, by Amy Wallace and Bill Henkin. I learned about psychic healing techniques that would not deplete me: how to use a "universal" energy source instead of my own. If I grounded myself—imagined a line going from my feet to the center of the earth—I could pull up earth energy. And, if I visually opened the top of my head to the energy of the cosmos, I could mix the two and have unlimited energy at my disposal. I understood the difference in technique. Using my own energy was like wearing out a battery instead of plugging into a more constant energy supply.

I was skeptical, but later in the day when I tried it, I was no longer exhausted; in fact, I was energized.

I also read the most powerful healings come from love.

Day 8—Today, I asked David how he wanted to be treated. I could not always tell whether I should pamper him or prod him.

David wanted me to treat him normally. He felt others were magnifying his pain.

"But you're going through the most extreme of circumstances."

"Don't you understand that the way I cope is by acting normally? Treat me as you always do. I'll let you know my limits."

"Seeing you tied to all those bottles. Watching the poisons destroy your spirit. Staring at your puking every ten minutes is just not normal. So you're saying that the easiest way for you to deal with this is denial."

"If that's what you want to call it."

I started to confuse denial, indifference, and courage, wondering what was real and what was performance.

I consulted with Doug. I asked him if it was healthy to deny. He said, "Who said life is healthy?"

Day 9— All the tragedies in the hospital which I've so far tried not to absorb have seeped into my skin.

The engineer with four kids who underwent open heart surgery, his wife complaining that they didn't warn her that her husband would look like a corpse after the operation.

The incontinent new roommate pissing on the floor, his rotund wife kissing him gingerly.

The woman in solitary confinement across the hall who has leukemia—frail, beautiful and bald—listening to her doctor talk about her low white cell count.

The ranting, incontinent alcoholic next door with the DTs.

The woman no one visits, who stares at me blankly and plays cards.

Another cancer patient who walks with her tall husband holding her tightly: she had been told she would never go home.

I've tried not to see. I felt it wouldn't help them. It wouldn't help me: pointlessly draining more sympathetic energy. I tried not to smell the death around me. The act of decaying. The rotting. But I did harbor a secret horror about the success of not seeing: I thought I would never see or feel anything again.

But today, it has crept inside while David experiences his last day of nausea. Chemotherapy is so crude, so hideous, so medieval. While he pukes his poisons, he too looks like a corpse. I turn my eyes away and stare blankly at the Charles River outside the window, trying desperately not to see.

·   ·   ·

Given experiences like these, it is no wonder that some witnesses not only desire escape, but actually leave.

·   ·   ·

In his practice, Doug encountered a husband who seemed nonchalant about his wife, who was having a psychotic episode. Perplexed by his wife's behavior, the husband dropped his wife off in the psychiatric unit of the hospital, left the premises, and went home to watch a baseball game.

·   ·   ·

Is this good? Well, it might be better than screaming at her to change, or abusing her, or not getting her help at all. In fact, he is practicing a medical dictum: "First, do no harm." The husband had judged he was unable to do anything else, and he felt his presence wouldn't help. To some, he may seem uncaring, but perhaps it is best not to judge. His actions may be betraying what he is feeling inside. After all, he became a spectator to his wife's illness. What his wife needed was medical attention and medication, not necessarily empathy.

Worry

Whether present with the patient or distant, witnesses are often plagued with the inability to escape from persistent worry.

• • •

The night I learned my friend Rebeccah went out of remission, that her Hodgkin's disease had returned only two months after she gave birth to her daughter, I became very sad.

The next morning, I awoke with a migraine, which broadcasted the full extent of my concern and stress. My headache went away when my cousin, a cancer researcher at the National Institutes of Health, called and told me she still had a 95–100% chance of recovery.

Yet the sadness—the worry about how she would get through chemotherapy and care for an infant—nagged me. I had a hard time ignoring my feelings. Living four hours away, I felt powerless and relatively unable to help. Was I an obsessive worrier? Or did it mean I was a loving friend and merely human?

When I deal with my emotions, I realize they can be unpredictable, constantly challenging my ability to be rational and productive in a crisis or even in the face of bad news. My emotional terrain resists control.

It may be dangerous to accept myself as a yardstick for normality, but I've come to realize that coping does not mean hiding the truth of my emotions. If I'm lucky, I can be distracted from them by actions, I can be soothed by kisses, satiated by eating, absorbed in writing about them, entertained by movies or comedians, but my emotions have their own life and their own timing. They grow, they blossom, they wither, and sometimes they blossom again.

•   •   •

Witnesses are unremittingly encouraged not to worry. Yet when people tell witnesses not to worry, they don't always mean exactly what they say. There are multiple subtexts in this piece of advice: people sometimes mean that worry will not change anything; people might feel witnesses are squandering time, energy, and the opportunity to do something other than worry (though sophisticated worriers are quite capable of doing anything *and* worrying at the same time); people might want witnesses to relax and feel better; or people might not want to hear about or acknowledge what witnesses are thinking or feeling.

Despite the confusion about what "don't worry" really means when people use the phrase, worry *is* a scarcely recognized coping mechanism. Worry is often mistaken for thought, and worrying and thinking are natural and necessary for the witness in the process of coping. Countering the conventional wisdom that worry does not accomplish much, worrying, in fact, may be essential.

The word *worry* is derived from the Anglo-Saxon *wyrgan*, meaning to choke or strangle, injure, or violate, and has evolved to mean to feel troubled, uneasy, anxious, and distressed. To think means to keep continually in the mind, to be obsessed with; to consider the welfare of; to work out, solve, discover, or plan by thinking; to ponder; to think about until one reaches a conclusion or resolution. Worry may simply be the affective experience, or the *feeling* attached, when *thinking* about the person who is ill.

Like other emotions, worry often has its own timetable and its own needs. For some, no amount of reasoning can force worry's demise. Worry is easier to deal with than panic, more tolerable than depression, and a resting place until change or adaptation can occur. In witnesses, worry or concentrated thought may be a productive tool for contingency planning: devising action and alternative options for any future outcome. Of course, there are extremes of worry. As a form of anxiety, worry can be pervasive for many witnesses, causing an inability to work or do anything at all. Obsession is an extreme form—

if unrelenting, the witness becomes unproductive, and even detrimental, in pointless occupation with meaningless, repetitive thoughts.

Guilt

Just as worry and thought can be mistaken for each other, so too can guilt and regret. Witnesses often talk about feeling guilty when what they really may be feeling is regret. Regret acknowledges the wish that we would like the patient's suffering to diminish—to feel better, heal faster—without implicating ourselves as the guilty party. Regret allows us to feel sorrow or remorse over something that has happened without feeling culpable, deserving of blame or punishment.

Accurately identifying and expressing feelings—always a semantic challenge—has a beneficial psychological effect. Words have an enormous strength and impact on ourselves and others. "I feel guilty" has much more negative emotional charge than "I feel sad." Many researchers are now examining the toll that so-called negative emotions—frustration, rage, fear, hopelessness, hostility, anger, dejection, defeatism—take on our bodies as opposed to the effects of positive emotions—purposefulness, determination, love, hope, faith, perseverance, will to live, festivity. Most of the studies tend to be focused on the emotions and recovery of patients, but these negative emotions also have an impact on the body of the witness. Witnesses suffer enormous emotional wear and tear. That is why it is so important for witnesses to understand their emotions. Though emotions are often hard to control, perhaps witnesses can be persuaded to work toward a healthy balance of feelings—by clarity of thought, by distraction, or by relaxation techniques.

At the same time, the words *positive* and *negative* carry unfortunate judgments about emotions, for both types of feelings are as natural as night and day. Neither is right nor wrong. The trouble is that this labeling can lead to harsh self-judgments, which might then compromise self-esteem.

Some people think that coping well or efficiently under deeply stressful circumstances is abnormal, but it may be impossible to judge one's coping abilities. There are no universally accepted standards for normality. Coping may become unproductive, or even unhealthy, if the witness is self-destructive or is abusive to others. What about those who cope by overeating, drinking too much, playing too much golf, overindulging in sex, doing too many drugs, or spending too much money on retail therapy? What can be said? We may be guilty of all of those things at some time in our lives. On the other hand, successful coping does not mean witnesses will be able to take care of business without any resistance, backtracking, procrastination, mistakes, or pain.

Successful coping may even include retreating. Not doing anything at all may, in fact, be a coping mechanism or a healthy strategy for regrouping and coping in the future. Not taking action can be especially important if the patient's words, manner, or relationship to the witness are as harmful as a lethal weapon. If witnesses have the ability to escape—with the goal of self-preservation—doing so may well be a healthy, necessary, and realistic choice. Because our society's ethics tend to favor self-sacrifice and personal suffering, there will be the consequence of disapproval—and personal guilt—if witnesses abandon someone who is ill. However, the martyrdom of staying can be psychological suicide in some cases. What will appear to be successful coping to many, most likely, has come about by compromise: the witness weighs the needs of the patient with his or her own needs.

Despite confusion about what constitutes successful coping, as witnesses cope with a crisis, they may review how they have acted. Self-appraisal is a normal process: evaluating the lessons learned, rethinking how situations might be better handled the next time. Yet, in this particular exercise of self-analysis, witnesses need to remember that this judging process can easily summon guilt ("I didn't do well enough; I could have done better") and crush self-esteem ("I'm a horrible person; I can't do anything well") at a time when energy is at a premium. Moreover, many people will feel they are "coping failures," despite evidence to the contrary. What is perfect coping anyway?

. . .

It was Easter Sunday at 4 in the afternoon when David started having severe pain in his lower left back.

At first, I hoped the pain would magically go away, especially because as soon as David announced he was sick, I immediately experienced sympathy pains. That's why our first guess was food poisoning. But soon, we realized it was more serious. We both guessed at another diagnosis: he might have been passing a kidney stone.

Because David's father had passed two kidney stones, we called his parents. His father related his experience, and his mother promptly got sympathy pains as well.

I then got angry. Though my anger surprised me, I soon figured it out. Of all times to be sick, David "picked" a holiday. But worse, it was the anniversary of a bad memory. It had been twelve years ago when David was near dying on the second day of chemotherapy (described earlier in this chapter).

Luckily, we were able to speak to our doctor through her service. She gave us instructions, and said if we could locate an open pharmacy, she would call in several prescriptions so David would not have to go to an emergency ward.

After making many calls to pharmacies that were closed, I called a local hospital. A nurse told me about an open pharmacy a couple of towns away, and after calling to confirm this fact, I immediately retrieved the medicine.

The pain killers put David to sleep, and I stayed up and watched his breathing as long as I could.

Our doctor called early the next morning, and David had still not passed the stone. He stayed in bed, and I stayed with him, giving him psychic healing while he napped.

Before noon, he passed the stone.

He was elated. He perked up, recovered his energy, and decided what he wanted to do the rest of the day. I knew what I needed. I needed a nap. **It took me more than 24 hours to get over his illness.**

My delayed recovery, I learned later, was typical of disaster syndrome, *the emotional effects of great catastrophe or tragedy on the survivors of a trauma.* Most people seem to function well during a crisis, but as soon as the crisis point diminishes, they crumble physically and emotionally, sometimes becoming "nearly stuporous."

More troublesome than the exhaustion was my internal critic. I was plagued with guilt that I didn't cope well during the crisis. I thought about being angry at David for being ill (and the bad *timing of his attack), feeling scared and helpless, feeling sympathy pains, and feeling shameful about collapsing afterward.*

On the other hand, I knew intellectually that David and I both did what we needed to do to make the stone pass. What was going on here? Why did I feel so conflicted?

Within a few weeks, while I was doing other research, I was relieved to learn that my feelings were typical of those felt by people who had experienced helplessness in the past.

Learned Helplessness

Martin Seligman defines helplessness as "the psychological state that frequently results when events are uncontrollable. . .when we can't do anything about it, when nothing we do matters." Generally speaking, experience aids our ability to repeat a task or conquer similar territory. (Remember the adage: "Practice makes perfect.") However, in cases of replaying past events of feeling helpless, experience can be a hindrance. If closely associated with hopelessness and futility, helplessness can rapidly lead the witness down the path to depression.

Seligman's thesis about helplessness is especially of interest to those witnesses who have encountered repeated traumas—past instances of feeling helpless, or witnessing illness where they were unable to relieve suffering. The ability to react in a present situation might be compromised: motivation to respond to trauma might be diminished by past traumas. Moreover, even if witnesses do respond, and the response is successful, they might have a perceptual "blind spot"; they might have trouble believing that the response worked. In other words, the experience of past uncontrollability or helplessness distorts a future perception of control. This is called *learned helplessness*.

•   •   •

The kidney-stone episode with David not only involuntarily linked me to the past; it reminded me of a time when despite my best efforts, my actions were nearly futile and a breath or two away from lethal for David.

I have no doubt that this memory, this past feeling of helplessness, found its way to my consciousness in an entirely different emergency. It is also linked to why I felt that I didn't cope well during this crisis, despite evidence to the contrary. Though self-criticism is hard for me to control, I have finally accepted that it is useless to rate how I cope like a midterm exam.

. . .

If witnesses have experienced previous traumas or incidents during which whatever actions they took seemed futile, they can expect to feel more emotional than usual and lacking in motivation when confronting a similar situation. They might ask questions like: Why should I try? Why bother? These, in turn, might lead the witnesses to depression, thinking their actions might be in vain, that they will not be able to nurture or relieve suffering. However, understand that this may be a learned behavioral response from the past. Every person, every instance of illness is different, even though on an unconscious or emotional level, it might not feel that way.

CONCLUSION

It is crucial for witnesses to realize how important they, as caregivers, can be in aiding and maximizing the healing process for patients. Though ultimate success (cure) cannot be guaranteed by anyone, witnesses make a sizable contribution in the healing process, significantly improving patients' physical and emotional well-being.

Coping is hard work, annoying, and scary. Flexibility and adaptability with grace, humor, and resilience are, no doubt, assets in facilitating coping. Yet, perhaps we need to accept that the coping process will be messy with anger, sadness, and grief.

4

BECOMING
AN ADVOCATE

*The real issue is the strength of human will and the ability to focus
that will under the most unimaginable of circumstances. . . . It isn't that
every painful experience offers ultimate awareness of life's intrinsic
values. It's that the most extreme conditions require the most extreme
response and for some individuals, the call to that response is vitality
itself. . . . The integrity and self-esteem gained from winning the battle
against extremity are the richest treasures.*

– Diana Nyad
Other Shores

THE WITNESS AS ADVOCATE

In the context of witnessing an illness, an advocate can be a family
member, a lover, a friend, or a colleague who supports and/or works
on behalf of a patient during some or all phases of an illness. To some,
the words *witnessing an illness* may imply distance, observing rather
than doing. However, more often than not, witnessing requires active
participation. Patient advocacy is one of the most important roles of
the witness. Witnesses can plead a patient's cause, offer counsel, or
defend a patient from harm.

An advocate or advocates (there can be more than one) can act
as a watchdog, mediator, negotiator, or nonmedical supervisor of the
patient's medical regimen, when the patient requests this service or
when the patient is physically, emotionally, or psychologically unable.

An advocate can offer help, caregiving, advice, coaching, or a sympathetic ear, facilitating or delegating work that needs to be done for the patient.

The witness as advocate can potentially help with many tasks or responsibilities. For example, an advocate can help the patient to:

- optimize the patient's well-being and the healing process by accompanying the patient during all (or some of) the important phases of the illness;
- establish a role with medical professionals to help the patient deal with hospital or outpatient care;
- research the illness and all available treatments, including current, standard treatment and alternative therapies;
- comprehend the technology that is likely to be involved in the treatment or evaluation process;
- find the best available medical personnel and facilities;
- solicit a second medical opinion, when possible, needed, or desired;
- understand the patient's medical and pharmaceutical regimen, learning the possible side effects of medication, and supervise treatment, if a patient is unable to do so;
- coordinate communications with family members, friends, and colleagues, particularly during critical phases of the illness;
- create a patient-care diary to track laboratory tests, procedures, surgery, drug use, drug side effects, drug interactions, and interactions with all medical personnel;
- research the financial and insurance issues, setting up files and records;
- alleviate worries about external responsibilities, by overseeing the patient's accounts and paying the bills, tending the house or apartment, taking care of the children, and so on;
- delegate responsibility for other needed tasks.

In addition to meeting the patient's needs, witnesses who become advocates may find that this role helps *them* to cope, diminishing feelings of helplessness and hopelessness. A cautionary note, however: this role can get adversarial at times—for example, challenging medical professionals when it appears the patient is not getting the proper care.

In this chapter, we will be discussing the need for advocates and their tasks, concentrating on helping the patient to research the illness and on the caregivers' relationship with medical personnel.

THE NEED FOR ADVOCATES

Advocacy is not always a matter of choice. It is often a crucial life-or-death necessity. Though not always effective in preventing problems, advocacy helps insure that mistakes and misjudgments are minimized.

•　　•　　•

Only in retrospect did I realize that I should have been an advocate when my mother first complained she was ill with an upset stomach and intestinal distress. Our family doctor said it was nothing. My mother died five months later. She was 53 years old. I was 20.

Should I have insisted that my mother pursue a second opinion at the onset of symptoms? With hindsight, it is easy and painfully obvious to say yes. But at the time, I did the best I could, as did my father, my mother, and the rest of the family who witnessed my mother's illness. We trusted the opinion of our doctor.

With my husband, David, I was a better advocate, yet his recovery from testicular cancer was scarred by multiple life-threatening mistakes made by doctors.

The first mistake was during his first checkup with his family doctor. Even though David had noticed a lump in his testicle, his doctor said there was no problem. Thus, the tumor continued to grow without any early medical intervention.

The second mistake came months later. After the tumor had enlarged, David's doctor at a large urban university hospital performed immediate surgery, diagnosing the cancer and recommending a 30-day course of radiation. We insisted on a second opinion, but our mistake was that it came from a colleague of the first doctor, a surgeon. Neither doctor thought to recheck the pathologist's findings. A year later, we found that the pathologist had misread David's cancer-cell type—a cell that did not respond to radiation treatment. We realized that David had been subjected to unnecessary daily radiation, with its immediate side effects of nausea and the long-term effects yet to be seen. This mistake also facilitated the continued spread of David's cancer.

The third mistake came a few months after David's initial surgery and radiation (but before the discovery of the misread slide).

David had complained of a cyst in his breast and promptly went to the hospital to have it examined. The doctor and the surgeon insisted nothing was wrong. They implied David's problem was psychological. They said he was merely frightened, even cancer-phobic, because of his previous bout with cancer. Impatient and condescending, the surgeon told David he would appease David's fears by removing the cyst, performing the gynocomastectomy. The cyst was, in fact, benign, but we found out later—not only from subsequent doctors but in a public information booklet published by the American Cancer Society—this symptom had been an important marker or clue that the cancer was still in his body. The gynocomastectomy had been unnecessary and stupid, underscoring both physicians' failure to understand and keep current with David's illness.

Worse yet, when the correct diagnosis was made by David's new doctors, the previous set of doctors pleaded with the new ones not to reveal the error to David. This infuriated his new doctors and influenced us to proceed with a malpractice suit.

The accumulation of the first three medical errors caused David's cancer to spread throughout his lymphatic system. He needed more serious surgery—a periaortic nodal dissection, which would leave a two-foot scar, and aggressive chemotherapy, which would last over two years. The delay in a proper diagnosis moved him into Stage 2 cancer, which meant he had poorer statistical odds of remission.

As I wrote in the previous chapter, there were more errors during chemotherapy. The first was a dangerous chemotherapy overdose. Then, there were the allergic reactions to antinausea medications. Twice, David lapsed into anaphylactic shock, and both times, he was seriously neglected by the medical staff until I aggressively fought for help. Without strong intervention from his witnesses, he might not have survived.

. . .

Patients and witnesses need to be intimately and actively involved in the process of getting medical treatment. Doctors are neither gods nor monsters; they are human, and they make mistakes. Often, patients are under too much stress to do more than deal with the physical or emotional pain of the illness. This is why witnesses can be so useful—and sometimes even lifesaving—by becoming advocates. Here is another case.

. . .

A friend's father, Nick, is a retired businessman in his late 60s. Ten years ago, a highly regarded oncologist treated him for a melanoma, and Nick remained in remission.

When Nick went back to the oncologist to check on a suspicious skin mole, the oncologist insisted there was nothing to worry about. The doctor had recently published an article about his research findings on the recurrence of melanomas in patients, which made him certain that Nick had no problem. Nick, though still concerned, respected his doctor's authority and expertise, and decided to do nothing more.

At his daughter's insistence, however, Nick went to get a second opinion. The second doctor rushed him into the hospital and removed a melanoma the size of an egg. The first doctor Nick saw had a blind spot, or what might be called a premature cognitive commitment. He was not open to a diagnosis that did not fit his research.

Nick recovered from the operation, but died a year later.

. . .

Unfortunately, there are many stories about iatrogenic illnesses and complications, by definition caused by physicians. Doctors can misread or misinterpret data. They can also be misinformed, even within the multiple fail-safes of modern medicine, which, in turn, is limited in its power to heal. Moreover, professional policies of solidarity may hide a physician's incompetence or professional history.

To be fair, most doctors work hard to interpret data correctly, to determine the best treatment plan, and to forecast the future course of illness. Ideally, physicians should keep current with new medical treatments, continuing their education, reading studies and articles, or doing extra research, especially when confronted with a patient with a particular type of illness. Or, if the illness is outside their area of expertise, they ask for consultations, or refer patients to specialists.

However, the ideal does not always fit reality. It is important for patients to be cautious about selecting physicians and about the treatment plans prescribed for their illnesses. Too often, patients give their doctors enormous power: the full authority to make decisions about the patients' bodies without giving this choice much thought or research. Doing this can be a fatal error.

TASKS OF THE ADVOCATE

Witnesses as advocates can help patients work through the often daunting process of finding the best medical care and treatment. Except during obvious limitations of youth or physical impairment, anyone is capable of acting as an advocate. However, some advocates will be more successful at some tasks than at others. For example, if a patient needs to choose an advocate—or witnesses need to choose among themselves—it will be helpful to select someone with the right sensibility for the task. Someone who is diplomatic, assertive, and persevering will be good for relating to medical personnel in and out of the hospital. If research is what is needed, someone who is diligent and aggressive may be most successful making telephone calls, visiting libraries, and seeking out the facts from whatever source is needed.

As mentioned before, there can be more than one advocate to share the tasks that a patient may require. Usually primary witnesses have the most to do, so if they can learn to ask others—secondary or distant witnesses—to help, they will ease their own burden and give others who are eager to do *something*, a chance to do anything useful. For example, a distant witness who is anxious to contribute and lend support might be able to do needed research.

ACCOMPANYING THE PATIENT
DURING ALL IMPORTANT PHASES
OF THE ILLNESS

One of the most important jobs of the advocate is to be *present*—to provide physical support, emotional support, and simple company. At the very least, an advocate should attempt to be present—or arrange for someone else to be there with the patient—during the news of diagnosis, postsurgical treatment at the hospital, or any emergency. Especially in hospitals, advocates can help patients cope with the "foreign" environment and the often fragmented, technological, and dehumanizing medical care.

Being present with patients during the diagnosis of an illness is more than merely a courtesy. If the diagnosis is not good, patients may not be able to ask questions or listen to the details of their illness while they grapple with the news. Ideally, after a diagnosis is made, doctors will talk privately to patients and their families, offer time for questions and discussion, and mutually decide on a treatment plan. Unfortunately, physicians who are tired, busy—or insensitive—have been known to deliver bad news or "death sentences" inelegantly.

·　　·　　·

For example, a writer and academic in his late 40s was told of his inoperable brain tumor while he was standing alone in the hallway of a hospital. The doctor saw him, told him, and left, asking the patient to call the next day for details. He didn't even offer the patient a seat.

In a similar case, a witness found her sister, a 40-year-old elementary-school teacher, hysterical in her hospital room. She had also been alone when the physician told her she was about to die of a brain tumor.

Both patients were not only devastated by the news, but needlessly ill-treated by their physicians. The writer's wife and the teacher's sister needed to work hard to restore the emotional equilibrium of their loved ones.

·　　·　　·

Bad news often represents a failure for physicians, since their goal is to heal. This disappointment can manifest itself in a hastily delivered diagnosis. However, besides the insensitivity, delivering a diagnosis that produces panic or depression can compromise patients' health by weakening their internal healing resources. Norman Cousins wrote

91

that the "psychological devastation caused by inartistically delivered diagnosis may be no less serious than mistakes in medication or surgery...a [terminal] prediction can have the effect of a hex and impair effective treatment."

Sometimes, a surgeon will talk to the family while a patient is still in the recovery room after an operation. Doing this helps to alleviate the anxiety of the family and friends, and can also aid the patient, who might want to hear about the outcome of surgery immediately after coming to consciousness. Waiting for the doctor to come to the patient's room to relate the news can cause the patient unnecessary anxiety in addition to postoperative physical distress.

· · ·

Before David's third surgery, he urged me to ask the surgeon a few pointed questions when he came to the waiting room to discuss the outcome of the operation.

Unfortunately, the night before his operation, David had a visit from another patient on the same floor in the hospital. This patient, who was also recovering from testicular cancer, told him about his experience with the periaortic nodal dissection. The operation had made him impotent. In fact, he was in the hospital for corrective surgery: to implant a prosthetic device to pump up his penis.

None of the doctors had told David about the risk of impotence. Thus, he was furious, and very worried about the outcome of his operation. Here is a portion of my journal after I had been waiting for news after the 5-hour operation.

The surgeon just left, after he conferred with David's parents and me. I tried to take notes, but all I have is a bunch of words. I can't really quote exactly what he said. Embryonal carcinoma. Venae cavae. Lymphatics. Embryonal cancer had spread from the testicle into his lymphatic system. They removed his stomach during the operation to get to the venae cavae region, where some 50 lymph nodes were excised. The doctor thought the operation was a success.

David will require "adjuvant aggressive chemotherapy." I wrote down the names of the drugs mentioned: vinblastine, bleomycin, actinomycin. Side effects: leukopenia, nephrotoxicity, myelosuppression, nonseminomatous germinal neoplasms, teratoma, alopecia.

What the hell is he talking about? I wondered. *Nonmedical intelligence is of no help here. He's not translating. David's parents are nodding. I think they understood more than I did, but I also guess they think asking questions of a busy surgeon is inappropriate, a waste of his time. I kept interrupting: Could you spell that? Could you tell me what that means?*

Finally, the surgeon snapped at me as he stared at my notebook: "Who do you think you are, Barbara Walters?"

When I asked the doctor whether David would be impotent, the doctor became enraged and acted as if I had insulted him. The subtext of his anger was that he felt David's sex life was not the important issue: he was focusing on David's life. Though I understood that, I was glad I asked. I knew how frightened David had become. I knew that if I could tell him his sex life would remain intact, he would have more energy to fight. The doctor finally answered that David would not be impotent.

I hated being intimidated by him. I find myself hating doctors. I am angry. I have a right to ask questions. I want to know precisely what is going on. I want to talk about the illness intelligently. I want to do more research. Yet, as I sit and quietly think about it, this man might just have saved David's life.

Years later, I learned to go through this process better with my friend Molly, who was having an oophorectomy to prevent the ovarian cancer which was so prevalent in her family history.

This time, I went to the surgeon with Molly for her presurgical checkup. I was introduced as her advocate and witness, and the surgeon knew I would be the person to speak to after surgery and for any emergency. In a living will, Molly had given me a medical durable power of attorney to act on her behalf.

Molly explained to both the surgeon and me what she wanted to know, so I could relate the news to her after she woke up. As they discussed what kind of postoperative medication she would prefer, I promised I would be in her room to see that her wishes were carried through.

Though I might have given the impression that this meeting was an easygoing session, that, in fact, was not true. Both the surgeon and Molly had reservations about the extent of the surgery, postoperative problems and prognosis, and drug therapy. There was a time when we all cried. We all acknowledged the procedure was a radical and primitive way to prevent cancer.

After the surgery, the surgeon found me in the waiting room. He and I were comfortable chatting. There were no problems, and surely that helped, but I believe the communication process went smoothly, because we had established a prior relationship.

.   .   .

Because of the current nursing shortage in hospitals, it can be particularly important for someone to be available to care for patients when they are in pain, critically ill, or at the time of an emergency. Being aware at all stages of medical treatment, the advocate can help guard against possible mistakes that could harm the patient. In this capacity, the advocate should become familiar with the medical and pharmaceutical regimen of the patient, learning the potential side effects of the medicines, and checking with the nurses to make sure that the proper doses, or the proper medication, has been given at the right time. (See the section on patient-care diaries later in the chapter.)

On the other hand, it may not be a good idea for witnesses—because they are anxious about the patient—to nag the nurses or pharmacists. Witnesses can be overprotective, causing another set of problems.

.   .   .

A male patient in his 20s and his family were complaining so frequently to the staff that the hospital's clinical psychologist was called in for a consultation.

The patient was unhappy, and the patient's family members were so upset about his condition that they were frequently calling on the nurse to get him more medicine, but the medication did not help his emotional state.

In questioning the patient, the psychologist found that the patient was disgruntled because he felt disempowered by the overzealous attention of his family. He wanted to be the one who asked for his medication; he wanted to be in control. Once he was allowed more control, his health and spirits improved.

.   .   .

The lesson is to let patients do as much as possible for themselves when they are able. At the same time, it is still wise to pay attention along with the patient. Here's a brief example of a pharmaceutical error, a story about a patient who was recovering at home after a hospital stay.

•   •   •

Rebeccah's father, a man in his 70s struggling with heart and lung disease, suddenly degenerated: he lost all his strength and could barely move or talk. His doctor decided to lessen the dosage of his heart medicine, while he continued steroids for her father's lung condition.

The strategy did not work, and Rebeccah and her mother were sure he was going to die. The family went on a constant 24-hour vigil, preparing themselves for his death.

When Rebeccah's mother went to give her husband his steroid pill, she suddenly noticed that the pills in the steroid bottle looked just like those that were in his heart medicine bottle.

She immediately called the doctor and the pharmacist. The pharmacist, in a rush on Christmas Eve, had made a mistake and put the heart medicine in both prescription bottles. Rebeccah's father was getting too much heart medicine, and dangerously went off his steroids cold turkey—a very hazardous mistake.

Luckily, they caught the mistake just in time.

•   •   •

During emergencies, a witness being present is sometimes a life-or-death necessity. Consider this example.

•   •   •

A concert cellist, Peter, and his pregnant wife, Victoria, suddenly became alarmed when Victoria started to miscarry. They rushed to the hospital. Peter pulled up to the emergency room and got out of his car to be with his wife.

The security guard told him to move his car, but Peter refused. "Tow the damn car if you want," he said. "I can't waste my time moving it."

Inside, he was stopped at the emergency check-in to fill in the necessary forms. There was no wheelchair for Victoria so he threw down his wallet and said, "Here, all the information is in my wallet. You figure it out." And he ran off to tend to his wife.

Once they were in a hospital examining room, no one came by. A nurse came in and said Victoria was just fine, but Peter knew she was in danger. Victoria's color was draining, and she was quickly getting weaker. Alarmed and enraged, he started screaming, "I know what my wife looks like, and something is terribly wrong."

Getting no action from the nurse, he ran out into the hall, found an anesthesiologist, and physically dragged her into the room. The doctor became alarmed, called in other doctors, and started a workup. The doctors estimated that Victoria was about 10 minutes away from dying.

Had Peter dawdled with parking the car or filling out forms, or had he listened to the nurse and not hauled in a doctor, Victoria might have died.

· · ·

We are not advocating leaving a car in a no-parking zone, but this story illustrates the importance of advocacy, and especially being present during emergency situations. Though this is an extreme case, making a fuss when the situation demands it is occasionally good judgment. Strong advocates refuse to accept less than thorough information, examinations, and explanations, despite reassurance or even possible intimidation. The patient's life can depend on it.

RESEARCHING THE ILLNESS AND TREATMENT OPTIONS

Assuming that both the witness and the patient are in agreement about the witness's role, the advocate/witness can help the patient understand the physical nature of the illness and its impact on the patient's life. Basic concerns of the patient—important everyday issues and questions, for example, about diet or exercise—too often get left out or overlooked as being unimportant in the interchange between the patient and the health-care professional. The patient needs to understand the illness to make pertinent decisions about treatment, discuss options, and feel in control.

During the news of the initial diagnosis, though advocates—like patients—may be distraught with worry and fear, advocates are more likely to be clear-headed. Even if the patient is in control of the interview with the doctor, an advocate may help in this process, asking questions the patient may have forgotten or disregarded.

Timing is important. When a patient receives a diagnosis and treatment plan, advocates should, if possible, immediately search for information. Afterward, they should bring that vital information back to the patient so the patient feels involved, and so that any panic is lessened.

Patients may—alone—want to conduct research about their illness: a healthy, empowering, and enlightened decision. In fact, Bernie Siegel, in his book *Love, Medicine & Miracles*, contends that "exceptional patients"—approximately 12 to 15 percent of all patients—who take control may have more successful recoveries. Characterized as feisty, positive thinkers, these patients conduct their own research, use visualization and meditation techniques, clear up old and interfering personal business, and love themselves.

Such exceptional patients should be applauded, but most patients—even if they are extraordinary people—will need or can use the help of an advocate. The additional pressure on the patient to be exceptional may be an excessive and needless burden. The goal to be exceptional is similar to the competitive pressure to become "A" students, though the stakes, here, are higher. The implication—that the exceptional patients are the ones who get cured, the ones who cause miracles, the ones who do not die—is dangerous to patients who are genuinely unable to do research or quickly transform their personalities to fit the exceptional patient profile. Whether patients are urged by well-meaning health-care professionals, family, or friends, this pressure to perform can cause body-damaging stress if the patient does not measure up. Moreover, patients simply may not be capable. Maybe they have had a stroke. Maybe they are in too much pain. Maybe they are postsurgical and bed-bound. Maybe they do not have the skill. Maybe they are busy with other problems. Or maybe they are exceptional, but have learned the wisdom of delegating authority. While the goals of becoming exceptional are obviously worthwhile, some ordinary patients may feel shame, depression, guilt, and inadequacy at the very time when they need to expend their energies and emotions elsewhere in self-healing instead of self-loathing. Labeling patients "exceptional" or "unexceptional" is unfortunate, because every situation and every personality cannot fit into such a categorization. Patients will have dissimilar needs—and can be extraordinary or exceptional without being in total control in every area.

In some cases, the advocate will be more interested in the research than the patient is. It will depend on the patient's personality, the advocate's personality, and the circumstances of the illness.

• • •

David was not really motivated to do research, because he said he was "living his illness." He didn't want to read more than cursory information. He was not able to concentrate. He was too busy fighting the pain. He said he relied on me to fill him in on anything important.

Being highly motivated, I went to work. I contacted the American Cancer Society for all available material concerning David's illness. When I found out the name of David's chemotherapy regimen and where it was developed, I called Sloan-Kettering Hospital to find out the results of statistical studies dealing with his type of cancer and chemotherapy. David's brother found and copied dozens of articles from medical journals.

I read everything I could find, though I had a hard time understanding it all. I asked questions, learned about how David's cancer was "staged," and studied the possible present and future side effects of chemotherapy. I also researched alternative forms of therapy and healing techniques, going beyond the purely physical into psychological and spiritual healing, researching diet, meditation practices, prayer, and even psychic healing. I was open to looking at or examining every clue that crossed my path. I felt I had to do everything I could to maximize healing.

Reading all the research materials might have undermined David's spirit. The facts were indeed horrifying. While I did not lie, I withheld some information that could not possibly be helpful—

details like all that could go wrong, the stories of the failed cases, the seemingly unending list of putrid chemotherapy side effects. I did not want to add any needless fear or create unwarranted pessimism.

.   .   .

Sometimes, sharing research with patients can cause arguments.

.   .   .

Linda, a middle-aged high school counselor with advanced colon cancer, was not interested in the technical details or statistics of her illness. However, to feel more in control, her husband did extensive research—collecting studies and reports. Whenever he found a pertinent piece of news, he wanted to tell his wife, but she wouldn't listen. Her lack of interest caused frequent arguments between them.

Hillary, Linda's daughter-in-law and also a distant witness, learned about a treatment that was potentially more effective than the one her mother-in-law had chosen. She knew Linda didn't like to talk about her illness, and she knew her mother-in-law was happy with the treatment, despite the poor prognosis.

Hillary found herself in a tough spot. She wanted to relate her information, but she didn't want to cause further dissension in the family. She didn't want to upset her mother-in-law, yet she found she did not want to ignore the news of the possible alternative treatment. Hillary was sure she could not live with the guilt if this information could save her mother-in-law.

She finally solved her dilemma by calling Linda's brother, a physician. She told him about her research, suggested he check it out and tell his sister. He did this.

This solution satisfied Hillary and protected her from family discord. Linda didn't change treatments. She died a few months later. In retrospect, it is clear that no new treatment would have saved her. In this case, the decision about treatment was made by Linda, as it should have been, because she was able to be in

*control. On the other hand, her family—who acted as advocates—
did all they could to help her; the result was that they felt no guilt.*

• • •

In both cases, the advocates clearly needed to do research. However,
from these examples, advocates should learn to be sensitive to patients'
wishes. Some patients cope by not wanting to hear about the technical
details of their disease or condition.

The most logical starting place for getting information about the
illness is the family doctor, the attending physician at the hospital,
or the surgeon, if one is involved. Be aware that certain questions are
easier to answer than others. Questions about the emotional impact
of an illness on a patient may be tough for a physician who is chiefly
technologically oriented and who does not know the patient personally.
It is also difficult for doctors to answer questions about prognosis,
though they are important questions to pose. Most likely, answers about
prognosis will be a kind of educated guess, based upon statistics.
However, statistical information is limited; numbers can be manipulated
and viewed from many perspectives. Physicians will often feel uncomfortable providing an answer with confidence, because what the future
holds for an individual is so unpredictable.

While the doctor explains the patient's condition, ask to see a model
or a diagram to help visualize the affected body part or system. Also
ask for explanations for all medical terms that are not common. For
those outside the medical profession, unfamiliarity with medical
vocabulary is almost universal. Some terms are not even contained
in standard dictionaries. Take notes, ask questions to insure understanding, request illness-related informational handouts, summarize
the pertinent details of the discussion, and, at the end of the conference, make plans for the next steps, confirming what the patient
will be doing until the next conference with the doctor.

Communications with physicians about medical issues can be
potentially quite confusing and frustrating.

• • •

*Elizabeth, a woman in her middle 30s, was having difficulty getting
pregnant. She went to an infertility specialist, and then spoke to Doug.*

Elizabeth sat on the sofa and looked across the room. "The infertility specialists are not known for their humor any more than the rest of you doctors," she said ruefully.

"I was dressed in a paper garment. I had just finished a whole day of complicated tests when the doctor decided that it was time to explain their outcome and the next steps to take.

"I thought that I was ahead of the game. I'd brought a friend along, because I knew that I'd be in no shape to understand him when he started in about how the adrenal was connected to the thyroid and the hypothalamic-pituitary axis, blah, blah, blah."

She shifted her position to emphasize, "That miserable s.o.b. I hate him. There I was in this paper towel. I asked him to give me a chance to put my clothes on, and invite my friend to come in. I told him I wanted her with me so she could hear what he had to explain to me.

"Do you know what he said? He asked me if I had a hearing problem!

"You doctors are really something. You explain all this medical mumbo jumbo to a patient who is scared, tired, and nervous. The patient says, 'I don't understand. Would you please tell me again?' And all you guys do is use the same words, but say them louder."

• • •

If communications between the patient, advocate, and a given health-care professional are difficult, find a different professional whose communication style is more comprehensible. Not a minor issue, relaying information and directions is key to a patient's health. Similarly, physicians should be comfortable with patients' having advocates available for care and support. If doctors are not comfortable with the arrangement, a more compatible patient-doctor fit should be found, if possible.

Unfortunately, communication with health-care professionals is not always easy. Many physicians are harried, curt, or short-tempered. Unrealistically, they may expect patients and advocates to comprehend their explanations and instructions immediately, somehow divining their meanings, when, in fact, doing this is often difficult for the lay person. If more information is needed about the illness, and the doctor is the right professional for the patient, there are other ways to find information.

Independent of asking the patients' doctors, there are a number of strategies available for seeking out information. Here are some suggestions:

- Ask the attending physician or a nurse to recommend a social worker or medical librarian, if the patient is in the hospital. A phone-call authorization will help gain access to other resources.
- Network by asking family members, friends, or colleagues if they know someome who is a doctor, nurse, or social worker who can provide extra information or physician referrals for second opinions.
- Consult with local pharmacists for information about medications.
- Contact the American Medical Association and other professional groups like the American Cancer Society or the AIDS Action Committee in addition to using the local library and medical society.
- Call the state Office for the Aging, or the local area Agency on Aging for issues and problems related to senior citizens.
- Review available health books and references in the library or in bookstores.
- Investigate alternative therapies and medicines. Explore a diversity of healing ideas and options by reading, visiting health food stores, or calling alternative healers. Small, alternative newspapers often list local holistic treatment centers and practitioners.

Having an outline of issues and questions will help organize research, planning, and the problem-solving process for both the patient and the witness. The following list suggests information a patient is likely to need.

Information about Diagnosis

- What are the technical and lay explanations of the illness?
- What is the accuracy of diagnosis?
- Is there an approximate timetable of the illness? Are there expected acute or chronic phases of the illness?
- What are the short-term and long-term effects of the illness?
- What is the prognosis?
- Is there a need for additional consultants or specialists?

Treatment

- What are the benefits and risks of the most effective treatment: statistical evidence, best and worst outcome, expected outcome considering patient's age, medical history, and physical condition?
- What are the recommended treatment options, with their prognoses—their plan and their rate of success, chances of stabilization, improvement, cure?
- Are there alternative treatment options? Explore the treatment plans, and their rate of success. Can alternative treatments be used as a secondary treatment in conjunction with the primary recommended treatment? Are the alternative treatments covered by insurance? What is their expense?
- What is available to control pain or discomfort from the effects of treatment?
- What is the wisdom or harm of waiting to initiate treatment?
- What is the surgical procedure: the surgery's process and goal, patient's preparation and anesthesia, recovery room time, approximate time in the hospital?
- What happens if surgery is delayed or rejected?
- Are there any problems to be expected with a patient's compliance to treatment?

Medication

- What are the types of medication needed: their names, purposes or goals, effectiveness?
- Are there any generic medications available?
- What is administration—the dosage and timing—for each medication?
- What are the normal and the dangerous side effects of medication? What can be done about them?
- Are there foods, drinks, medicines, or activities to be avoided or encouraged?
- How can medication go wrong: drug interactions, and so on?
- When is the suggested time to stop medication? What is the timetable for results?
- Are there articles, studies, or written information on the drug?

Testing

- What is the reason for the test: diagnosis, determining prognosis, and/or choice of treatment?
- Are there alternative and reliable tests that are less invasive, less strenuous, or less expensive?
- What are the risks of the test?
- What is the best timing for the test—time of day, risks or benefits of delaying the test?
- What is the preparation for testing—food, liquids, how to handle current medication being used?
- What is the meaning of test results?
- Is there a need for verification of results or repetition of tests at a later date?
- Are there follow-up procedures if the test is negative or positive?

Care

- What are the problems the patient might need help with during treatment?
- Are there dietary restrictions, suggestions, limitations?
- What kind of exercise is suggested: how much, how often?
- Will there be special needs for sleep or rest?
- What are the explanations and reasons for restrictions on physical, emotional or social behaviors?
- What is the emotional impact of surgery, treatment, medication, illness?
- What are the expected needs for continued outpatient care and/or visiting nurses?

Resources for the Patient and Advocate

- What are the local, state, and national organizations, and hot lines dealing with the specific illness?
- Where are the local institutions: hospitals (closest emergency room), hospice centers, nursing homes, walk-in medical center, closest pharmacy, closest twenty-four-hour pharmacy?

- Who are the medical specialists, physicians, counselors, social workers, home-care consultants, visiting nurses, alternative therapy practitioners, accountants, insurance agents who will help?
- Are there any books, medical studies, articles that will be useful?
- Are there local support groups for the patient and the witness?
- Is there any patient with the same illness who can be a support or positive role model?

In sum, researching the physical, social, emotional, and financial impacts of the medical illness on the individual and family, and identifying resources to handle all illness-related issues or problems, may be one of the more concrete and tangible means of providing patient support.

Assuming that the patient and advocate/researcher are acting as a team, they may want to meet with trusted friends or family to discuss care and treatment options. Alternatively, the patient may need time alone to process information. Advocates can aid the patients to explore which treatments are best for the patients' health, comfort, and well-being, but ultimately patients, if capable, must choose what is right for them.

The patient may choose not to accept treatment of any kind, allowing disease and possibly death to proceed naturally—without technological intervention.

. . .

Reinhart, a 47-year-old man with serious heart disease, discussed his options. It was likely his next heart attack would be his last one.

"My brother died in Viet Nam. He was 22 years old. He was shot in the head. Died just like that." He snapped his fingers. "It was his time.

"My father died at 62. My mother's time was 65. She was sick with diabetes and kidney disease. She was sick, and it was her time."

He paused. "A heart transplant. It's expensive and risky. I don't know if I want it. If I have two years or five, maybe I should just live out my time. It's hard to know what's right. Maybe it's my time. My wife's strong. My kids are almost grown. They will adjust.

"I don't want to spend my time in a fancy hospital. None of us are immortal. I can't see draining my family's resources by going through heroic medical procedures."

Reinhart opted against a heart transplant. His family respected his wishes.

·   ·   ·

This option may create complex ethical and emotional dilemmas for witnesses. If the patient is cognizant, and competent, *and* has chosen to refuse actively any treatment, advocates can only express their opinion. Most likely, the patient will encounter great resistance from friends, family members, and the medical profession. However, advocates should try to give as much emotional support to the patient as they can and respect the patient's decision, though this may be difficult.

If the patient is in a coma—or incapacitated in any other way—in the hospital, the situation becomes much more complicated by hospital and governmental laws and regulations if no medical directive has been given by the patient about life support systems and resuscitation. New laws mandating medical directives may ease this dilemma if the patient has made choices before being admitted to the hospital (though surely unanticipated problems and special circumstances may still arise). The decision to continue life support systems can become a legal and public battle and, in fact, go *against* what the patient may have wished and what the family desires, if no prior living will, medical directive, or durable power of attorney has been signed. It is, therefore, a good idea for all people—patients and witnesses alike—to take care of this business before it is too late to make a choice.

DEALING WITH MEDICAL PERSONNEL

Choosing the Doctor

Advocates should try to convince patients that it is in their own interests to be happy and confident about their choice of doctors. Patients' faith and belief in a doctor's ability can contribute to their healing.

The *American Medical Association Family Medical Guide* suggests physicians should be well-trained, competent, accessible, organized, compassionate, and ethical with a good reputation, an acceptable hospital association, and with Board certification. The editors also suggest thinking about personal preferences, for example, whether there is a preference for a male or female doctor, or a physician who is older or younger.

Some physicians are mainly technicians; some physicians are humanists as well. Some physicians are politely adroit; others have the personality of a proverbial barn door. During the first visit, witnesses should be able to determine if the physician is a good "fit."

Physicians who seem to be primarily "technicians" are often quite accomplished and gifted in their technological skills, but may not be as talented as others in comprehending emotions. Everyone is susceptible to crankiness; however, detached, gruff, or insensitive behavior is potentially irritating to the patient and witness.

• • •

At a party celebrating the cancer remission of a mutual friend, I met an emergency room physician who seemed to fit a stereotypical portrait of a "technician." We talked about his work and his views about medicine.

He said if it were up to him, he would abolish intensive care units. He argued that because the cost was too high for each person, the "greater good" would be better served if the money were put into research.

I then asked him what he would do if his mother needed intensive care after a heart attack.

This upset him. He accused me of getting personal.

Getting personal was not what he was interested in at all. When I backed off and asked him about his work, he told me that talking to patients and their families was the most dreaded part of his job. His fascination, rather, was with science. His patients' recoveries or demises were seen as wins or losses. He said he rarely felt sadness.

• • •

Some might argue that "technicians" do not make the best "healers." Norman Cousins described the ideal doctor as one who should provide "responsible reassurance"; identify the causes of illness; educate the patient about the healing and regenerative qualities of the human body; emphasize that no one can make a precise forecast, that remissions are possible; stress the challenge of illness; identify resources—psychological, emotional, physiological; present the current medical treatment, and avoid false hope or creating false fears.

On occasion, advocates and patients will wish to be assured that the doctor is indeed human and does feel pain and sorrow. Other times, perhaps when on the operating table, advocates and patients will want to be sure that their doctors have icewater flowing in their veins and will make no mistakes even though their hands are bloody up to their elbows. However, even the best of medical care providers, the humanists who are also skilled technicians, often need to be professionally "detached" in their own fashion, using mental boundaries that limit and define their investment of emotional energy with each individual patient. This is one way physicians cope with the continuous assault of illness in their lives.

Patients—on occasion along with witnesses—must decide for themselves what is most important. Sometimes the technician's skills will be more important than attending the patient's emotional needs. If the patient needs emotional support, it is possible to ask the physician for a reference to a colleague or support group that will help the patient cope with the emotional issues of the illness. Physicians may be able to get a counselor or psychiatric consultation for the patient arranged the same day of the request, if there is an immediate need. Or, if necessary, find a technician who is a humanist as well.

Forging an equal partnership between patient and doctor is not easy. In some cases, patients can be subtly foiled in their attempts to be in control of their medical decisions.

.   .   .

Kathy, the 50-year-old wife of a heterosexual man who contracted HIV (the human immunodeficiency virus) during a blood transfusion, had been HIV-positive and was now beginning to get sick. Her

*T-cell counts were worsening, along with the frequency of minor in-
fections. One other symptom of the increasing severity of her illness
was that her skin was bothering her.*

*John—a friend of hers who was an AIDS Buddy, a volunteer
caregiver for people in various stages of the illness—told her it looked
as though she had Kaposi's sarcoma lesions, a condition often affect-
ing AIDS patients.*

*She went to her doctor, asking for a diagnosis and some treat-
ment. She had learned Kaposi's sarcoma was being relieved by some
new medicines.*

*Her doctor snapped at her, "Women do not get Kaposi's sar-
coma," as if the issue were shut.*

*As her friend and advocate, John suggested that she find another
doctor. She went for treatment to another physician, who accurately
diagnosed her Kaposi's sarcoma, and her conversion to AIDS, the
severe manifestation of the HIV infection.*

*In another illustration, Eric and Adam, a gay couple in their mid-40s
who had been together for over 10 years, went to the doctor for their
regular checkup. They had used this same doctor for years.*

*The doctor told them the news. "Adam is HIV-positive. Eric
is not." He continued, "I have a group I want you to go to. It's a
support group for couples like you. You know, one infected, one not.
It's called the Discordant Couples Group."*

*He went on to say—with a hint of pride and familiarity—he
was able to pinpoint the moment Adam contracted the virus. While
Eric puzzled about this comment, Adam suddenly spoke up, "I'm
hungry. I think I have to leave now."*

*Eric was pleased at Adam's taking the news so well, thinking
that if he was hungry, he was coping admirably. But once outside,
Adam told Eric what he really felt. "I want no part of any group
called the Discordant Couples Group, no matter what," he said.
"Any group that could be so stupid as to call themselves that is
not worth going to. We're not discordant, and we don't want to
become that way in the future, either."*

*Eric agreed, adding, "I also wonder how he knew when you
became HIV-positive. He may think he knows his statistics, but that
doesn't account for the many people who lie when it comes to relating*

their sexual history. The people who give lip-service to safe sex are the same people who are part of the statistics."

Soon after the visit, they went out for a drink. They talked and cried. They decided to change their doctor to one who was an AIDS specialist. He was more sensitive to their needs.

In both cases, the patients were disturbed by their doctors' arrogant certainty and lack of humility in their opinions and suggestions.

Interestingly, both patients chose not to confront their doctors directly, and both were subsequently advised by their advocates, who listened to them ventilate about perceived offenses in the course of their treatment and persuaded them to try another physician. Both patients changed doctors.

They were much happier when they found physicians with whom they were more compatible in communication, philosophy, and style.

． ● ●

If a patient does not like or has lost faith in the physician, help the patient to explore options. For those patients associated with HMOs, control over choice of doctors is limited, but not impossible. Changing physicians is a delicate decision based on many factors, including the nature and personality of the patient, and the medical personnel involved. If, after consideration, it is clear that there is so much unhappiness with a given working relationship that a change in medical personnel is necessary, find a more suitable physician. Ask friends first for recommendations, or if in a hospital, ask the nurses whom they would recommend or use themselves. Or, call a local medical society.

Seeking Out a Second Opinion

Seeking a second opinion is becoming more routine, with many insurance companies now mandating it before any major medical intervention. It is, nonetheless, a good idea in all critical or life-threatening cases, and before any non-emergency invasive procedure.

· · ·

Jan, a young professional woman in her 30s, noticed an enlarged lymph node in her armpit. The doctors at her HMO all concluded that she needed surgery: the node had to be removed. Frightened, Jan called a friend, who suggested that she try getting a second opinion from her previous family doctor outside the HMO. Her old family doctor then discovered she had a sinus infection, undetected by her other doctors.

Although the doctor was not sure the two were connected, she told Jan she should treat the sinus infection first, and then wait and see what happened with the enlarged node.

Sure enough, when the infection disappeared, the enlarged lymph node shrunk. The woman did not need the surgery, and her family physician learned something new about lymph nodes.

· · ·

A second opinion can be sought through the primary physician, who is aware of test results and preliminary diagnosis and has questions that should be asked of the consulting physician. When the primary physician chooses the consultant, there is a risk that the second doctor, having been suggested by the first, will support the first physician's interpretations, because of professional loyalty or friendship. A second opinion by an unassociated doctor may be more advantageous. In knowing as little about the case as possible, the doctor may offer a new, unprejudiced, and unbiased view. With the latter choice, discussing this option with the first physician is an appropriate courtesy. Few physicians turn down a chance to be informed by a second opinion.

In seeking a second opinion, there is a danger of offending the first attending physician, even though the aim is to make an informed decision. Sometimes physicians complain that the patient is lacking in trust. Many patients are quite sensitive to their doctor's feelings, and thus hesitate to get a second opinion, because they fear the doctor's anger and rejection. However, if patients—or advocates—calmly explain their need for additional information and express their respect for their doctor, patients should be able to maintain a positive relationship with their doctors and take the right medical action.

When the second opinion is in direct opposition to the first, the patient is the ultimate arbiter. The only exception to this situation is when the patient is unable to make rational decisions. It is possible to seek out a third opinion, or to keep getting opinions, until the patient is satisfied. Often the choice becomes intuitive. One doctor or one treatment plan will feel better, make more sense, or seem more comfortable. The patient must have trust in the doctor personally as a human being and professionally as a diagnostician. Very rarely will the patient's intuition be wrong.

Patients' Rights

The Patient's Bill of Rights, written by the American Hospital Association, allows patients and their families access to information about diagnosis, treatment, and prognosis. While researching the patient's illness or while caregiving during the treatment process, questions might come up about the advocate's rights to information concerning the patient. According to the Hippocratic oath, physicians have an allegiance first and foremost to their patients. Technically, patients have a right to a copy of the data in their hospital medical chart and medical files—the physician's record or file of the patient, which is owned by the doctor or the institution. Most physicians are, thus, comfortable with the idea of reviewing the information with the patient, blood relatives, or a spouse, but not necessarily with the nonconventionally related advocate, because of the patient-doctor rules of confidentiality and privacy. **Patients, therefore, will need to communicate with the physician if they wish advocates to have access to information concerning their medical care.**

For the most part, physicians feel comfortable sharing information with their patients' biological families. This preference can cause conflicts for the patient's friends, colleagues, and lovers, who are sometimes unfortunately regarded as "outsiders." The patient's immediate social network—those who are sometimes the real "family" to the patient—might need to anticipate this problem and work harder to establish a relationship with the health-care professionals involved. Sometimes, however, caregivers can encounter situations they might not anticipate.

. . .

Jane complained, "It is unbelievable. She's in one of the best hospitals in the world, and we can't get any information from them!

"Remember that I told you this wonderful neighbor of mine lost her husband recently? We were all in Boston for a special dinner, and she had chest pains. We took her to this big city hospital, and they put her in the ICU.

"When we asked to see her, they wouldn't let us. They have this rule that only family can visit.

"Well, her husband is dead, and all the kids live hundreds of miles away. We had to call the son to call the doctor. Then we called him back to get the news thirdhand.

"The next day, I visited the hospital and said I was her daughter. What were they going to do? Tell me I'm a liar? How can they make such stupid rules?"

. . .

To prevent this type of complicated situation, advocates who are not close family members might want to discuss the option of getting a durable power of attorney for health care from the patient. This would allow the advocate to become a proxy or agent to make decisions the patient desires even if incapacitated or otherwise unable. Usually, a legal consultation is appropriate before this step is taken.

When the concept and role of "primary witness" becomes more widely understood, perhaps this problem will get easier. However, sometimes even family members have difficulty getting information, as in the dilemma outlined in this case study.

. . .

Grace, a divorced mother of two, brought her six-year-old son, Paul, into the hospital for a hernia operation. Right before the operation, Grace saw the surgeon and pleasantly wished him good luck. "I don't need luck," he said.

Grace felt put off by his arrogance, but said nothing.

After the operation, when Paul was recovering in his hospital room, he experienced severe vomiting and nausea. Grace concluded it was a bad reaction to the anesthetic.

When Grace asked the anesthesiologist the name of the anesthetic, so her son could avoid repeating this bad reaction, the anesthesiologist turned his back to her and walked away, refusing to give her any specific information. "It's not important," he said.

Grace asked the surgeon. He said he didn't know. Then she asked the assistant anesthesiologist who also refused to tell her.

After bringing Paul home, Grace continued her quest to discover the name of the offending drug. The anesthesiologist wouldn't return her calls, so she called the nursing department. The head nurse spoke to her and said the information was in the computer and in Paul's medical history.

Grace said, "I am his medical history. I'm his mother. What if I'm in another city?"

The head nurse said she would get the anesthesiologist to call.

The anesthesiologist called her back, and he told her he gave her son a "general" anesthetic.

When Grace asked him to be more specific, he laughed at her. Finally, he told her names of some drugs, but admitted the records were not in front of him.

Grace finally called her family doctor. He called the surgeon and later related to her the specific types and amounts of anesthetic.

• • •

When rebuffed while trying to get information, especially when a patient's health has been compromised, advocates are likely to feel angry and frustrated. While certainly understandable, the challenge is—when confronting the patient's doctor about lack of information, or suspected medical misdiagnosis—to continue to speak clearly about what information is needed and why it is important in an unthreatening way. Witnesses will often find that using a family doctor to retrieve medical information from another specialist or consulting doctor is a path which more often leads to success.

Many people are intimidated by the authority of doctors. If patients don't feel capable of asserting their rights, they can conceivably be placed in medical jeopardy if they don't feel they can take control. Witnesses and patients alike need to remember patients have a right to refuse or delay treatment.

Suggestions for Successful Interactions

When a busy surgeon comes to discuss the results of a patient's operation, the surgeon may not have time for a lengthy conference, because other operations may be scheduled afterward. If more information is needed, ask to schedule a follow-up appointment. Likewise, in the hospital, catching doctors on rounds can be a challenge. The doctor may be facing unpredictable delays due to emergencies, surgery, or bloated schedules with other patients. To avoid frustration, call the physician's office or ask the nurses when to expect the physician. Be there, and then expect delays. If the doctor is unable to answer questions at that time, ask for an appointment. Before an emergency occurs, find out how best to reach physicians by discussing their communication policies. Some doctors have office policy handouts that discuss this.

To get the clearest response from the physician, prepare questions ahead of time. If the witness does not know the doctor well, it is a good idea to take time for an introduction, explaining the relationship to the patient and why the witness—in addition to the patient—needs to get questions answered. Try to ask questions and approach the doctor dispassionately. It may be hard to be calm and rational when worried or angry, but if witnesses are not in control, they may receive "emotional" rather than rational responses to questions or complaints.

When dealing with obviously ill-tempered medical professionals, digress and try a sensitive approach, asking how they are. Acknowledging their state of being might make them more open. Medical staff often feel underappreciated. Small courtesies may surprise and relax them.

However, if advocates sense they are still not communicating adequately with the physician or with any other medical personnel, they might have to confront the offending person, and politely insist on what is needed. Or, it is possible to back off, apologize, and attempt to start all over again. Apologizing can be effective in re-establishing the reality that the witness is there to work together with the medical staff. Apologizing does take energy and concentration—qualities witnesses might find in short supply during stressful or angry situations—but it is often worth the attempt. If tired and unable to apologize, try clarifying the information at another time, or enlist someone else to help.

Understanding the Physician's Point of View

To facilitate cooperation, communication, and negotiation in the doctor-patient-witness relationship, understanding life from a physician's point of view can be helpful. Society, patients, and advocates often place unrealistic expectations on the doctor as healer—the curer of *all* ailments, physical and psychological—when being that is simply not possible at our stage of medical knowledge. The misconception about medical power is understandable. Doctors are trained to "act" the role of a physician, inspiring trust and confidence. Even doctors' uniforms or "costumes" contribute to the persona, as can their language, manner, gesture, and tone of voice.

Physicians are not free of worry: economic problems, institutional pressures, or personal conflicts abound. In running their businesses, they confront such complicating factors as the bureaucracy of the Medicare system, state systems of support, individual insurance companies, running an office, and general administration. In their practices, they often encounter challenging patients who upset them. In an article in the *New England Journal of Medicine*, James E. Groves, M.D., identified and defined four types of patients that physicians dread to treat:

1. **dependent clingers**: patients who tax a doctor's stamina by excessive demands of attention and affection;
2. **entitled demanders**: patients who intimidate and insult the doctor, often threatening nonpayment or litigation;
3. **manipulative help-rejecters**: patients who are so unrealistically pessimistic that they are sure no treatment regimen will help;
4. **self-destructive deniers**: patients who glory in self-destructive and suicidal behavior.

Not having been taught how to cope with patients who have difficult personalities, Groves said that doctors can have feelings of guilt, aversion, avoidance, malice, and exasperation, thus adding the burden of working through unwanted or negative feelings to the heavy technical burdens of their daily practice.

It is also sometimes a challenge for doctors to work with some witnesses. Patient advocates who take a long time to deliberate about the right medical action—in their earnest efforts to make the right decision—can cause a patient to suffer. A kidney specialist related this story.

·　　·　　·

Nadine, an 84-year-old woman in pain, was brought into the hospital by her daughter, Alice. She was easily diagnosed by her doctor as having a stomach abscess, which needed to be drained. Nadine was unable to talk.

The attending physician explained to Alice that there were two possible courses of action to drain the abscess—a procedure using a tube or another using surgery. Either procedure required quick action. Nadine was in severe pain.

Alice didn't know what to do, so she started making calls. It took her 12 hours to satisfy her need to do the proper research to make a decision.

The original doctor, exasperated over having to wait, turned the surgery over to another doctor, who operated at midnight. Nadine survived the operation.

·　　·　　·

The doctors in this illustration both worried about the patient advocate's interfering with their job and art. They questioned the antagonism that resulted in this type of transaction. Should physicians be thwarted in treating their patients by delays that witnesses might demand? What happens to the patient in the process? Does this type of delay imply a lack of trust in physicians, and if so, how can they perform their work with the tension this lack of trust produces? On the other hand, though the doctors have a compelling argument about

117

being given the time, freedom, and space needed to practice their art properly, their canvas is a loved one's body. What is clear, however, is that it is imperative that all parties place the patient's needs first.

In order to improve and rebalance doctor-patient-witness relationships, witnesses and patients need to demystify doctors. The "godlike" images of a doctor are fading. Though patients and witnesses want doctors to be perfect, many already know that physicians are mortal, fallible, and sometimes impatient and cranky. For physicians—and all medical personnel—the emotional impact of interacting with sick people all day is enormous. There are also times when physicians act with great courage and integrity. With the AIDS epidemic, some doctors face difficult moral, political, ethical, and personal dilemmas when they treat their patients. Some risk infection to themselves—and their families—despite precautionary measures.

•　　•　　•

Mark, 40, an orthopedic surgeon in California, began a long and difficult treatment with John, an HIV-positive patient, when a plastic surgeon referred the case to him.

John had been in a motor vehicle accident. An uninsured driver smashed into him on his motor scooter, causing John to lose his leg below the knee and sustain a hip joint and femur fracture. John was overweight, in a wheelchair, and his other hip was arthritic. He couldn't walk. He also had no medical insurance.

Mark devised a medical plan designed to get John walking again. He needed two operations: a hip replacement and another operation to repair the poorly healed hip and thigh fracture.

Mark knew the risks that surgery would pose to the entire surgical team. In the hip replacement surgery, there would be aerosolized blood and bone in the air from the use of power equipment needed in the procedure. During the operation, the whole team would wear "space suits" with built-in air filters, and special, reinforced gloves.

Though the operation went well without any complications to the patient, Mark became contaminated. His glove was cut, and he received multiple cuts on his hand. John's blood had splattered onto his bare skin.

Mark began to lose sleep worrying. He had a wife and two young children who depended on him, and there was another big surgery to perform on John. Mark became increasingly nervous, because it, too, was a risky and long operation. There would be hardware removal, bone fragments, and more potential for cuts.

Mark first talked to his wife. She was against his performing the operation. She understood his moral reasons, yet she was terrified. Her health was at risk.

There was also a bit of medical administrative "craziness" she didn't understand. A recent ruling disallowed any HIV-positive physician to operate on patients. For most, this is a sensible ruling, but it also eliminated a possible practical solution to Mark's dilemma. One of Mark's colleagues, an orthopedic surgeon with HIV, could not take over the case. To Mark and his wife, it made some sense that someone with HIV could operate on an HIV-infected patient, without increasing any further risk. However, with this option closed, this ruling also meant that if Mark became HIV-positive from taking on John's surgery, he could realistically expect to lose his job and his life. On the other hand, it was unethical to deny a patient's treatment, not to mention that Mark would be in legal jeopardy if he refused to treat John.

Mark talked openly to John about how he was feeling. He told him about his nervousness and fears about risking his own health. John, in turn, was sympathetic. He understood Mark's risk to his family; John said he didn't want to do anything to hurt them. Mark told John that he needed the surgery, that other doctors would not touch his case, and that he would consent to do the surgery, despite his reservations.

Mark always knew he would proceed with John's treatment. "I couldn't live with a decision not to operate. I couldn't accept that, because I knew I could fix him. I could make him walk." As a doctor, he also admitted to the pride and the power of achievement he feels when he practices his craft. It is why, he says, he wanted to become a doctor in the first place.

Mark performed the second operation, which lasted five hours. There were many parts to the operation, and each phase went well. Because of the surgery, John was able to walk; however, because of his weakened physical condition with HIV, there were a couple of postsurgical complications: a blood clot and a wound infection. Both *were handled successfully for John, but these had more consequences for Mark, who had to go through the political pressure of peer review.*

Each patient complication automatically receives a peer review, and for both, Mark was called in for academic questioning. However, all physicians involved in the case supported Mark with letters and testimony and defended him strenuously. Even John wrote the chief of medical staff and the executive committee of the hospital about his treatment, because his ability to walk surpassed any surgical discomfort. Any question of Mark's mishandling the case was squelched, but Mark was uncomfortable during the process.

A year after the operation, John developed AIDS symptoms, but both hips worked well, and he was still able to walk. Mark gets tested for HIV every six months and remains clear of the infection so far. He received no money for working on this case.

• • •

Physicians want to diminish pain and transform illness into health, but doing this is not always possible. This dilemma produces conflicts. Facing the expressed and unexpressed pressures of the patients and families who want the physician to cure or fix the impossible is difficult.

Placing importance on patient advocacy does not mean that all physicians are bad and need monitoring. There are many fine, caring physicians whose stories go untold. When people complain, they speak about the bad times.

In the process of both physicians' and witnesses' becoming sensitive to each others' needs, there will be times when doctors will feel abused by patient advocates demanding too much time, attention, or information, and advocates will feel neglected. **However, to maximize teamwork, advocates need to remember their goals are usually common with their physicians: to help the patient.** If the goals are not shared, it's time to find another doctor.

Creating Patient-Care Diaries

To help keep track of medical procedures, especially when patients are not able to or interested in doing this, advocates might want to organize a patient-care journal to help them supervise medical care.

Pertinent details of the diary might include: names and addresses of all physicians involved; dates of office visits; names and dates of all medical procedures and their outcomes; diagnosis; prognosis; treatment plan; lists of medications, their names, dosage, schedule, and potential and real side effects; outpatient care; national, state, and local resources; financial information; insurance policies and bills; research and literature about the illness or disease; and future important medical calendar dates—appointments, tests, examinations, and so on. In other words, the detailed story of the patient's illness and the research accumulated.

This journal may later become a valuable record of the patient's care or a ready reference for the future. For example, it is easy to forget names of the patient's consultants, and in the future, patients may want to find them or their records; also, a journal can be a health-protection resource by tracking the patient's use of medications. On-going research studies periodically reveal important information about medications, like previously unknown side effects or delayed complications of certain drugs.

AREAS OUTSIDE THE ADVOCATE'S RESPONSIBILITY

It is important to emphasize that patients have the final say in their treatment. Advocates should always respect the patient's wishes, especially when they are not in agreement.

Advocates do not bear sole responsibility for the patient's progress in the recovery or the outcome of the illness. The outcome is decided by a combination of factors, including, but not limited to the severity of the disease, the state of medicine, the skill of the medical team, the patient's physical shape, mental outlook, genes, and immunological system, and elements that are harder to pinpoint, like the patient's faith, luck, or unknown agents in the body or in the environment.

Some witnesses may harbor impossible personal expectations about what they can do for the patient. This desire can lead to an overpowering sense of guilt if there is failure. Yet advocates cannot wish their patients back to health, just as patients cannot will their illness away with positive thinking alone. Advocates are there to help in whatever way they can as contributors and participants—with limitations.

The level of advocacy will be different for each individual. One person may not be able to achieve all of the tasks outlined here. However, an active role as advocate might assure witnesses that they helped to maximize the healing process, and increased sensitivity to these issues will create better health care consumers.

CONCLUSION

It is no longer advisable to grant too much authority to the medical profession. Authority, power, and responsibility need to be put in a proper perspective: the patient is responsible, the advocate helps or takes over when the patient is not able, and the doctor is another part of a team effort. All participants must interact in a very complex system, and each must respect the need for balance among all members of the healing team.

The role of witness-as-advocate is still evolving. Witnesses should be prepared for some resistance, and perhaps for only a limited alliance with some doctors. This should not deter witnesses, however, if they remember that their goals are to get the best medical care and to maximize comfort and healing for patients.

Advocacy is an enormous task: devoting time and effort to the patient can be a full-time job, especially in addition to the responsibilities of a normal daily routine. For this reason, witnesses should consider getting help: delegating or sharing the authority of the advocacy position with friends or family members.

For witnesses in the advocate role, emotion occasionally will cloud reason. At the same time, emotion is often the heart of insight, invention, and resourcefulness. It may be inconceivable for witnesses to think that there may be something good for them in this role; however, life is filled with contradictions. Advocacy may bring rewards in addition to the frustrations. The act of selflessness brings gratification, and contributing caregiving time usually makes a patient's healing go smoother or faster. There is reason for witnesses to feel a sense of self-esteem and pride in caregiving—even if the job goes by unnoticed or without thanks.

5

THE ESSENCE OF CAREGIVING

The act of caring is the first true step in the power to heal.
– Phillip Moffit
The Power to Heal:
Ancient Arts and Modern Sciences

Relationship is both a psychological and spiritual opportunity when it is based on compassion—the shared bond of empathic understanding.
– Joan Borysenko
Guilt Is the Teacher,
Love Is the Lesson

Caregiv[ing]. . . begins by doing things for ill persons, but it turns into sharing the life they lead.
– Arthur Frank
At the Will of the Body

DEFINING CAREGIVING

The word *caregiver* is relatively new, and not yet included in most standard dictionaries. A check of its etymology shows that *caregiver*—meaning the person who provides care for the very young, sick, and elderly—made its first known appearance in 1970. Since then, the definition of caregiver has expanded to include "a person who helps *prevent* [emphasis added] or treat another person's disability" and "a parent, foster parent or medical or service professional who provides care to an infant or child."

These definitions can miss the heart and soul of caregiving, which also involves elements of shared participation, emotional connection, and a spoken or unspoken dialogue or exchange between the caregiver and the patient. In short, the essence of caregiving is *empathic partnership*.

Though caregiving includes the performance of traditional and alternative medical treatment, as well as patient advocacy, the focus in this chapter will be on the nature of empathic partnership and its role in caregiving.

THE ROLE OF EMPATHIC PARTNERSHIP

During an illness, patients often suffer from more than just the disease. Illness may cause patients to feel out of control, powerless, and depressed, and, in turn, may cause them loss of self-esteem and confidence. Additionally, an illness may force a drastic change in life-style.

While the patient's physical problems are being attended to by medical personnel, witnesses can monitor the patient's emotional well-being and help cope with the psychological trauma often brought on by an illness by working as an empathic partner. As an empathic partner, witnesses can function as teachers; outside sources of information; sounding boards or mirrors; allies or supporting coaches; or simply as persons to help the patient comply with recommended treatments. Sensitive, benevolent, and dedicated to enhancing the patient's well-being, an empathic partner can try to listen, understand the patient's emotions, and facilitate problem-solving. All of these activities help.

It is tempting to explain the role of empathic partnership as one of mere friendship. Close friends, indeed, are the ones who usually do act in this capacity. However, not all friends are capable of this special type of intimacy. There are many levels of friendship—from casual acquaintances to "soul mates" or deep friendships within love relationships—but this particular partnership requires patience, compassion, intellectual identification, and insight.

The two words *empathy* and *sympathy* are often used interchangeably, because they share the root word *pathos*, meaning feeling. However, the Greek word *empatheia* means affection, passion; whereas the Greek word *sympatheia* means like or fellow feeling. To make the distinction clearer, **knowing** what someone is feeling is empathy; **feeling** what someone is feeling is sympathy. Empathy is an "insightful awareness," understanding the meaning and significance of feelings, emotions, and behavior of another person. In contrast, sympathy may require no emotional ties to the individual with whom we feel sympathetic; yet to be sympathetic is actually to experience the same feeling another person is feeling, like crying along with a victim of tragedy. The emotions can feel authentic, and are often fatiguing. Feelings of concern or interest—commiseration, compassion, pity, tenderness, and condolence—can essentially remain internal in sympathy.

One of the most common definitions of empathy is to understand how someone else feels by imagining how we would feel in the same situation. This is not easy. Professor Eric Cassell writes about suffering:

> We can never truly experience another's distress. . . . Suffering is private. . . . To know the suffering of others demands an exhaustive understanding of what makes them the individuals they are—an awareness of when they feel themselves whole, threatened, or disintegrated.

Ironically, an advantage in empathic partnership is some emotional distance. Because the partner is a step away from the patient's experience, the partner is able to think, act, and view problems from a different perspective. This distance also allows empathic partners to conserve energy for more important tasks: to help patients to manage stress, to encourage relaxation, or to work on other therapeutic choices.

While maintenance of mental health begins with patients themselves, their state of mental health is no doubt influenced by the friends and family who surround them. Within the patient's personal network of relationships, there is a tremendous opportunity for witnesses and empathic partners to optimize the mental health—and thus physical health—of the patient.

The link between the witness as empathic partner and the patient's health and well-being is the essence of caregiving. Empathic partnership is an approach to the problem of managing the stress of illness in another and in oneself. The witness as empathic partner becomes an adjunct to the medical staff and the treatment, one who will concentrate on optimizing the patient's psychological well-being to conquer the illness, helping patients to free their minds to cooperate in healing.

Stress, hopelessness, and loneliness distract or preoccupy the mind. In helping to relieve these weights, the mind and body can concentrate more on healing itself. The fields of psychoneuroimmunology (PNI) and behavioral science have conclusively linked the body and the mind working in connection. Emotions affect the immunological system. Sandra Levy, a psychologist at the Pittsburgh Cancer Institute, found that the strength of natural-killer cells—one type of immune cell—is affected by psychological factors such as a person's perceived social support and ability to cope with stress. In the Mind/Body Clinic at New England Deaconess Hospital in Boston, the behavioral scientist Dr. Herbert Benson has proven that the patient can *contribute* to the process of healing by using the relaxation response—a behavioral therapy especially effective for illnesses involving high blood pressure, migraines, ulcers, insomnia, colitis, the immunological system, and pain.

Thus, the witness can supplement conventional medicine and encourage the patient's healing process by:

- providing social contact and positive emotional support;
- increasing the patient's self-confidence and esteem;
- finding the source of a patient's stress and attempting to help reduce its severity;
- helping a patient gain control over his or her environment;
- aiding the patient's psychological resilience;
- joining the patient in problem-solving;
- encouraging the patient to be assertive, express feelings, and take an active role in the management of treatment;
- teaching the patient meditation, the relaxation response, or the principles of guided imagery.

Additionally, witnesses can learn to monitor what they say and counsel others about the importance and the powerful effects of communication.

NOTE OF CAUTION: Most of this chapter is based on the assumption that the patient wants the witness to help in the healing process. Thus, before taking any action, it is wise to reassess the relationship with the patient. Find out if the patient really wants help through empathic partnership and is willing to share this aspect of living through, surviving, and growing from the experience with illness.

Not every patient will want witnesses to become intensely involved, or a desire for involvement may change from day to day. If patients prefer to work out their illness in solitude, respect their choice. They may feel better alone, or they may be empowering themselves by working through the process without any help. There may be many other reasons. Whatever the rationale, spoken or unspoken, don't push.

The process of empathic partnership—a *nonprofessional's* version of the patient's and therapist's relationship—might work only within certain conditions and limits:

- if the patient is physically capable—cogent, past any kinds of postsurgical traumas, and not heavily medicated—and wants to be involved in this special kind of intimate dialogue—*and asks for it*;
- if the witness recognizes the distinction between the roles of professional therapist and an empathic partner;
- if the witness does not "analyze" the patient or force change—avoiding making judgments and offering opinions without sufficient professional training;
- if the witness works with the patient as a guide and companion, but not as an authority figure;
- if the witness can genuinely feel "unconditional positive regard" for the patient, "prizing" the patient and accepting positive and negative feelings and experiences;
- and, if the witness is the right person to work with the patient.

The last condition is perhaps the most difficult to determine. Any friend, associate, or family member who has had a good and positive relationship with the patient will be able to improve the patient's psychological well-being—sometimes merely by a supportive presence. However, to investigate and discuss privately the patient's deep concerns, the empathic partner will most likely have had a history of intimacy with the patient: a relationship where problems and triumphs had been shared.

The empathic partner can be a primary, secondary, or distant caregiver. A patient must be comfortable with the person who acts in the capacity of empathic partner (and there may be more than one person). Patients need to be able to reveal the truth about their primary needs and wishes. Many times, this need means that a special close friend or relative plays the empathic role—as opposed to a primary caregiver, such as a spouse or parent. Sometimes the primary caregiver is too traumatized by the patient's illness or too close to the patient to have the needed distance. Sometimes there is no primary caregiver available.

. . .

Marilyn, an AIDS outreach volunteer, works with homeless, addicted, and runaway teenagers on the streets and in a neighborhood church. She provides counseling, anonymous HIV testing, education, but also a place to hang out, watch videos, listen to music, and eat pizza.

"It takes patience, perseverance, and creativity to educate teenagers about different and safe styles of intimacy. Sex is so life-affirming and natural that it's hard to layer in the threat of death.

"Often, teens don't understand the future implications of taking care of themselves. They deny they are at risk; they feel invincible and immortal. They want to be independent, yet they want to conform. They also use sex, drugs, alcohol, and other self-destructive behaviors to cope with the enormity of their problems. This, of course, does not improve their chances of survival.

"Many of these young adults are without parents. Some parents are dead, out of the picture, abusive, or don't care. These teenagers thus face problems of violence, identity, and self-esteem.

"We try to work with them in a nonjudgmental way, but so much damage has been done that it can be hard to make a difference in their lives. For example, there is Janet. She's 17, HIV-positive, her boyfriend died of AIDS, and her one child was taken away from her. We were talking together, and she said, 'I can't believe it about Magic Johnson getting HIV. He's such a good person.'

"I asked her, 'Does that mean you feel you're a bad person, because you got HIV?'

"Janet nodded.

"I told her, 'You wouldn't feel like you were bad if you got chicken pox. You have a virus.'

"Janet remained silent and unconvinced."

. . .

Empathic partnership is not always immediately successful or successful at all. Even if the witness appears to be the right person for patients to talk to, a patient might not want to open up to anyone. Some people with illnesses carry complex psychological or psychosocial problems. During an illness, patients also often act atypically; they can be hypersensitive, moody, or emotional. The writer Anatole Broyard, a patient with prostate cancer, wrote: "A critical illness is like a great permission, an authorization or absolving. It's all right for a threatened man to be romantic, even crazy, if he feels like it. All your life you think you have to hold back your craziness, but when you're sick you can let it out in all its garish colors."

Even when patients have agreed that they want help from empathic partners, they can still be antagonistic. People have needs to withdraw, to deny, to rebel, to be alone, or to be distracted. Witnesses cannot expect that every moment will be filled with an active, productive working relationship.

There are other potential problems. Each patient's experience of illness will be different and will require creative strategies of care, defying any formulaic approach. Witnesses may feel that they don't have the right answers—or any answers—to questions posed by patients. Many times, caregivers will need to be intuitive, creative, and adaptive in speech and action. Witnesses might encounter issues that are too complex for them to manage, and they might feel they need additional support, or a professional consultation to sort out the problem. However, even professionals are constantly challenged, as Doug found when he attempted to be an empathic partner with his father.

.   .   .

My father, Monie, declined into a state of lassitude, losing strength four years after his first heart attack. My father was suffering from complications of coronary artery disease: weakness from the medications, depression, and anxiety. My mother was distraught—narrowly avoiding auto accidents and forgetting two-thirds of what doctors and friends were telling her. My parents needed me, and I needed to be with them. I flew to Florida.

My father pleaded, "If these doctors can't help me, find out who I see next." Ashen, with his head sunk to his chest, he struggled to say, "I don't want to go on this way."

I became a medical advocate for my father. He listened to all the directions, but he did not take to suggestion. As gentle, kind, and honest as he was, he wanted to do whatever he wanted in his own way.

At the same time, I tried empathic partnership with him. We shared time and company, but I found a big gap. He did not share his feelings easily. I ran into the boundaries of a father-son relationship.

Of course, he had no energy by that time. He was not responding to any treatment. Nonetheless, because he was a reserved man, his privacy was the enemy of our intimacy.

I attempted to get closer, but the content of our conversations was superficial. I don't know if he had a fear of death. If he did, he didn't talk about it, and I chose not to confront him.

In essence, we struck a silent deal. I didn't invade him. In turn, he didn't reject me, openly disagree, or devalue me.

This was a peaceful empathic compromise. He and I had little unfinished business. He gave me permission to be successful. I gave him permission to die.

That was no small thing for him or me. He died about six months later.

•　　•　　•

Even if a witness may not be the right person to act as a close empathic partner, this chapter will help caregivers cultivate more compassion and strengthen their responsiveness to the patient. In learning how to become a more effective caregiver, witnesses will discover methods to:

- help learn about what the patient needs;
- learn how to listen to and observe the patient;
- become psychologically responsive, contributing to a patient's health—even in small ways;
- recognize and be sensitive to the balance of helping neither too much nor too little;

- appreciate the natural process of the patient's resistance to change;
- understand the importance of caring, yet empowering patients to solve their own problems.

THE PROCESS OF EMPATHIC PARTNERSHIP

The work of an empathic partner involves a process that is similar in many ways to the psychotherapeutic process. Many of us perform psychotherapeutic acts without being aware we are doing so. If we boost another's morale, if we help another look at a problem with a new vision, if our words comfort and renew another's spirit, we have performed a psychotherapeutic act of healing. Though not trained as a psychotherapist, the empathic partner can increase a patient's self-esteem or self-confidence and encourage and support the patient's competence. Michael F. Basch, a psychiatrist, defines a *psychotherapeutic transaction* as "an event where one of the individuals receives a new self-image, one that has a beneficial effect on his life, changing his feelings about himself and his behavior with others."

The most poetic and elegant definition of *psychotherapy* is "nurturing of the soul" derived from the Greek words *psyche*, meaning soul or mind, and *therapeia*, nursing or curing. Precisely defining psychotherapy is more complicated, considering there are now approximately 150 types of psychotherapeutic techniques, including psychoanalysis, Jungian, cognitive, and Gestalt therapies.

Psychotherapy is a kind of conversation or dialogue between two people. The difference between conversation and psychotherapy is that in psychotherapy there is a contractual agreement between a psychotherapist and a client. Generally, the two work together to diminish the client's suffering. Having been unsuccessful by mere will, introspection, or through the help of friends and relatives, the client, along with the therapist, attempts to change how he or she feels, thinks, or behaves.

Psychiatrists, psychotherapists, or psychologists guide their clients to look within themselves and to observe and to understand the patterns of behavior and thinking which motivate them. Basch suggests that "the underlying motivation for all behavior...is the striving for *order, competence and esteem*...it is a person's self-image or self-concept that furnishes both the potential and the limits of individual existence."

As patients decide which patterns of their behavior are inappropriate, unhealthy, unproductive, or limiting to their potential, therapists may help them to understand what types of stress trigger the patterns, help them to cope with their daily pressures, and consider alternatives in their behavior, thoughts, and feelings. Therapists thus *facilitate* patients to solve their problems. Basch contends the therapist does not "do anything *to* the patient," but investigates "*with* the patient what has gone wrong with his or her problem solving behavior and what the patient, not the therapist, may be able to do to make things better...the goal [being] to permit the patient to achieve the experience of competence."

During the process of therapy or change, there will be impediments to progress. Therapists call these opposing forces *defenses* and *resistances*. In other words, there will be days when the client wants to change, and days when the client does not *feel* like doing so. The therapist expects, acknowledges, and accepts this as part of the process.

Psychotherapy, then, is like any other learning process, more typically a gradual method of change and learning how to feel better. On occasion, there are blinding flashes of insight ("By golly, I never saw it that way before"), but much more commonly, it is "Oh God, we talked about that thirty-seven times already, and I'm still doing it the same way. I wonder if I'll ever learn."

In examining some aspects of empathic partnership that are often parallel or analogous to the psychotherapeutic process, the witness can extract and use some of its common sense, wisdom, and practices to help learn what a patient needs. The goal of a witness and psychotherapist, after all, is similar: to help a patient return to health.

ASPECTS OF EMPATHIC PARTNERSHIP

Setting the Stage for Intimacy

Though finding privacy may be difficult in a hospital setting or in the midst of family or friends, for a therapeutic transaction to occur—

like a heart-to-heart talk—privacy is necessary. When a patient goes to a therapist, the therapist attempts to provide a private, nurturing physical environment where, without distraction, the therapist and client can discuss and begin to understand the feelings, thoughts, and behaviors that are at issue. Like therapists, empathic partners need the right environment. Sometimes they need to ask others for privacy, plan for it, or create it, or occasionally they "make do" by "stealing" some moments. "Alone time" with patients—with no distractions, if possible—is crucial for the patients' relaxation and for the revelations of how they are *really* feeling. When their need for "acting" cheerful or brave is released, patients will be more able to reveal their needs during this time of intimacy. For example, in the following case, a patient revealed the cause of her tension with a nurse during a private moment.

•　　•　　•

In a quiet consulting session in a hospital room, a woman in her 50s suffering with lung cancer made a request. She asked Doug to tell her attending nurse to change her daily greeting. Each day, this young nurse began their day with a smiling "How are we today?"

Doug learned this patient disliked the greeting, because "we" made her think of the nurse and her health. She did not want to envy the nurse's obvious vitality. Nor did she want to be reminded of her own pain and disability first thing each morning. Insensitive behaviors are magnified when someone is ill.

When Doug told the nurse how her behavior affected the ailing woman, she easily changed her greeting to "hi," "hello," or "good morning." They liked each other better after this simple change.

•　　•　　•

Simple courtesies can help set the environment for intimacy. Bringing a gift—no matter how small—can be a material demonstration of care and intimacy, especially if the gift is meaningful to the patient. Bringing something to eat, something to read, a flower, or something the patient requested increases the patient's relaxation and self-esteem by the generosity and thoughtfulness of the witness.

Small acts of kindness also benefit more formal therapeutic alliances where—to make a session productive—the therapist tries to release or reduce the client's anxiety, though, in general, there is no tradition of gift-giving between therapist and client. Here is an example of how Doug intuitively created a supportive milieu for one of his patients.

· · ·

Before a session with a patient began, Doug craved a doughnut. He asked his next patient if she also wanted one. Doug knew this patient had suffered great difficulty with feeling properly nurtured by herself and within her family. She agreed, asking for a chocolate doughnut.

At the store, Doug wondered if the Boston cream chocolate-covered doughnut would be okay. It was the biggest, and he figured that maybe giving her the biggest doughnut would be right. When he gave her the doughnut, she told him it was her favorite kind and visibly lost much of the tension that was observable in her face.

The session that followed was one of the most productive and easy sessions they had shared in over two and a half years.

· · ·

Thus, creating a nurturing environment—where one feels filled instead of depleted, good instead of bad, liked rather than rejected—enables the work of healing.

Learning What the Patient Needs: Asking Questions and Listening for Answers

For the empathic partner, conversation is the equivalent of the psychotherapist's search for diagnosis and information, an opportunity to understand how the patient feels and what the patient needs. If witnesses have a history of intimacy with the patient that would not make probing awkward, encourage the patient to go beyond the mechanics of the illness. Together, try to enter the realm of feelings where fears can be explored as well as hopes and needs: listen to the process of coping and try to understand the impact of change as a result of illness.

> For a seriously sick person, opening up your consciousness to others is like the bleeding doctors used to recommend to reduce the pressure....What a critically ill person needs above all is to be understood. Dying is a misunderstanding you have to get straightened out before you go. And you can't be understood, your situation can't be appreciated, until your family and friends, staring at you with an embarrassed love, come to know, with an intimate, absolute knowledge, what your illness is like.
>
> – Anatole Broyard

Sometimes empathic partners will know what specific questions to ask patients to allow this interchange. At other times, witnesses who act in this role will be stuck, not knowing how to approach the patient. Therapists often use open-ended questions to discover what a client thinks is important. To facilitate dialogue, empathic partners, too, might want to try open-ended questions, because they give people great range in choosing their responses. "How you are feeling?" will produce more of an answer than the closed question "Do you still have a headache?" which could be simply answered yes or no. Other good examples of open-ended questions or queries are:

- How can I help you?
- What do you need?
- What can I do for you?
- Tell me what's wrong.
- Tell me what's bothering you.
- Tell me what's on your mind.

Once the questions are asked, listening carefully to the answers is crucial to understand and learn more about the patient's needs. Therapists try to listen to what the client is not addressing directly, paying attention and listening carefully for what is going on between the lines, the underlying meanings of the dialogue, and what is left unsaid. Thus, while listening, the therapist—like the witness—grapples with the complexity of conversation and looks for the levels beneath consciousness. Often, people can be indirect, masking what they are thinking and feeling, and saying things that they don't intend.

Sometimes, empathic partners will find the subtext apparent to them. "I don't want to go out" may mean "I don't want to spend time with your brother." Or, "Go away" may mean "I don't want to talk about my illness anymore." If the subtext is not apparent and witnesses are not satisfied with the answer to an open-ended question, they can follow up by trying more specific questions like "What do you mean, you don't want to go out?" or "Do you really want me to leave?"

Listening is not a passive enterprise. In the process of our education, rarely have we been taught how to listen. When Ralph G. Nichols and Leonard A. Stevens tested listening skills, they learned that the average person remembers only about half of what was heard. According to their study, attention wanders while one is listening, often because of boredom. This apparent lapse in concentration occurs because we are capable of thinking faster than people normally speak. To improve listening skills—redirecting the "spare time" available when our minds wander during a conversation—Nichols and Stevens suggest that the listener:

- try to anticipate the speaker's thoughts;
- judge whether the speaker's arguments are compelling, convincing, or complete;
- mentally summarize the speaker's thoughts;
- pay attention to nonverbal communication for additional meaning;
- be aware that our emotions affect our listening (we hear best what we agree with and filter out disagreeable information).

The researcher and author Samuel Trull also offers tips to enhance listening:

- encourage the speaker by silent nodding and voicing "neutral" semiverbal "uh-huhs" or "ums";
- repeat an answer to a question to influence an expanded version of the reply (for example, "So, you don't think this treatment will work." If you pause, the patient may enlarge the explanation, "Well, the treatment won't work, because it didn't work for my sister.");
- periodically summarize information for clarity;
- state the general conclusions and the action to be taken, if any.

It is important to emphasize silence as a useful tool for witnesses. Silence allows time for observation, noticing and reporting any important or radical changes in the physical appearance and behavior of the patient. For example, here are some basic physical observations to consider:

- functional mobility: Is the patient able to sit, stand, walk, or only stay in bed?
- communication skills: Is the patient speaking and using body language in a way that is consistent or inconsistent with his or her overall physical condition?
- personal hygiene and nourishment: Does the patient appear clean and well-fed?

In addition to permitting observation, a conversational lapse also allows the patient to think and consider an answer.

Frequently, responses to questions will be vague or equivocal: "I don't know," or "I can't think now," or some other effort at not answering the question. There are many reasons for not answering: fear, anxiety, confusion, indecision, distrust, exhaustion. A question may hit on an issue the patient does not want to touch. Accepting help from others is often difficult: independence or feelings of self-worth may be challenged. On occasion, witnesses will find that patients will not want to reveal what they want or need. Sometimes, patients want to test empathic partners in their ability to be prescient, to guess their needs: to measure their love or loyalty. Witnesses might be expected to perform tasks or meet needs that have purposely gone unexpressed.

. . .

Judy, an unmarried 40-year-old accountant, needed to arrange for someone to be with her in the hospital after her foot surgery.

She had been living with a man for a year, yet she didn't want to ask him to come to the hospital.

Psychologically astute, she felt she knew the problem. "It's too hard for me to ask. It's involved with my childhood. Asking and not receiving."

Her close friend Sharon said, "It sounds like a test to me."

Judy agreed. "I want him to come without my asking. I'm afraid if I ask, he'll say no, and I can't bear it."

Sharon told her it wasn't a good time for a test. Judy was placing herself in physical jeopardy. If she didn't have her boyfriend at the hospital, she would need to ask someone else.

Judy relented and asked her boyfriend to·be with her. He had
no problem doing that, and Sharon joined him.

•   •   •

This type of situation may be hard for empathic partners to avoid.
It's not easy to be a mind-reader; however, it might be a good idea
to ask about periodically and try to anticipate the patient's needs, and
if possible, surprise the patient by doing little things that are unexpected. This may help to circumvent caregiving "tests."

Patients who are insecure or fear being abandoned may push their
friends and family into other, more difficult tests. Some may fear their
witnesses are loyal merely because of a sense of obligation or pity, and
may consciously or unconsciously try to alienate those around them
by being abusive, picking a fight, or flinging insults.

•   •   •

Linda and her husband, Bill, went away for a weekend to visit
their friends Amy and Roger. Linda, a New York financial analyst,
was undergoing chemotherapy for ovarian cancer. She was bloated
from steroids and had lost all her hair, though she still looked quite
attractive in her stylish bandana.

Soon after they arrived at Amy and Roger's house, Linda snapped
at Bill, "You bring our luggage upstairs. I've got cancer."

As soon as Bill complied, Amy pulled aside her longtime friend,
and told her she wouldn't have tolerated that if Linda had said
that to her. "If you had asked me to help you, I would have, but
you are perfectly capable of lifting your luggage, even though you
have cancer."

"Bill is only staying with me because I'm sick," Linda said.
"He doesn't really love me."

Amy said, "He won't love you if you keep acting that way."

Later, Amy talked to Bill alone. He told Amy that Linda hated
being dependent, and the more dependent she got, the angrier she got.

"I take the abuse, because I love and understand her," Bill said.

Amy reminded him it wasn't without cost. He was chronically exhausted and suffered from an undiagnosed digestive problem.

•   •   •

This test of loyalty is a no-win situation. What to do about it is tricky. Recognizing the situation, questioning it, thinking about options and discussing them is one strategy. Yet sticking around might mean taking abuse; leaving might produce guilt from abandonment. However, underlying this sort of conflict is often a love that keeps patient and witness together, despite the pain. Some people might be tempted to classify this relationship as "co-dependency in a patient-witness context." Yet the complex circumstances surrounding serious illnesses defy such simplistic categorization. Medication side effects, fear of death, fear of loss, anxiety, anger at life's seeming injustice—all contribute to the understanding of how such transactions can occur. Sometimes superhuman patience is required to endure the hardships that strain relationships.

Encouraging patients to fully express their feelings, most of which will not be positive, should help the process of understanding. While listening to a patient's story, empathic partners can ask patients to elaborate about their past. In revealing more about medical, familial, marital, work, and sexual issues, patients will be helped in shaping their lives into a meaningful personal story. This often helps patients find clues that will give them insight into identifying or solving their problems. By listening and witnessing, empathic partners can help patients sort out and validate their feelings and find value or significance in the experience.

Experiencing illness can be lonely and wretched, especially for the chronically ill, as the psychiatrist Arthur Kleinman describes:

> *The undercurrent of chronic illness is like the volcano: it does not go away. It menaces. It erupts. It is out of control. One damned thing follows another. Confronting crises is only one part of the total picture. The rest is coming to grips with the mundaneness of worries over whether one can negotiate a curb, . . . make it to a bathroom quickly enough, eat breakfast without vomiting, keep the level of back pain low enough to get through the workday, sleep through the night, attempt sexual*

intercourse, make plans for vacation, or just plain face up to the myriad of difficulties that make life feel burdened, uncomfortable, and all too often desperate.

While listening, empathic partners should try to accept the feelings of the patient—no matter how emotionally intense they appear. Patients must be able to express their feelings—without editing or censorship.

If the patient is visibly upset, a hug or some other type of physical touching may be the best response. Sometimes a touch on the upper arm or shoulder will do just as well. After an appropriate pause, empathic partners may then want to offer how they want to help: from offering the primary needs of survival (food, clothing, shelter) to helping the patient relax.

It is easy to underestimate the benefits of listening. Simply listening to the patient—encouraging the patient to tell the story of the illness—alone is therapeutic. In addition to the physical assaults of the disease, illness affects all aspects of a patient's life, often creating severe emotional turbulence. Goals might need to be altered. Relationships may change. Losses can be staggering: loss of control, independence, financial stability, identity, privacy, appetite, libido, bodily functions, body architecture. Adding to the burden, some illnesses—those that are disfiguring or life-threatening like AIDS and cancer—carry cultural stigmas that some witnesses cannot overcome.

.   .   .

Danny, a 40-year-old artist with AIDS, found that he and his father strengthened their relationship during his illness, but he was devastated by his mother's reaction.

While he was home during a visit, she wouldn't let him put his laundry in the washing machine. She said he could put his dirty clothes in a bucket of bleach.

When he suggested they go out shopping together, his mother told him he couldn't go out. Danny said he wasn't that sick; he was capable of walking.

However, that was not his mother's concern. "You can't go out, because the neighbors will see you. They will know you have AIDS."

Danny called a friend to tell him the story, "Imagine. My own mother is so afraid and ashamed. I can't bear this."

.   .   .

This societal pressure not only demoralizes patients; it sometimes causes social poverty: family members, friends, or colleagues may retreat.

. . .

Arthur, a homosexual veterinarian in his mid-50s, was avoiding his lifelong friend Ken, a successful boat builder.

Arthur was suffering badly from the news that two of his friends had just died from AIDS—both in the same week. Arthur's longtime companion was also HIV-positive. Arthur desperately wanted to go see Ken and his family to be nurtured and cared for and to talk about the events of the week, as he had done so many times in the past, but this time he didn't feel as if he could or should.

Ken, who was married and a grandparent, was HIV-positive. He contracted the virus during an adventurous, but ill-fated, one-night liaison at a sales convention. His wife became HIV-positive as well.

Ken, realizing something was wrong since he hadn't heard from Arthur in quite some time, went to visit Arthur at his office and grilled him. "What's up? Why are you avoiding me?" he asked. "Didn't you have your AIDS test a while ago? Don't you have the results by now? Why aren't you telling me?"

Arthur sighed deeply. "I'm avoiding you, because I'm fine. I didn't want you to be jealous. I'm HIV-negative, and I feel guilty about it. Everyone around me is sick or dying, and I'm depressed. I wanted to talk to you about all these deaths in my life. I wanted to talk to you like we've always talked. But not now. You have enough problems without hearing about more people dying of AIDS."

"I'm still alive," Ken said. "Don't shut me out. Let me continue to be your friend. I couldn't be happier that you're okay. Someone has to be around to take care of all of us."

. . .

Conceivably, empathic partners are way ahead of therapists in already understanding the patient's issues or problems. However, a degree of humility is useful; witnesses may not know as much as they think they know. Most people have secrets. Initial information patients offer is but a suggestion of what therapists might discover. Patients frequently reveal surprising historical tidbits. Illness is often a time of autobiographical revelations for patients—a time to unburden guilt, release memories, and ask for forgiveness.

In their quest to understand patients, empathic partners need to remember that, during an illness, common problems in communication can arise: from anger, anxiety, denial, a desire for privacy, unwillingness to share feelings, confusion from medication, aggressiveness, a conscious or unconscious covering of real needs, depression, or an unwillingness to ask for help—just to name a few. Sometimes patients will feel a general malaise and not be able to express their problems or complaints.

An empathic partner's need for understanding a patient is secondary to the patient's needs. If the patient does not want to talk, shift the focus: diminish the stress and pressure. Unless there is a pressing need for information, back off, be calmly resigned, and try again another time.

Communicating with Insight and Compassion

On occasion, empathic partners will want to coach patients when patients' spirits are low. Many sports coaches use positive thinking to pump up a team's energy; their principle: If athletes think they are going to lose the game, why fight to win? Or they use the strategy of encouraging the team to get them going.

For empathic partners, this strategy can translate into inspiring hope and expressing unconditional support and solace—a gentler kind of coaching that is comforting and consoling. Or empathic partners, like coaches, can also get tough, giving all the reasons (including selfish ones) why the patient should get going and fight, like: Get up and exercise. You're not working hard enough. You're not done yet. You can do it. You can beat this. You have more work to contribute. Your family and friends need you. However, this approach has been known to backfire with some patients.

At the same time, empathic partners need to learn to monitor what they say and to counsel others about the powerful and influential effects of communication. Words affect the body. Bad news can upset normal bodily functions like appetite, the digestive system, and sleep. An argument can increase blood pressure. A compliment can cause a facial blush. Words can also "disturb the cardiovascular system, endocrine glands, autonomic nervous system, skeletal musculature, even the digestive system of the listener, with effects ranging all the way from increased heart rate and blanching of the skin to regurgitation and even loss of consciousness."

Though physically they are only a slight disturbance of airwaves, words are powerful and potentially healing or destructive if used undiplomatically. For example, before a friend is going into surgery, relating an encouraging story about someone who has survived the surgery and is doing well can bolster the patient's courage. On the other hand, pre-surgically recounting a horror story about a similar surgery can cause a patient unnecessary and potentially damaging tension.

Offering platitudes or advice to patients may boomerang, despite well-meaning motivations. This impulse to say something to make life better for the patient is so natural, it is almost reflexive. However, platitudes—like "Pain is necessary in order to feel the joy of life"—are often hollow-sounding statements meant to express why bad things happen. While they are mildly interesting to contemplate, rarely do they help those who are suffering, since they often sound trivial and insincere. Hearing the seemingly empathic sentence, "I know what you are feeling," can anger patients who know it is not true, since all that is possible is *imagining* what experience is like for another. Similarly, telling a patient, "Don't worry about work; your job is getting well," may not wash for a patient whose identity is strongly tied to a career.

Likewise, there are times when advice can feel like criticism to the patient, judgmental rather than consoling. Telling a patient that exercise will help could sound condescending, suggesting the patient doesn't already know this. In a similar vein, recommending another type of treatment can imply the patient is incapable of making sensible medical choices. Because they are vulnerable, patients may be hypersensitive. If witnesses have advice or suggestions they would like to offer, they might want to ask patients if they want to hear it. A sensible approach might be: Do you want my advice or do you want me just to listen? Or, I have a suggestion. Would you like me to tell you about it? Is this a good time to discuss it?

What is sure to help is a dose of compassion, acknowledging life *as it is* for the patient, confirming the struggle, despair, and sorrow of suffering.

There is no question that communications can be difficult even for sensitive caregivers. Often they don't know what the sick person wants to hear. Sometimes coaching is too positive, sympathy too negative. In some cases, only listening may be "just right," though that may be difficult to know in advance.

· · ·

Gail, a breast cancer patient in her 40s, discovered that one of her lymph nodes was enlarged in her neck. Her doctor thought it was no problem, but neither she nor her doctor was 100% sure. Gail remained concerned, so she called two friends to talk about it.

One friend reacted with reassurance, telling Gail that there may never be a time when she is 100% sure about anything. But for the moment, she advised Gail to remember that she was okay. She didn't need to take further action. Her friend said she thought the doctor was making the right decision by just waiting and observing. She ended in celebration. She said, hooray, this crisis appeared to be over for the moment.

Gail's other friend reacted more soberly and cautiously. She wondered whether the doctor was right. She said she was concerned and sorry that Gail even had to think about such things in her life. Then Gail's friend said this all made her sad.

Gail started to console her friend, but found she was getting angry, because the focus of the conversation switched to her friend. Gail lost patience, as she felt she was the one who needed assurance and comforting. What Gail realized she wanted was support and cheering: something like "You've been doing great, going through all the doctor's visits and tests."

Gails's second friend felt frustrated, because she soon realized she didn't say the right thing to Gail. However, she stood her ground and told Gail that she was entitled to her own feelings, too.

· · ·

The point of this story is the difficulty of never absolutely knowing the right thing to say. The two friends could have asked what Gail needed to hear, but even Gail would not have known, as she discovered what she needed in retrospect. Neither friend was right, or wrong, or insensitive. However, one friend was slightly "off," inaccurately guessing Gail's needs, misfiring a sentence or two that angered rather than soothed her.

When patients and witnesses communicate, subtle misinterpretations can occur. It is almost inevitable for good intentions to go wrong: words spoken in the wrong tone, witnesses being in the wrong mood to suit the patient, and so on. Caregivers want to make illness less bumpy for patients, but they can contribute to turbulence inadvertently. Both the witness and the patient want reassurance; neither can know exactly how to give it or what to do all the time. Sometimes all we can hope for is that what we say will help, and, if we don't help, that our relationship is strong enough to withstand a little tension or a small mistake. As a precaution, empathic partners can apologize in advance for miscommunications, pledging to be open about correcting them, but it is the rare caregiver who will escape the process of witnessing illness without some kind of semantic disagreement.

Denial

There are many ways that patients deal with the problems of their illnesses. Denial, a legitimate coping method for many patients, is one of those methods. It is often an unconscious or conscious wish to avoid painful feelings, ideas, or situations. For some, it may be the only way to get through the illness experience.

There are many types of denial. Some patients deny (to themselves and to others) that they have an illness at all and will not seek treatment, or they ignore a professional diagnosis. These types of denial can be dangerous, potentially harmful to the sick person, and frustrating for witnesses to watch. Denial like this is most often associated with people who have alcohol and drug-related illnesses. In fact, the term *denial* has been so popularized in this context that many assume denial is an altogether inappropriate or negative behavior.

However, other forms of denial may, in fact, be adaptive and healthy: a normal, productive function of how we think and process information.

. . .

Martha, a children's book illustrator and mother of two young boys, was in a state of shock when she learned her husband had a brain tumor and needed surgery.

Early in her crisis, her babysitter took her aside and strongly delivered some advice, "You have to pull yourself together. You shouldn't worry. It won't do you any good. And it won't help the children either."

Martha then quickly snapped out of her state of anxiety, took care of her husband and children, and later learned the power of her denial during her caregiving experience.

After her husband's surgery, one side of his face became paralyzed, causing half of his face to droop. The doctor told Martha his face would clear up in two days, and Martha thought it did. However, when she looked at photographs during his recovery, she noticed his face had not improved for months!

Eventually, his face returned to normal, and he has fully recovered and gone back to work.

. . .

Some patients, while getting treatment, deny to others that illness is a problem and appear nonchalant about the experience. Some deny they have pain or fear. Arthur Frank, who wrote about his illness experience, contends that patients who deny their needs, illness, or impending death may be acting in response to their family or attending medical staff, who prefer them to be quiet, amiable, and undemanding. Their denial is an act of self-preservation to insure that caregivers will not be alienated and will not leave. It is also possible to confuse hope and denial. If patients say, "I know I will get better," they are not necessarily denying the problem; they may merely be expressing hope.

Denial may also be a stage of digestion, when patients are quietly absorbing the reality and consequences of their illness. This stage of processing and accepting information may be necessary for some patients, and empathic partners should try to respect the silence. Consider this example, a story about both denial and the occasional frustration of empathic partners.

• • •

One night, Sue, a 30-year-old artist, called me, feeling frustrated and distraught. Sue's friend was scheduled to have a hysterectomy the following week, and during Sue's pre-op call, her friend apparently refused to talk about any of her feelings about the upcoming surgery.

A veteran of group therapy and a child of alcoholic parents, Sue complained that her friend was in denial, not dealing with the fears or consequences of the surgery. Sue asked me if I could recommend any books to send that would help.

I asked Sue if it was a good idea to force her friend to face her feelings. Maybe she was not ready to talk. Maybe she wasn't scared. Maybe she saw no reason to be scared. Maybe she didn't want to think about the surgery for reasons of her own.

Sue said she normally played the role of empathic partner, encouraging her friend to talk about her feelings. With her friend, this was the way Sue helped or felt she mattered. Having that role taken away from her made her feel helpless and disempowered. The problem, then, she realized, was more hers than her friend's.

Weeks later, Sue's friend recovered from surgery well. When Sue visited her, they then talked more fully about the operation.

• • •

Professional therapists are cautious about getting their patients to reveal information too soon. Though empathic partners may think that probing patients about their feelings will help them eventually come to a peaceful state of mind, they may want to adapt to a more flexible tolerance toward denial, allowing patients their own timetable to cope with and understand their feelings. Emotions—usually anger—do spill out when tampering with denial. Any strong outburst is a sign to stop, apologize, state a wish to support, and move on to something else. Eventually, the anger should subside.

In its psychological definition, denial is considered to be a "defense mechanism, operating unconsciously, used to resolve emotional conflict and allay anxiety by disavowing thoughts, feelings, wishes, needs, or external reality factors that are consciously intolerable." Denial, then, can be productive, because it enables people to concentrate and to continue normal activities until the problem can be faced; it may be a natural process on the way to problem solving. On the other hand, denial can become problematic if the person is stuck in that stage, especially if people somehow endanger themselves, us, or others. Witnesses will usually know when the denial is too dangerous to the patient to allow it to go unchallenged. However, most commonly, denial moves from a rejection of reality, refusing to accept, believe, or embrace the truth, to its gradual acceptance. From a state of conscious acceptance, people are then capable of identifying, confronting, clarifying, solving, and working through problems.

Confrontation and Clarification

Dialogue helps to expose and identify problems. When the stories of problems are shared, people can confront and clarify their emotions and conflicts, examine the issues, and review decisions with the goal of self-understanding or reaching some resolution. For example, in this next case study, Mary, a witness to her ill husband, confronts an emotional conflict with the help of Doug as her therapist. Mary was confused, plagued with doubt, ambivalence, and a feeling of hollowness, and she needed to explore the reasons for her feelings.

• • •

"Since my husband, Ben, had his surgery for his brain tumor, everything has been different," said Mary. "Ben is disoriented and confused, and his recent memory is extremely poor."

After Ben's short hospital rehabilitation, Mary and her two sons decided to supervise his continued rehabilitation while he worked in their family business.

Mary and her sons felt good about their shared goal of rehabilitating Ben. The two single sons, ages 25 and 28, had clearly enjoyed a positive sense of family and work relationship with their father. They were justifiably proud of their patience and fortitude in joining Mary in the effort, which worked well.

A year later, Ben had a setback. After a seizure, Ben was put on Dilantin, a medicine to prevent seizures, and he lost his confidence. He became insecure and childlike, fearing Mary's absence.

"He had been driving, and now he can't," Mary said. "He'd been working pretty much unsupervised in the shop, and now he won't. He wanders off, leaving jobs half started, and gets nervous when I mention I'd like to take a day-long shopping trip with my girlfriend. The boys and I are working 70 hours per week, and they really need him to work in the shop when they go out on calls. It's been quite a strain on us.

"The problem is that I'm just not getting to do anything for myself. My husband says it's okay for me to take some time, but he's so forlorn when I go away. He never used to go to the market with me. He never used to miss me when I went to my cooking classes, he never used to get such a puppy-dog look when I told him I was going to the city to go shopping for the day. It's disheartening and burdensome for us."

Doug chose not to investigate the subtext of Mary's complaint— for example, what were Mary's own concerns about abandonment and separation? In Mary's past, did she suffer from a traumatic loss? Instead, Doug proposed that Mary actually take a day off and see how Ben and her two sons fared. Afterward, she would discuss how she felt about the experience.

Vitality slowly replaced her visible feelings of oppression. They discussed this option, and Mary agreed to try it.

In their next session, Mary said the experiment had worked without problems, and she and Doug did not need to explore for further clarification.

·   ·   ·

The concepts of confrontation and clarification are hard to separate. In fact, clarification essentially means that both parties in the dialogue agree that they understand each other, looking at the same thing at the same time. In psychotherapeutic terms, clarification "aims at placing the psychic phenomenon being analyzed in sharp focus. [The problem] has to be made evident, has to be made explicit to the patient's conscious ego. The significant details have to be dug out and carefully separated from extraneous matter. . . singled out and isolated." This process of clarification usually goes on at all stages of normal communication—and in therapy as well.

In the process of confrontation and clarification, therapists most often deal with the surface before they approach a client's subconscious depths. A professional psychotherapist moves very slowly in helping people look at unconscious mechanisms, which are, by definition, not immediately available to conscious inspection. This priority respects vulnerability, lessens the risk of offense, and builds a working relationship. Empathic partners should exercise similar caution for the same reasons. The unconscious is not their province. Instead, stick to problems that are immediately available to conscious inspection, allow professional therapists to explore the patient's deeper feelings, or wait until the patient wants to talk more intimately.

It is important to remember that a therapist does not act the role of a friend. Therapists and their clients have an agreement to change behavior to help the client realize a fuller and happier life. In contrast, empathic partners, as friends, need to encourage patients when they are ill. It is usually not appropriate to bring up a patient's pathologies or self-destructive patterns. Instead, empathic partners may want to emphasize a patient's positive traits to revitalize self-esteem—or protect a patient by quiet, subtle empathic actions.

. . .

"Before Greg became HIV-positive, we shared one razor," Paul explained. "When I talked to our doctor, he said it would probably not be a good idea to continue doing that.

"So I bought a new razor. Every morning, I now wait until Greg leaves the house for work. I take the razor out from a drawer, shave, and then put it away.

"I can't bear him watching me use the new razor. I don't want him to see me withdraw our intimacy."

. . .

On the other hand, empathic partners usually know when they can confront a patient they have known for a long time. Sometimes, empathic partners feel compelled to speak directly about a problem. For instance, witnesses might want to tell patients to seek some therapy to work out a perplexing issue that has had a long history. However, patients are responsible for understanding and acting on what is said. Witnesses should speak their truth, and if patients are not ready to listen, they will probably need to hear it again from someone else, or go through another experience to drive the point home. In other words, don't violently force a message.

Interpreting another's feelings or behaviors is tricky, though many people unabashedly offer their views. Sometimes conjecture has good results.

•   •   •

Nikki, a beautician in her late 20s, listened to her client complain about her recurring sore throat. Nikki asked her client if this was a pattern, if she got the sore throat when she had trouble communicating or when she was repressing some anger. Nikki had read Louise Hay's book You Can Heal Your Life, *which lists illnesses and their possible psychological or spiritual causes.*

The client suddenly had insight, and told Nikki she was right. It was true there was a pattern: she suffered from a sore throat whenever she was angry.

Some time later, she told Nikki her sore throats had cleared up, and she continues the practice of communicating more freely.

•   •   •

This is a lovely story; however, such successes are not always the rule. This type of interpretation, a guess at the psychological or spiritual cause of illness, may encounter an angry backlash from people who are ill.

•   •   •

Nancy, a 30-year-old mother of two, was about to undergo surgery to treat her glaucoma. She feared the operation. She had just signed a consent form that disclosed the operation might not work, that indeed she might become blind. She worried, too, about the care of her children, as she knew her physical mobility would be decreased after the operation, in any case.

A friend of hers, a believer in a New Age philosophy that attributed physical symptoms and illness to psychological causes, told Nancy she had glaucoma because she wasn't currently looking at something in her life clearly.

Nancy became enraged and hurt. Though Nancy has recovered successfully from her operation, her relationship with her friend remains fractured.

. . .

Though this type of interpretation can be fascinating to contemplate, its truth is hard to prove, and it appears to be another version of blaming the victim for illness. The many spiritual healers who have worked in the tradition of clearing up psychological or spiritual problems in order to enhance or accelerate the process of healing may be on the right track. Scientists who are working in the field of psychoneuroimmunology are probing and successfully proving the connections between the mind and the body. However, even if there is truth in elements of this theory of causation, it may not always be helpful or healing for the patient to hear. Who is the right person to talk to a patient about this? When is the right time? Did Nancy's friend really think that by making her examine her life's blind spots, Nancy's glaucoma would magically disappear? While illness may provide a welcome and necessary opportunity to explore the depths of character pathology, it is also a time to be nurtured, rather than accused, confused, and enraged.

Perhaps it is best to be cautious, and not too attached to speculations. Sigmund Freud suggested that interpretations are nothing more than "conjecture awaiting examination, confirmation or rejection, [requiring] no direct agreement from the patient." He said the situation would become clear in future developments. Moreover, even if speculations are correct, empathic partners might not generate positive feelings. The patient might have mixed or even negative feelings about what is said and resent the accuracy.

Solving Problems and Working Them Through

Empathic partners might be tempted to pressure patients to change self-destructive patterns; correct faults in their emotional architecture; and achieve a more "positive" or healing state of mind. While behavioral adjustments may be a worthwhile goal for the patient (and for the witness), patients may need encouragement more than being forced into a life reassessment. The process of change takes much time and energy, resources often missing in patients.

Instead of suggesting massive personality changes, empathic partners might find it easier to inspire patients to use creative problem-solving strategies to view their situation differently and invent solutions to pressing problems. In a problem-solving partnership, empathic partners and patients can work together, exploring answers to questions like:

- What actions can the patient or witness take to maximize the healing process?
- How can the patient revitalize energy?
- What are some ways to relieve stress?
- What can the patient do to have fun?

In other words, given the present condition, what can be done to make the most of the situation? It takes courage, support, and creativity to cope with illness.

Empathic partners can provide the support to launch the patient toward the creative problem-solving process. The state of mind during the creative process—a kind of concentrated, alert meditation—may be healing alone. The act of creativity is engaging. Time passes quickly. Childlike leaps of imagination resuscitate and regenerate us, and the new options that emerge—the illumination, the "ah-ha's" that revelations bring—are energizing. Creativity can be a vacation from the stress of too much analytical, left-brained thinking, provided there is no pressure about the outcome of the exercise. If the patient is willing and able—experiment.

Here are some steps to optimize and facilitate problem-solving:

Step 1: Relax.

A proper state of mind for the both witness and patient is essential. George Prince, an innovation and creativity consultant, suggests opening up to experimentation by:

- taking risks, being intuitive, impetuous, curious, and open to everything, not minding being wrong or confused;
- playing, seeing the fun in things, breaking rules, enjoying surprises, and making impossible wishes;
- making connections, visualizing, imagining, speculating, using dreams and seeming irrelevance.

In other words, lighten up and try to have some fun with the process. This may be a challenge, considering the normal circumstances of illness, but try.

Step 2: Formulate the problem.

Step 3: List all possible solutions.

Classic problem-solving techniques start with free associating or *brainstorming*; that is, draining the brain of *all* possible solutions to the problem or question without regard to practicality, sensitivity, decorum, logic, or any other rational constraint. Either patients can look for answers alone, or empathic partners may join in to spark additional creative tangents. In either case, make sure to write down all ideas. No solution is too silly or outrageous.

Preconceived solutions or fixed thinking can block innovative answers that come from the freedom of creativity.

· · ·

For example, Lorie, a single, professional woman in her 30s with a chronic back problem, looked for ways to relieve stress in her life. While brainstorming, some of her more outrageous solutions were to scream obscenities at her boss, blow up her vacuum cleaner, or live on a beach in Hawaii.

Later, these playful solutions led to a practical plan of action: discussing ways to ease tension in work with her boss; hiring a cleaning service; and taking an extended vacation or leave of absence.

· · ·

Step 4: Review answers to the problem.

Sometimes the right solution is not immediately forthcoming. Often artists, scientists, or creative thinkers come to a dead end that is accompanied by anxiety or frustration. However, the mind works in mysterious ways, and sometimes it just needs a period of rest or incubation to arrive at an answer.

Frequently, after the brain has worked on the problem on its own time, the solution comes to consciousness at a moment of relaxation. Niels Bohr, Albert Einstein, and other scientists solved their problems intuitively and visually first before explaining their discovery in words. Similarly, answers to questions are often received in a dream state.

Step 5: Illumination.
When the brain is freed from editing out the unacceptable, creative and spontaneous solutions can be born from the newly opened pathways of uncensored thinking.

This problem-solving strategy is a life-planning tool for coping when the time is right. Some patients will not want to solve problems or even try to cope with illness. Others will not be able to use this process, especially during a serious crisis. However, patients and witnesses will do better if they are creative, flexible, and adaptive in facing any problem they both encounter—no matter what method they choose to come to a solution.

The final operation in psychotherapy is called *working through*, which means that the patient takes in new information, makes something out of it, and faces reality. Working through refers to the "repetitive, progressive, and elaborate explorations of the resistances which prevent an insight from leading to change." Patients understand their behavior, and now struggle to replace old behaviors with new ones, sometimes battling with the persistence and ease of old habits. Insight does not always mean no mistakes will be made. It means there is now the capability to reassess behavior and think about ways for change in the future.

Therefore, even after a solution to a problem is found, the process still continues. Action must be taken, and in the course of action, there may be obstacles that are encountered and need to be worked through. Often after a therapist and client define their goals, they will next look into what gets in the way of achieving the goal. What will oppose the process of self-exploration, change, or healing?

Empathic partners should understand that patients will resist change. During the process of working through problems, patients may feel guilty for failing to change. However, self-forgiveness is more healing than self-flagellation. Likewise, for the frustrated empathic partner, it may simply be prudent to smile at the humanness of imperfection. It is also a good time to remember—and forgive—the times that caregivers have fallen short of their own expectations.

Though these questions might be best left for a professional to work out with a patient, therapists often ask their clients why they resist following suggestions that might make them feel better and if they are experiencing fear of change. There are sound psychological reasons for opposing change: self-preservation, self-control, and a stubborn sense of identity, to name a few. Other reasons may not be as rational, such as refusing to face reality or simply not wanting to grow up.

Patients resist change in many ways. For example, one patient is told his cholesterol is too high, and he must give up dairy products, but he does not really want to give up cheeseburgers, pizza, or chocolate ice cream, because he will feel deprived. Another patient is told that after twenty years of smoking, he really should give it up, but he still likes to have a cigarette after sex. A heart attack patient is told that exercise is important, because her job is sedentary. But with the demands of the job and her family, she does not feel she has the energy to get to the gym three times a week. Another patient refuses to remember taking his high-blood-pressure medication. Witnesses will surely encounter these and other opposing forces in patients: the desire to have fun at any cost, the desire to be naughty, the desire to rebel, and the desire to do whatever they damn well please, no matter what anybody tells them. Change is perhaps the most difficult thing for human beings to undertake.

Though this might not work, empathic partners may want to try to point out to patients that they are not helping themselves as they had agreed, that perhaps some negative forces are at work that need to be identified and confronted as part of the treatment process. This approach may help patients understand the natural process of their ambivalent feelings and resistances, but if not, try to persuade patients to get additional help or therapy.

In trying to understand and share the difficulties of change, empathic partners might want to express how they think the patient feels or ask further questions about their observations. Some examples:

"It's hard for you to break your smoking habit, isn't it?"

"Because you were so active before the illness, slowing down must be very hard for you now."

"I can see you are feeling poorly. Is that why you don't want to get out of bed? Or are you depressed?"

"Why don't you want to go back to the doctor? Is it the doctor or are you afraid of what he might tell you?"

"Why are you looking so glum? Are you missing work? Or are you just feeling lonely?"

While negotiating through conversations with patients, periodically stop, paraphrase what the patient has said, and ask for clarification, like: Did I understand what you meant? Did that sound right to you? Am I off base? It is important not to get into the trap of competition: I know what's bothering you, and you don't. If you would only listen to me, and do it my way, you would be better. Empathic partners should take care that their manner is not perceived as unduly assaultive, aggressive, or demanding, but rather as nonjudgmental, persistent, and attentive. It will then be easier to help patients discuss options to cope with or solve their problems.

Caregivers should not feel obligated to force patients to confront their slow adaptation to change. It is not a caregiver's responsibility to make someone else change. Unless the person is ready, change is not possible. If patients are continuing a life-threatening behavior, empathic partners may feel a moral responsibility to express their opinion, but should also acknowledge the patient's choice. Like the psychotherapist, the empathic partner or caregiver is different from a "fixer." A fixer takes something that is broken and says, "I'll mend it." In essence, the caregiver says to the patient, "I'm going to keep you company while you're trying to fix yourself. I might have a few helpful hints along the way."

Insight is often considered the first step needed in changing behavior. Insight is self-understanding, the extent of a person's understanding the origin, nature, and mechanisms of attitudes and behavior that were previously unconscious.

Occasionally, patients will be enlightened by the mutual search for insight, and perhaps begin to make the appropriate behavioral changes to aid the healing process. Their doing so can be a rewarding sensation for caregivers. In other cases, a patient may not be able to "hear" what the caregivers are saying and may be presently incapable of change. Sometimes, a patient's denial is so strong that he or she can actually fail to understand what another person is saying. Or in other instances, a patient's ideas are so strong that listening to another point of view is out of the question. Witnesses may also encounter a patient who is not a willing partner and co-explorer, but who expects to be cared for, pushed, pulled, and guided through life.

CONCLUSION

In therapy—as in life—resolutions are not usually neat. Insight does not necessarily mean that change will occur. Sometimes we change, sometimes we adjust—or sometimes we do neither. Patients are not necessarily cured or freed from conflict. Most likely, new problems will appear and old conflicts will arise in new guises. For example, a patient's stress that was handled poorly in the past, and made manifest in migraine headaches, may have been conquered. Then suddenly, as the patient experiences a new stress, she or he develops a different stress-related ailment, like ulcers. Having gone through the process of problem-solving, however, the patient may be able to adjust and cope more easily with potential conflict and its stresses when they are confronted, clarified, interpreted, and worked through.

Thinking about people in his practice who have made successful progress in resolving their problems, Doug has noticed they have an intellectual curiosity and willingness to:

- learn about themselves and their feelings;
- make use of what they learned;
- change relational patterns;
- endure the changes that have been thrust upon them;
- own their feelings, thoughts, and behaviors;
- grow in new directions.

With a sense of humility, these clients also knew that they would have to cope with continuing emotional challenges and obstacles.

Not all social support or attempts at empathic partnerships are successful. In a study of cancer patients, Gayle A. Dakof and Shelley E. Taylor from the University of California discovered that caregiver actions that provided self-esteem and emotional support are what patients rate as most helpful. More specifically, the actions translated into physical presence, expression of concern, empathy, or affection, accepting illness, or being a positive role model. Patients also found getting information about their illness useful. What patients found most distressing was the opposite: criticism, avoidance, failure to understand the impact of the illness on the patient, unwanted practical assistance, or incorrect advice.

Different patients have different preferences for care, and choosing how to act can be tricky. What one patient needs for emotional support may be repulsive to another. There are plenty of potential booby traps. If the behavior is too cheerful, the patient may find it inappropriate, dishonest, or offensively perky. If it is too negative, the patient may become depressed or angry. If empathic partners want to deal with the illness and the patient's feelings straightforwardly, the patient simply may not be in the mood, preferring to talk about other things for diversion. On the other hand, avoiding talk about the illness might make the patient feel betrayed by the aversion. Thus, witnesses can conceivably be offputting by underinvolvement or over-involvement, withdrawal or overprotection.

Despite the challenges, studies are beginning to hint that the act of helping others may be important for our health and survival. In a study conducted by the University of Michigan Research Center, researchers found that regular volunteer work correlated with increased life expectancy. Men who did no volunteer work were two and a half times as likely to die during the study as men who volunteered at least once a week. But perhaps the most poignant argument for community or communal effort comes from Terrence Des Pres' study of concentration camp survivors. During hundreds of interviews with the survivors, he was repeatedly told, "Nobody survived without help." He thus concluded, "Survival is a collective act, and so is bearing witness. Both are rooted in compassion and care, and both expose the illusion of separateness."

Caregiving requires the risk of involvement, the search for behavioral clues, the temerity to ask questions, and the courage to be intimate. One must discover the patient's changing needs, while taking care of one's own needs. Doing this often requires negotiation. If successful, empathic partners can help the patient feel in control of his or her treatment and environment, complete "unfinished" business, empower the patient to solve problems, or relieve sources of stress that distract the patient from getting to the business of healing. If caregivers can console, inspire hope, and increase a patient's self-confidence, they have increased the patient's chances for a healthy outcome, or at the very least, improved the quality of the patient's life. That is, indeed, a great accomplishment. Though the process may be difficult and wearing, the empathic resources of responsiveness, insight, compassion, and understanding are some of the more powerful healing tools presently known to humankind.

6

THE WISDOM OF
SELF-NURTURANCE

I grieve to see how many pleasures I pollute with worries about obligations I momentarily left untended.

– Patricia O'Toole
"Alice through the Hourglass"
Lears

The hunger of imagination which drives men to seek new understanding and new connections in the external world is, at the same time, a hunger for integration and unity within.

– Anthony Storr
Solitude: A Return to the Self

The great surprise of human evolution may be that the highest form of selfishness is selflessness.

– Robert Ornstein, Ph.D., David Sobel, M.D.
Healthy Pleasures

Life can be like an undigested tuna sandwich.

– Alexandra Johnson

THE NEED FOR SELF-NURTURANCE

Nurturing ourselves during the process of witnessing an illness tends to be the last priority. Though this inclination is understandable, it is not wise. Witnesses can live in continuing turmoil for long stretches of time as illness eclipses normal routine. As one witness said, "It's like watching a movie that's not going to end."

Stress, in and of itself, is not a bad thing, nor is it pathological. Everyone experiences differing intensities of stress from either internal thoughts or feelings, or from external events. How the stress is processed will determine how disturbing it might be. For some people, getting a traffic ticket will spark enormous stress, while others can handle it by laughing it off. Yet, when a situation tramples us and challenges our strength to handle it, stress appears in one of its many guises— even in dreams.

*   *   *

Morris, a real estate agent in his 50s, was caring for his wife who had multiple sclerosis, and his father, who was recovering from a broken hip. To supplement his income, Morris was also doing consulting work for a computer company, because the real estate market was gloomy.

He felt he didn't have enough time in the day to do everything he needed to do.

After a long day of work, he had a dream about his time pressure stress. "I had a dream I was at my doctor's office. She had a very solemn expression when she told me the news of the diagnosis. I had N.F.E. along with C.G.F."

Like a good patient, he asked her to explain. She said, "Morris, you have Not Fast Enough, along with Couldn't Go Faster."

*   *   *

The stressful life event of witnessing illness often disrupts and upsets a caregiver's equilibrium. Witnessing illness causes stress by changing life's normal routine; challenging the expectation that things will remain constant; and forcing the witness to work at understanding all the nuances of life with an ill person. Caregivers will commonly feel the pressures of time, unending practical chores, confusion, emotional saturation, limited patience, focused and unfocused anger, and fatigue. There are other potential stressors: financial difficulties; the shame of not measuring up to personal ideals of caregiving; being revulsed by hospitals or the nature of the patient's illness; disagreements between caregivers or family members; and the inability to make plans or to complete personal goals.

Integrating all the emotions and changes that witnessing illness brings takes time, especially because new information or daunting challenges are often a daily proposition. The inability to understand immediately and process all that is new is in itself a major stressor.

Since unabating stress can compromise physical and emotional health, witnesses need to pay extra attention to their health. Even the sturdiest individual will have good and bad days and be vulnerable to the inevitable exhaustion chronic stress brings. Sick caregivers are no help to patients. Caregivers should not be a work force of "co-dependents" who selflessly work to care for another without taking care of themselves or at the expense of their own well-being. In the context of caregiving, self-nurturance is not a wholly selfish act. **Developing self-nurturing skills helps to prevent personal pathology or illness that would deplete the ability to give care**.

It is easy to ignore the signals of caregiver overload. Witnesses might think they are doing just fine, performing the tasks needed, even feeling a sense of mastery in conquering a difficult situation. They might have no idea why people are asking them how they are doing. This phenomenon can be called *altruistic denial*; that is, while the witness is serving another, his or her own needs can remain unnoticed.

Mihaly Csikszentmihalyi's concept of "flow"—the state in which people are so involved in an activity that nothing else seems to matter—may account for the reason why "martyrdom" is so prevalent among caregivers. Though they are in the midst of a crisis, they have a clarity of purpose, focus, and perspective about what really matters to them. This clarity lends them an equanimity that makes inconsequential stress—like a traffic jam—simply unimportant. That a problem exists at all may escape the notice of the caregiver who is operating from adrenaline-like energy that being in service to another often brings. Perhaps this vigilant or even hyper-vigilant energy is the gift of altruism. Unfortunately, it can also mask the emotional and physical needs of the caregiver. Even those in flow need to take breaks.

. . .

The first time I was a primary witness, to my mother, I took a certain amount of pride in being adult and responsible, doing everything I knew at the time to be helpful. I was an energetic caregiver and felt full of strength.

I steeled myself for the job, allowing very little emotion to get in the way. I remember I even earned a 3.75 grade point average in college during the semester when my mother was dying. What I didn't know was the extent of my apparent emotional repression. Even as my mother died, I was able to tend to her, close her eyes, pick out her dress for the funeral and her coffin without great shows of emotion.

But then, at the funeral, things changed. As my last job, I wrote my mother's eulogy, but the rabbi concluded my mother's service without reading it. Instead, he invented things to say about my mother, because they had never met. I was furious. After the service, I confronted him. Why didn't he read it? He said he forgot.

His act of omission, insensitive as it was, ruptured my emotional reserve, and I quickly lost control. An aunt of mine still talks to me about it. I cried, without stop, for about five hours. All I had held in, burst with torrential force.

Some 20 years later, it still rains.

·   ·   ·

Witnesses often deny the extent of the emotions that are building as they responsibly go about the business of caregiving. Witnesses may feel that they are in control and coping extremely well. But later, when the caregiving experience is over or a crisis ended, having worked at their maximum energy for an extended period of time, witnesses might feel the exhaustion: the physical and emotional fatigue that they did not have time to stop and notice. Suddenly their bodies take stock, only to find that the imbalances and the strain have taken their toll.

The danger of caregiver overload is that eventually the emotional dam will break. Sometimes it is with tears. Other times, the results are more internal, possibly creating fatigue, a lowered immune system, or actual physical damage caused by stress. Long-term stress can lead to alcohol and drug abuse, increased blood pressure, cardiac arrhythmias, coronary heart disease, depression, digestive problems, gastrointestinal upset, duodenal and gastric ulcers, chronic headaches, backaches, panic disorders, sleep disorders, and chronic anxiety. Stress can even increase susceptibility to flu viruses and build tooth plaque.

A rather daunting list of stress symptoms includes: absenteeism, excessive alcohol or drug use or dependence, chronic anger, argumentative behavior, backaches, boredom, rapid shallow breathing, car accidents (or near-misses), compulsions, depersonalization, diarrhea, dread of getting out of bed, dependence, dysattention, dyspepsia (upset stomach, gas, heartburn, acid stomach), fatigue, headache, hyperexcitation, hypersomnia, imperiousness, impulsiveness, inefficiency, frequent infections, insomnia, irritability, low self-esteem, malaise, muscle aches, obsessions, pain without physical causes, palpitations, poor judgment, rigidity, sexual dysfunction, sinking stomach, smoking, social withdrawal, tardiness, tearfulness, grinding teeth, trauma, and frequent urination or vomiting.

To prevent stress symptoms, witnesses need to stop periodically to rest, relax, and take time out for self-nurturance. In addition, a change in thinking has also been prescribed by many practitioners dealing with stress. This has been called mental toughness, learned optimism, or mindfulness: controlling stress by reconstructing how we think about events in our lives. (We will be talking more about this later in the chapter.)

People who are experiencing a period of life that is filled with complicated and multiple types of stress may be immune to any self-help measures. For example, they may be all at once caring for a dying parent, working on a career deadline, moving homes, and coping with a personal threat of recurring cancer while in a difficult pregnancy. These are concurrent stresses that observers can't imagine bearing or surviving. People who are in the midst of off-the-chart stress may be unconsolable, for good reason, and may need just to get by, however they can. Sometimes their methods of coping won't appear smart—not eating well, not resting. For some, the only thing to do is to endure and hope the stress lessens and resolves with time.

Self-nurturance is necessarily personal. Most people have their own special strategies to make themselves feel better—if they take the time. But personal time seems out of the question for many witnesses. Caregivers might need prodding—and a stand-in—to leave a bedside vigil. Nonetheless, there are many self-nurturing strategies a witness can use *while* caregiving.

RELAXATION TECHNIQUES

Meditation is a relaxation technique to clear the mind of extraneous thoughts, reducing internal and external noise. A nonchalant concentration is used to focus on either a word or image to silence the chatter of the mind. Other ways to explain meditation is that it's a "formal exercise in turning off the negative ego's voice and quieting the critical, judgmental mind"; it "takes the mind out of its boundaries and exposes it to an unbounded state of consciousness."

Meditation and other relaxation techniques can be seen as preventive and curative. Meditation can preserve physical and mental health, and it is also a way to provide the body with complete relaxation, which can restore energy and aid medical treatment. Meditation is also said to expand the mind. This subjective benefit is hard to quantify, but it is a seductive technique, nonetheless, which enjoys widespread practice.

There is impressive evidence to support the use of relaxation techniques. They are by no means a cure-all. However, they can be useful to alleviate stress in general, and more specifically, they can help relieve tension headaches, anxiety disorders, asthma, high blood pressure, some types of pain (like heart-related chest pains), immunological disorders, backache, and other stress-related ailments. It has even been reported that meditation slows the aging process. Studying a geriatric population, Drs. J. K. Kiecolt-Glaser, R. Glaser, and others found that relaxation techniques practiced only three times a week can boost immunological systems.

There are so many books and tapes to learn how to meditate or perform the relaxation response that the method can seem intimidating to the witness who has never tried any technique before. There is transcendental meditation, as well as Zen, Tibetan, and Chinese meditation. There are variations on meditating like quiet sitting, body-scan meditations, walking meditations, and concentration or mindfulness meditation. There are meditations for self-healing, centering, aura cleansing, and dissolving self-limitations. Some meditations zero in on love, growth, forgiveness, grief, letting go, even connecting the heart with the disheartened. There are meditations using crystals as concentration objects or for specific healing rituals. Another method to achieve relaxation is *yoga*, from the Sanskrit word meaning "union" or "joining together," a system of self-development. Yoga exercises awareness of the mind and body through physical techniques (hatha yoga) and meditative techniques (raja yoga), employing physical postures called *asanas* and focused breathing.

However, basic meditation is quite simple and can be done anywhere. Though many techniques have been introduced and teachers use many methods, Dr. Herbert Benson, author of *The Relaxation Response*, suggests using these basic steps for getting into a state of relaxation:

> *Step 1:* Pick a "focus word," or sound, also known in some meditation traditions as a mantra, such as ōm, peace, one.
>
> *Step 2:* Sit quietly in a comfortable position.
>
> *Step 3:* Close your eyes.
>
> *Step 4:* Relax muscles.
>
> *Step 5:* Focus on breathing slowly and naturally, taking time to breathe in and out fully. Repeat the focus word as you exhale.
>
> *Step 6:* Notice what takes your mind off breathing and gently bring it back—without judgment. Try not to worry about how you are doing. When other thoughts come to mind, simply say to yourself, "Oh well," and gently return to the repetition.
>
> *Step 7:* Continue doing this for 10 to 20 minutes.
>
> *Step 8:* Practice this technique once or twice a day.

Physiologically, the body experiences a slower heartbeat and breathing; less oxygen is consumed. The metabolic rate may decrease, and meditators may produce alpha brain wave activity as demonstrated on electroencephalograms (EEGs). In meditation, the body can relax deeply, though not asleep, with an enhanced state of awareness.

Once learned, meditation is simple to employ any time. In fact, it is such an important healing tool—for the self and others—it can or should be an essential part of any first-aid repertoire of skills. There is no right or wrong method of meditation. Some methods work better than others for individuals, and there is plenty of room for safe, creative experimentation.

• • •

One afternoon while I was working, I received an emergency call from my neighbor, Ann, a therapist. She had just taken her blood pressure, and it was way too high. She had to go to the hospital immediately, and she asked if I would take her. A cancer survivor, Ann routinely monitored her blood pressure, as some of her medications occasionally threw it off balance.

We drove to the hospital where she worked, but found she had a long wait to see the emergency room physician. As she was feeling increasingly afraid and anxious, I suggested that we try out a relaxation and visualization technique to see if we could lower her blood pressure ourselves.

She agreed, though she had never tried it before. I told her to sit, relax, get comfortable, close her eyes, and start breathing deeply. I stood in back of her, put my hands on her shoulders, and I started to breathe deeply with her in unison.

Though I knew focus words would help her concentrate, I intuitively felt it was not quite the right method at the time. I thought it would take too much time to pick a word and try it out. Instead, I suggested that she visualize herself in the most beautiful and relaxing place she had ever been. All the while, I had her breathing more slowly and deeply.

We did this in unison for some 30 minutes until the doctor was able to see her.

When she came back to me in the waiting room, she excitedly told me we had lowered her systolic blood pressure by some 40 points.

Convinced that meditation worked (however clumsy it was that first try), Ann bought a simple biofeedback machine that looked like a small transistor radio. She used that to practice lowering her blood pressure, and then enrolled in a more extensive relaxation program sponsored by her hospital.

• • •

Meditation is such an excellent self-healing technique that it should be required education. Learning how to manipulate and control our bodies to manage pain can be crucial in emergencies, but also helpful in daily life when pain or stress gets in the way of functioning.

• • •

In my mid-20s, I started getting stress-related migraine headaches that were often debilitating for up to six to eight hours at a stretch. Medicine didn't work. I would have to sit in a darkened room, because light would hurt my eyes, and the only way I released the excruciating pain was through induced vomiting—a process I hated.

During my husband David's illness, Doug happened to phone while I had a migraine. He told me I could get rid of my migraine using meditation combined with a visualization technique.

Doug had known I was already using meditation to maintain and restore my energy. He also knew that while I was learning about alternative healing techniques for David, I had met an engineer who hooked me up to a small, portable biofeedback machine that mechanically helped me verify the extent of my willed relaxation.

I had told Doug that the experience surprised me. I learned that before I even consciously gave myself orders to relax, the machine's peculiar hum went lower. It was as if a car started braking before the foot depressed the brake pedal. Intention preceded my internal instructions; my mind worked faster than I had imagined. And it continued to descend. When my mind lost focus, the machine's noise increased, I refocused and it continued down to its next level, and then I turned off the machine. It was remarkably easy.

To cure my headache, Doug told me to sit comfortably, close my eyes in a darkened, quiet room, breathe deeply, progressively relax my muscles, and then visualize the blood in my brain migrating down to my fingertips.

"Warm up your hands, and keep warming them until your headache goes away."

I asked for a more precise visualization: the route the blood takes so I could visualize moving the blood along its path. Doug agreed and proceeded with a lengthy guided visualization. I knew I wanted the Fantastic Voyage *version (though I later learned the simpler version worked just as well).*

"The heart is at the center of your circulatory system. With each beat, the pressure in the arteries carries blood from the heart, through the neck, behind the eyes and into the base of your brain.

"From the base of your brain, the blood circulates to the front half of the brain from the carotid arteries and to the back half from the vertebral arteries. From the arteries, the blood is passed to the capillary network.

"Here is the problem. In the capillaries, imagine the slight pooling and eddying currents of the blood in the dilated or enlarged capillaries. The dilation creates pressure and leakage of fluid from the capillaries, which pushes the surrounding brain tissue. This, in turn, presses the brain tissue into the confining skull, and thus the headache.

"Now, let's correct the problem. Draw back the fluid into the capillary, flushing the excesses of fluid that have gathered around the capillary bed back into the circulatory system.

"Use the power of your mind's eye. Keep breathing deeply. Slow your pulse. Visualize draining the fluid re-entering the circulatory system. Aided by gravity, the blood will flow to the veins.

"The veins will carry the blood and the excess fluid back to the heart. It will pass from the right side of the heart, through the lungs where the exchange of gases takes place through the gentle, slow, regular, deep breathing. The blood then goes the the left side of the heart.

"Now, you will send the excess blood to your left hand and raise your hand's temperature. Your hand is an extremity that can allow for excess fluid by the reddening and expansion of your skin. There heat can be dissipated into the atmosphere. And the pressure from your head will be released and gone."

The headache disappeared.

For me, this procedure of guided visualization combined with progressive deep muscle relaxation and meditation, though simple to perform, can take from 30 minutes to up to an hour to stop a nasty, migraine headache. It takes solitude as well. Some might prefer a shorter visualization.

I have since added a sentence to the meditation/visualization when I know I'm having a headache related to stress: Nothing is worth getting sick over.

I have also discovered an effective medicine for migraines, but I still use the technique in combination with a pill.

•   •   •

In addition to the physical effects of lowering blood pressure and stress, meditation, guided visualization, or time for relaxation can be a chance for some quiet moments, an intimate exercise for both the witness and the patient.

MAINTAINING HOPE

Most people would argue that maintaining hope is a good idea. It is especially true for patients. If patients think a situation is hopeless, they may give up fighting, and by doing so unintentionally accelerate the illness. Hopelessness breeds helplessness, which then begets futility. The researcher and author Jean Achterberg contends that the absence of hope can be dangerous. She says, "Helplessness can literally be lethal, or barring that, significantly detrimental to the individual's health and well-being....Helplessness...is normally associated with severe depression, apathy, and loss of energy."

Maintaining hope is important for caregivers as well. How this is accomplished is not so easy.

Sometimes it is hard to face the fact that illness is a predictable human factor and that death is a necessary outcome of life. The reality of death, its various causes, and the utterly confounding factor of its unpredictability, make us feel completely out of control when we dare to contemplate it. Taking some positive actions might improve the length and quality of life, but we are nonetheless certain we will all have the same outcome as a conclusion of our lives.

Some people maintain hope by finding strength in their spiritual or religious philosophies, which provide a transcendent logic to events. Some people believe there is a reason for everything that happens. Some make peace with the mystery or the chaos of the universe.

Praying can help ventilate emotions, build endurance, and create a foundation for resolute persistence. As an additional bonus, a recent study about the efficacy of prayer has shown that the power of prayer has not been exaggerated as a healing technique. In a double-blind study of patients admitted to a coronary care unit, the cardiologist Randolph C. Byrd found that prayer, one of the oldest of healing therapies, had beneficial effect on patients. Unbeknownst to them, some patients were prayed for daily by a group of "born again"

Christians outside the hospital who knew their first names, diagnoses, and general condition; patients received prayers for a speedy recovery, and for prevention of complications or death (allowing those who prayed to be a bit creative in adding other elements). The patients and those who prayed for them were not matched by religious philosophy. Patients who received no prayer were set up in a control group. Those patients receiving prayer had less congestive heart failure, they required less diuretics and antibiotics, they had fewer episodes of pneumonia, fewer cardiac arrests, and they were less frequently intubated and ventilated; in short, they had fewer complications and better recoveries.

Some religions provide philosophies that explain suffering and offer comforting notions of heaven, eternal salvation, life after death, or reincarnation. For some, faith begets trust and an unshakeable equanimity. Other witnesses, in the face of illness, suffer from their faith being tested. Their God ceases to be of comfort. Some feel guilt for unknown sins. Some feel betrayed, for rarely does illness seem just.

Sometimes, hope is maintained by the strength that comes from friends who bind in support, or the strength comes from faith in the doctor or the medical system. In other cases, hope seems to come from introspection—an increased inner life activity that focuses on an eclectic combination of spiritual, religious, and secular guidance.

Many people use what could be called *enforced optimism*, looking at every event, every challenge, every situation with the certainty that everything will turn out all right. Doubt is the enemy. Sometimes this is a good strategy, similar to denial.

Optimism can help through treacherous times. It can be a catalyst to alter inertia and motivate psychological and physical change. Positive energy can enable problem-solving. Visualizing a positive outcome is a worthy goal to promote internal and external healing. However, it is unrealistic to expect optimism to anesthetize the experience of witnessing illness or to create miracles. It is easy to confuse hope with expectation. While it is true that optimism will *encourage* or *facilitate* positive results more than pessimism might, thinking optimistically will not necessarily *produce* the results that are expected by wishful thinking.

There are times when optimism doesn't help witnesses. Some people have joked that a pessimist is an optimist with experience, but optimism becomes a problem when it is a lie. A lie can endanger trust. Positive thinking also can be physically exhausting when it is a charade, when it counters the truth of feelings. Being falsely cheerful can be an immense pressure (and completely irritating to a patient who is not doing well and senses the dishonesty). In its extreme form, optimism may lead to a denial of reality, which may then cause inappropriate action or nonaction. However, in a more philosophical vein, ceaseless optimism may shield the fact that there are always positive and negative aspects in life. In fact, negativity is sometimes a positive force, necessary for growth or change.

There can be a balance. There is, after all, an inappropriate rigidity in being either optimistic or pessimistic all the time, although there are people who seem bound to certain types of thinking, because of their personality and style.

.   .   .

Woody Allen's character, Alvy, in Annie Hall *is a perfect fictional negative personality. In the bookstore scene, he warns Annie that he has a pessimistic view of life—dividing life into the horrible and the miserable. The horrible are people with terminal illnesses, those who are blind and crippled. Everyone else fits into the miserable category, and he tells her to be thankful they are miserable, because they are the lucky ones.*

.   .   .

Though there are people who love to complain, for most people positive thinking feels more energizing than negative thinking. Visualizing a positive outcome has been known to work as an adjunct to traditional medical care, and as a stress reliever for both patients and witnesses. Unfortunately, in some cases, realism and truth have become secondary virtues in the unflagging pursuit of positive thinking. Yet, if witnesses acknowledge that positive and negative feelings and events do exist, and that it is natural to experience the good and the bad, they will not get into the bind of inappropriate good cheer, or feel guilty about the inability to outlaw sad or negative feelings. This balance of thinking can be called *mindful optimism*, incorporating hope with realism.

In her book *Mindfulness*, Ellen J. Langer describes *mindfulness* as a limber state of mind. This definition could suggest that positive thinking or negative thinking is good in specific contexts. There are fewer examples where negative thinking is a good strategy; nonetheless, many people do use it successfully as a way to escape disappointment.

. . .

James, a biochemist and research scientist who depends on grant money to complete his projects, always takes the position that he will not get his proposal funded.

"If they give me the money, I'll be pleasantly surprised. I won't risk being upset, which could sap my determination to try again elsewhere."

He describes this negative thinking as a personal ritual to lessen the possibility of pain resulting from failure.

. . .

Similarly, actors and writers are coached to expect rejection. In a witness context, some caregivers feel more comfortable expecting the worst. They prefer to prepare themselves with a worst-case scenario first, then cope with reality, which may be less troublesome.

The power of mindfulness or mindful optimism is its flexibility. In a sense, this style of original thinking is a commitment to looking at every new situation with fresh vision, embracing uncertainty as part of the process. Each situation and context is viewed without previous automatic mindsets or incorrect generalizations like: All old people are senile or all cancer patients die. Those who are mindful avoid reflexive and thoughtless solutions in favor of rethinking old categories and creating new points of view. Jon Kabat-Zinn, in his stress clinic, teaches attitudinal factors in achieving mindfulness that he believes are crucial to balanced thinking: nonjudgment of self, using impartial observation; patience; a beginner's mind that is willing to see everything as if for the first time; trust in oneself and one's feelings; and acceptance of the present—letting go and letting things be as they are. It is important to remember that mindful optimism is an ongoing *process*, and a method of thinking that is neither automatic nor constant. For the witness, there will be days filled with doubts, conflicts, anger, pain, and sadness: normal feelings and normal lapses in strength and disciplined thinking.

Langer says that the rewards of mindfulness are sharpened judgment and increased self-esteem. When this process of thinking is specifically related to the process of witnessing illness, such advice as reframing events to change the way witnesses look at life (it could always be worse) or reinterpreting the situation (though it was hard to live through, this life experience taught me a great deal) or seeing life as a process rather than focusing on an outcome (taking one day at a time—the sage advice of Alcoholics Anonymous) makes enormous sense.

It still may be a challenge to maintain hope in the midst of a serious and life-threatening illness. Arthur Frank feels it is possible to have a "faith that allows us to accept whatever just happens and at the same time a will to bring about the change we desire." With hope, there is room for surprises and miracles. For some, hope is quiet and persistent, like a heartbeat not always noticed, but always there. Hope becomes a deep confidence that the patient will survive. Or, if the patient clearly won't survive the illness, hope becomes that feeling that the remaining time that is spent together will be as good as it possibly can be.

HEALTHY AND CREATIVE OUTLETS FOR EMOTIONS

As with depression or feeling hurt, we may cultivate guilt in order to blot out the awareness of our own anger. Anger and guilt are just about incompatible. If we feel guilty about not giving enough or not doing enough for others, it is unlikely we will be angry about not getting enough.

– Harriet G. Lerner

Frustration, impatience, betrayal, dishonesty, helplessness, disappointment, stupidity, greed, insensitivity, irrationality, and injustice can all lead to anger. Anger is a signal that could represent any number of issues. In her book *The Dance of Anger*, Harriet G. Lerner suggests other reasons for anger: hurt, something not being right, desires being thwarted, when there is more giving being performed than is comfortable, when others are doing too much at the expense of personal competence and growth.

Anger is a primal emotion linked to survival, and it has its personal and social functions as well. Emmy Gut contends that anger speeds up thought and action, quickens defenses, helps to express demands and complaints, helps to meet emergencies, persuades others to negotiate, give in, proceed more cautiously, or leave. Lerner postulates that "anger is neither legitimate or illegitimate, meaningful or pointless...anger simply is." She says, "We all have a right to everything we feel—and certainly our anger is no exception."

Anger, along with irritability, rage, and hostility, makes most people want to respond by taking some aggressive action, especially aimed at the offending party. Anger makes people calculate their responses differently: concern for others may decrease while the wish to hurt increases. Anger is so intense, preoccupying, and unpleasant that the desire to get rid of the anger overwhelms feelings about tolerance. Although most of us have been tamed and civilized, the veneer of civility is easily broken by intense emotion. Anger is frequently self-regulated, because of the power of anger's ability and desire to do harm.

Assertiveness is an adaptive way to channel anger. Using assertiveness, people become articulate, purposeful, and directed to achieve a positive action—that is, when there is an appropriate target or person for the appeal. When there is no target or the target of anger is inappropriate—as it might be for witnesses who can get frustrated with a patient who is not really at fault—learning what to do with anger can be more of a challenge. Specifically, the task is to try to avoid the self becoming the target of aggression for the lack of anyone or anything else.

Some people stew with their anger; others ventilate their anger by a direct confrontation. The danger of confrontation is escalation. Positions on both sides can become more rigid if the dance of anger continues indefinitely. Righteous indignation, and its expression, doesn't necessarily change things. On the other hand, sometimes a forceful confrontation not only works in getting rid of anger, but it may occasionally change a situation, as it did for Doug.

· · ·

On Sunday, I found myself angry with Mike, who himself was angry and anxious. He had been in the hospital for treatment of his psychiatric problems for many months. He was frustrated by his inability to meet me halfway, and I felt his dependency weighing heavily on me.

Finally, I confronted Mike. I angrily and emphatically insisted he recognize the limits of my power to cure him and my unwillingness to encourage his suicide.

Within a week of my assertions, he was improving miraculously. To be sure, he was still in the hospital and not able to care for himself safely, but the pieces were definitely pulling back together.

I didn't much like the unpleasant task of a controlled display of angry passion at the patient. But it was worth the gratification I gained in observing his reintegration to health. And it made us feel better. . . this time.

· · ·

Lerner suggests that simply venting anger is often not enough; instead she proposes trying to solve the problem, changing the circumstances that provoked anger, and changing one's own behavior instead of trying to change others.

Anger is only one of the many emotions witnesses will feel and need to air. The pain and drama of witnessing illness will awaken memories, emotions, thoughts, and actions that can make witnesses feel like strangers to themselves. Witnesses might find the need to process these feelings by talking about it, shouting about it, or releasing it in some way. Almost any creative act—from participating in the art of conversation to journal writing—can alleviate helplessness by exerting control and expressing emotion. The amusing Irish proverb about the inevitability of releasing emotions goes: "The more you cries, the less you pees."

With or without a therapist, the process of introspection and self-analysis may help work through the complex external and internal problems witnesses might face. Some witnesses may prefer to discuss problems with medical personnel, therapists, counselors, social workers, trusted friends, or patients. Talking about the experience of witnessing may make it feel more real emotionally. Sharing the experience helps witnesses understand their own feelings and be understood by others. The impact comes closer to the surface, and in fact, may be mirrored by the person who is listening, confirming the gravity of the situation. "Oh, I'm sorry," they might say. "That's awful." Moreover, the very act of translating feelings into words—the intellectualization and organization of the experience into a story—moves the witness into the process of analysis. Once this occurs, the event can be slightly removed, or distanced, and thus examined, validated, and discussed. Talking about the problem may diminish isolation, help clear the mind, ease the pain, and even result in getting information about coping. Often, people who suffer the most are those who get fixated or trapped in their feelings, remain in a state of helplessness and cannot or will not move out, sometimes because of a fear of change. Venting disappointment and unpleasant feelings more often leads to equanimity.

Of course, witnesses need to be careful about choosing the people who will listen to their stories. Those who respond with disbelief, criticism, or belittling comments might insult and injure witnesses who do not need additional victimization. Rather, witnesses should try to seek out family members, friends, colleagues, counselors, therapists, or a support group where empathic caring is more assured. A meaningful and trusting communion with others also serves to underscore the possibility that new relationships have their merits and that life is filled with rich experiences and the potential for healing and growth.

On the other hand, some caregivers might prefer working out problems in introspective solitude or by journal writing.

· · ·

Writing my journal kept me sane. Witnessing illness had staggering emotional repercussions for me. I was both enraged and deeply touched by what I witnessed. I wrote to cope and to find some time alone, away from the chaos, and sort through some of the complex flow of emotions that swept through and disturbed me.

Writing diffused my tensions and let me be privately aggressive. Writing particularly helped to release the intense anger I felt at times—anger at life, at the medical establishment, at helplessness, at injustices, at God. Not commonly given to outbursts of anger, I had felt hostage to emotions that felt out of control.

Carolyn G. Heilbrun, in her book Writing a Woman's Life, *wrote, "If one is not permitted to express anger or even to recognize it within oneself, one is, by simple extension, refused both power and control." She contends that historically, when women could not complain publicly, they took refuge in depression or madness; or if they did write, they were criticized as being shrill or strident. In my case, my anger, in part, propelled the inception of the book.*

Every witness will experience his or her own autobiographical landscape. While witnessing illness, absolutely, has common threads of feeling and experience, it is also intensely personal.

My story is just one of many.

• • •

A journal may be the only safe way to release feelings. Sometimes friends who have little experience in witnessing illness might have a hard time discussing or understanding the experience. Often people don't know how to react to the intense emotions of witnesses. They might not know what to say to ameliorate the pain, and witnesses might not need or want advice. Sometimes, too, there is no one around to talk to.

Writing in a journal is a positive, cathartic method to clear the mind and recapture some control. Transforming stressful events into a written story helps to organize and assimilate the meaning of the experience.

Emotions can be read instead of felt, resulting in a certain amount of objective distance and increased self-awareness. Indeed, in a study done by James W. Pennebaker and Sandra Klihr Beall from Southern Methodist University, confession in diaries or to close friends may improve the immune system and long-term health maintenance. Students in their study wrote about the facts and emotions of traumatic life events. Though at first, this storytelling heightened their blood pressure and negative moods immediately after writing, six months later, they had fewer health center visits. In their discussion, they theorized that people who had failed to disclose or discuss traumatic events in their lives had more health problems; inhibiting or repressing the event takes physiological work that might accumulate stress and increase the probability of stress-related illnesses. Carrying a notebook and writing in it when life gets difficult seems like an easy and cheap exercise in preventive medicine. Writing can also easily be done in the quiet moments of caregiving.

Sandra G. Shuman, educator and counselor, has written, "Being creative is a spiritual anti-pollutant, helping us gain our psychic equilibrium....The psyche registers every creative act as a birth." Any creative effort or imaginative enterprise that witnesses may try—art, music, clothing design, woodworking, model-building, gardening, for example—will surely nurture them.

BUILDING A NETWORK OF SUPPORT

Many caregivers, especially primary caregivers, are reluctant to seek support and instead remain alone in their suffering.

. . .

Nora, a painter and college instructor in her early 50s, found out suddenly that her husband had a brain tumor. But instead of seeking outside support, she stayed close to her husband and two children.

"I feel like a 'black cloud,' bringing with me the message of death and the image of an impending widow. I do not have the energy to comfort others who see me. I will not do the dance of denial for anyone's benefit."

Instead, she resolved to be strong. She coped within the intimate confines of her family, although she recognized the importance of one friend who called her every week during the ordeal.

. . .

Witnesses need time off, and it is hard, indeed, to persuade them it is necessary, especially when there is the ticking time clock of impending loss. However, witnesses might become overinvested in being the primary caregiver, wanting to do it all themselves, while in the process inadvertently becoming isolated (along with the patient). Whether this caregiving stems from love, fear, altruism, or lack of insight, witnesses need to tend to their health and the patient's need to feel connected with others as well. In other words, **witnesses should try to share the burden of caregiving**—even if only occasionally. It can also be an extraordinary opportunity—granted, a mixed blessing—for intimacy with select friends and family members. Building a network of support will be helpful to witness and patient alike.

Witnesses need witnesses of their own for emotional support.

.   .   .

Joseph, a newspaper editor in his late 40s, had just witnessed his daughter's kidney transplant.

During the crisis and for some time afterward, he received many calls asking how his daughter was doing.

He began to get annoyed. "Why isn't anyone asking me how I feel? I feel terrible."

.   .   .

Some witnesses will find comfort in their normal support group of friends, families, or colleagues. However, some find a support group of relative strangers who are going through similar problems more helpful to put matters in perspective. Witnesses may feel freer to discuss problems with others who are likely to understand the circumstances, who are not personally involved, and who lack the emotional tie of a shared history. There is evidence to suggest that being in a support group improves a caregiver's health. In a study of caregivers, J. K. Kiecolt-Glaser, and others found that caregiver participation in a support group increased the strength of the caregivers' immunological systems.

This support can be particularly helpful to counter feelings of rejection from the patient that can often happen during the course of illness. During mental and physical stress, a sick person may prefer to be alone and even ask for isolation to work through problems, gain strength and equilibrium through silence. This desire tends to be hardest on witnesses or friends who have their own needs to be of help and support (and to be acknowledged by the patient).

• • •

Harry, a physics professor, was about to have a prostate operation.
A week before the procedure, he expressed the desire to be alone
so he could be introspective and avoid the benign but constant in-
terrogation of some of his colleagues.

He confided in his close buddy and primary witness that he
was particularly worried about his department chairman, who
wanted to know the details of his upcoming surgery.

His buddy tried to explain the witness point of view: needing
information, wanting to express concern, feeling the desire to help.
Nonetheless, Harry still wanted a break from his job and needed
to protect his privacy.

His buddy suggested that he screen his telephone calls. Harry
created a message on his phone answering machine that he was
writing and would be available to talk one afternoon a week. In
this way, he could minimize intrusion without appearing to shut
everyone else out.

After the operation, when he was able to speak more freely,
he lifted the phone when he wanted to.

• • •

During a period of isolation, rejection, or abandonment, witnesses
can lose the pleasure of intimacy with the patient. This can mean the
loss of comfort, support, and shared storytelling that family, friends,
or loved ones often share with ease. Sometimes the rejection is temporary; other times, the separation signals a transition or permanent
change in the relationship.

The physical and emotional perils of rejection need more study
and exploration. Being refused, spurned, cast away, or forsaken surely
takes its toll on the body, much like stress. Rejection can be a form
of abuse, though it is not widely regarded that way. The conventional
wisdom to counter the effects of rejection is odd: don't take it personally. Yet, rejection *is* personal. What this statement really means
is: don't let rejection have an effect on you; it's not your fault; it's not
about you, or it's not *just* about you; it's about you and other factors
out of your control. The idea is to encourage strength and to restrain

despairing emotions in the face of what looks like personal defeat; in other words, the advice is to employ rationalization as a coping solution. For witnesses, this may be impossible; they may be too vulnerable.

For most witnesses, the normal reaction to feeling rejected is to feel hurt, disappointment, or at the very least, feel some vague, but tolerable pain. As the screenwriter and actress Ruth Gordon has written, "A kick in the pants never feels good." Although witnesses might understand the rejection, because of a patient's pain, agony, or need, it is rarely easy to accept it. Witnesses, however, may take comfort in the awareness that they weren't responsible for the patient's emotional state. Hurt may occur, nonetheless.

In the end, not taking rejection personally really means to honor and accept oneself, despite assaults, holding one's self-esteem sacredly intact. This is a goal worthy of pursuit. On the way to the goal, however, witnesses might want to restore themselves by turning to others in their network of support, helping another who needs their help, or helping themselves to a dose of unbridled pleasure—like a double-dip chocolate fudge sundae, or a day in bed under some cozy covers.

SETTING BOUNDARIES

Emotions can be contagious. Some people who are highly reactive to stimulus or overly empathic—who often feel like a psychic sponge— are more sensitive to this problem than others. However, most people have encountered times when emotions or moods are infectious. For example, at a dinner table, one person in a foul mood can contaminate the atmosphere, while someone who is inexplicably jolly can inspire good cheer.

In a similar way, a depressed person can produce distress in others. In a study exploring the effects of living with a depressed person, researchers at the University of Michigan found that 40 percent of the witnesses in their study became so distressed that they met the criterion for psychological intervention themselves. The witnesses—burdened with someone who was tired, listless, apathetic, worried, and lacking in self-esteem—became strained by being the "strong one," losing the ability to plan for or participate in a social life.

Being aware that the emotional state of patients can affect their own sense of well-being, caregivers might want to protect their emotional boundaries, thus safeguarding themselves as well as the patient. When the patient and caregiver are both miserable, life becomes more difficult. This is not to say that anyone should hide their emotions.

·   ·   ·

Ellen, a lawyer in her late 20s, was a Buddy to Roger, a fellow lawyer in his final stages of AIDS.

Roger was not an easy guy to nurture. He was cranky, selfish, and demanding, but Ellen liked him nonetheless.

When Ellen called before her normal visit, Roger asked for some homemade chocolate pudding. Ellen had never made it before, but she set herself to the challenge and arrived at Roger's several hours later.

"Where in the hell were you?" was Roger's greeting when she came into his apartment.

Ellen replied loudly, "Listen, this is the first time I've ever made this damn pudding or any other like it. I hate it when you're so ungrateful."

Roger calmed down, apologized, and then thoroughly enjoyed pigging out on his pudding.

Ellen felt better after she yelled at Roger, but she also understood him. "Roger's demands," she said, "were his way of asking if I loved him enough to do something special for him."

·   ·   ·

Even the suffering need to hear when they are trespassing boundaries. Truth is always the best way to maintain trust in relationships. However, when a caregiver is feeling emotionally weary or vulnerable or when events necessitate time to process and relieve emotions, caregivers should consider leaving and taking time to regroup.

Caregivers should also be aware of taking on the physical symptoms of the patient, commonly known as sympathy pains. Instead of feeling and confronting fears of separation, pain, or loss, witnesses may trap pains in their bodies rather than in their minds. Sometimes, this mirroring of symptoms may be out of the caregivers' control, unless they divorce themselves from direct and primary witnessing. On the other hand, sympathy pains sometimes arise from a sense of guilt. If the patient is unable to eat, often caregivers feel guilty about their appetite and promptly lose it.

While it is easy to suggest setting emotional boundaries, actually accomplishing the task can be a challenge. For some caregivers, this is why setting some physical boundaries—such as taking time off—becomes essential. However, some witnesses have learned that by conscious intention, they can separate their emotions from the patient. Some have even done this by visualization techniques—building an imaginary shield around themselves. Others picture an internal porous screen, honeycomb, or even a flow-through tea bag where emotions from others are consciously processed right through the body without sticking.

In the spirit of self-preservation, witnesses may also need to consider budgeting their time. How much time will be devoted to the patient: Will it be twenty-four hours a day—under what circumstances and for what reasons? Once-a-year visits? Weekly or nightly phone calls?

●   ●   ●

Carol, a 40-year-old mother of two grown children starting a new career, is a distant witness to her mother, who has become virtually an invalid through multiple illnesses. She is in a wheelchair and going blind. Carol's father is the primary witness. Carol has three older brothers.

Carol never got along well with her mother, whom she described as self-centered, distant, manipulative, and selfish.

Because of her mother's demands that Carol tend to her more frequently than her once-every-three-month visits, Carol is in conflict. She feels sympathy for her mother, who is helpless, but her mother is also thankless and ungracious, which makes Carol withdraw in anger.

Carol described an incident that illustrated her feelings. During a rare visit to Carol's home, her mother was given a wheelchair that friends had located. Her mother noticed that a part on the chair was missing. Instead of thanking the friends, she proceeded to insult and berate them for their stupidity.

Carol wants to be close with her mother. She wants to discuss the fears that her mother is experiencing about her handicaps and her serious illness, but Carol feels guilty that she can never quite seem to get to it. She admits, though, that they were never intimate.

Carol realizes it is she more than her mother who needs to talk. However, she still faces the conflicts over being far away, loving and hating her mother, and feeling guilty, ashamed, and angry. She has a desire to help her mother, and yet a simultaneous revulsion from her experience of being rejected when she tries.

Despite her mother's pleas for help, Carol has decided to remain within the boundaries she has set for her own mental health. These are boundaries that were always there for her.

·　　·　　·

A decision about how much time is spent may be negotiable; other times, a choice is made by circumstance or fate. Sometimes, choices about boundaries may become more dramatic.

·　　·　　·

"The only hope of the adult is that things will get worse slowly."

Richard, a talented wordsmith whose mother's stroke had made him a tired and beleaguered witness with his longtime companion, Dale, was having a particularly bad week. (A portion of Dale's witness journal, about her mother-in-law's stroke, was used in Chapter 3.) His truck was stolen in the midst of his mother's health crisis. Richard and Dale had already quit their jobs, relocated from their home in another state, and moved in with Richard's mother to take care of her.

"I'm supposed to view this as two discrete events, but I can't. This is my reward for tearing up my own life, leaving my home, friends, and crummy job to come down here and do the honorable thing.

"If I'd been selfish, and part of me wishes I had, I'd still have my goddamned truck instead of some illiterate, feral swine.... I hope I am soon successful in drinking and/or smoking myself to death.... But I just go on cooking three meals a day, emptying slop

buckets, being hopeful at the hospital, chilling out with the laundry, vacuuming, cleaning toilets, and generally spit-shining this museum.

"I am tired, and feel my life is over as if I were one of those poor old folk who spend their days shitting themselves and waiting for the Cosmic Comedian to pull the plug."

Compounding his problems was his mother's vitriolic sister, Florence, who did nothing but criticize his caregiving. Everyone who knew Aunt Florence disliked her. She was cranky, tactless, cruel, and clever, and thrived on abusing others. She was abusive not only to Richard, but also to Dale.

At first, Florence was merely menacing, making nuisance phone calls to them early in the morning, demanding that they perform certain chores as if they didn't already know what to do. Though they tried to ignore her, Florence started to make them feel incompetent and furious.

They then noticed that Florence was stealing her sister's valuable antiques, claiming them to be her own and perniciously taking advantage of her sister's weakened memory. She also started giving away her sister's knickknacks to her friends, in front of Richard and Dale, as if to anger them.

But then, their aunt's behavior started to affect their mother. Because Florence had an abrasive personality, she had already alienated a neighborhood doctor. She also interfered with medical appointments, canceling them without notice so she could be in control. In Richard's words, Florence had "a history of thrusting disastrous decisions on family members, derived from the turgid cesspool of her mental processes."

Florence, however, was not a simple menace. She acted like a truly concerned caregiver, bringing food and trinkets that disguised her malice. She had also gotten power of attorney from Richard's mother before Richard and Dale arrived.

Clearly on the offensive and waging psychological warfare, Florence called every member of the family, accusing Richard and Dale of being derelict in duty.

Richard, being a gentleman and quite respectful, tried to ignore his aunt's mean behavior. He was angry, but he and Dale kept the anger to themselves. However, Florence escalated her attacks, calling Dale a woman of ill repute.

Outraged, Richard started getting chest pains. He realized he was in danger, and this put his mother in danger. He decided to take control. He set his boundaries, and he did this by changing them. Within 24 hours, they packed up Richard's mother and drove her to their former home. There, they were able to take care of her in peace and with full support of their neighbors.

Fortunately, though the move was difficult, Richard's chest pains disappeared. His caregiving job is still hard. He wrote me, "Apparently my mother is to be spared nothing and will be required to die by inches. Sorrow and helplessness are added to the burden of physical exhaustion; it is hard to believe in a God who permits a blameless individual to suffer a death you wouldn't wish on a bad dog."

What was saving him was a genetic "Irish sense of the absurd," the ability to laugh at himself, which "keeps this flounder out of the rubber room."

Eventually, Richard's truck was found, and he apologized for what he called his outburst of self-pity. However, what really saved him was putting a limit to the abuse he took from his aunt, and taking control by leaving. Although he was sorry he had to relocate his mother, the move proved to be helpful.

Months later, with an active rehabilitation, his mother is recuperating from the stroke, though she still has some problems with her memory.

· · ·

Saying no, calling a halt to abuse, and taking care of oneself can be lifesaving. There are limits to anyone's energy, time, responsibility, and self-control.

Primary witnesses are especially prone to ill health after extended periods of nursing a patient's illness. By overextending personal, emotional, and physical resources, witnesses may also become depressed or suffer from other ailments that result from too much stress, fatigue, and sympathy. Moreover, becoming a martyr may not be entirely altruistic. Often, caregivers give too much of themselves to avoid dealing with their own problems.

Setting a boundary can be as simple as explaining what witnesses hope to accomplish during a visit. For example, saying to the patient, "I've come to visit, because I want to talk with you and share my concerns with you," sets some boundaries for expectations and tells the patient about the witness's needs. An open-ended approach would be to simply walk in, nod hello, not say anything, and to wait for the patient to tell the witness what he or she wants. Overattention can suffocate patients, not allowing them enough time to think, be silent, or heal themselves. However, setting a boundary can also be as complex as the decision to remain a distant caregiver or placing an Alzheimer's disease sufferer in institutional care. Setting boundaries will not always work, but the aim is not to feel totally powerless and burnt-out.

There is another kind of boundary: a boundary against the outside world. This is a time when patient and witness devote time to each other exclusively: no visits from others, no interruptions, no phone calls.

• • •

David and I would often take a day off from the world. I remember one day in particular. The week before had been wearisome.

We were trying to go about our normal business, but the chemotherapy side effects were taking center stage. Bleomycin had left brown streaks on David's shoulders, and a swelled and aching tongue full of mouth sores which made it hard for David to speak.

A week earlier, his hair started falling out. When we awoke, we noticed traces of body hair—pubic hair, leg hair, and head hair—strewn all over the sheets. And then there was silence. David just looked down at the pillowcase and started gently sweeping off the hairs. He went to the bathroom mirror, and I followed him. I assured him that I loved him. He went into the shower, and his hair streamed out of his scalp as easily as the soap drained off his body. When he dried off, he pulled the remaining strands of hair, testing for resilience. Maybe, he thought, some would stay.

During the week, David continued to look and feel awful. Along his muscled and hairless arms, his veins were clogged and discolored from the chemicals, resembling the track marks of a drug addict.

He had lost some 20 pounds, his eyes were sunken in ashen circles, his eyebrows and lashes greatly thinned.

David had lost all his hair. When there were only a few hairs left, he went to a barber to have his head shaved to get it over with. We shopped for hats. David didn't want to wear a wig.

Being bald wasn't easy for him. Aside from the obvious issues of vanity, there was the general public who didn't understand baldness in a young man. From being treated gently when he had a full head of curly hair, he was now crudely ridiculed. People called him a skinhead, sang hare-krishna chants as they walked by him, accused him of being in the military, and children pointed and jeered at him. Slightly kinder were those who just stared or thought he was a swimmer.

David took it in stride, though occasionally he had some revenge. In school, someone walked by and stopped to comment on his hair-cut. David told him the style was the result of chemotherapy. The guy, of course, slithered away.

It was time for an intimate vacation. As we cuddled together in bed, David cried for the first time as he faced the reality of his uncertain future. Soon, he would experience the rigors of another bout of chemotherapy, and he hated the prospect of being in the hospital again with peculiar roommates, the sterile environment, awful food, and strangers probing and piercing his body.

He said he had aged. His perceptions changed about institu-tions, his family, his ambition, his love. I didn't prod how. He spoke of efficient living, efficient dying, his body as machine, and the crudity of treatment. And the mistakes!

We held each other, soothed each other, made love, ate, read, played Scrabble, and listened to music.

We spoke softly, we stroked softly, and we knew this day was very precious. We acknowledged transience and agreed life teases with days like these when paradise is merely a cheek against a warm thigh while silence echoes the calmness of two loving spirits in refuge.

·   ·   ·

Exercising the power to set limits is a delicate procedure: a bal-ance between the needs of the patient and the witness. A medical professional witness talks about the nature of his boundaries.

•   •   •

Seth, a family nurse practitioner who specializes in adolescents with HIV, says, "I'm like a tightrope walker between the subjective and the objective, the personal and the professional. I give nurturance and care, yet I need to be objective enough to tell when someone needs something.

"I especially need to detach and put up a shield when I watch or help perform a painful procedure, but the boundary is permeable. I can't be cool and aloof entirely. If I ever lost my heart connection, I'd get out of this work.

"Though the work is sometimes painful, it is also satisfying. I like to help teenagers improve the quality of their lives, no matter how long they have to live.

"For example, one of my 17-year-old patients, Derek, who was in the final stages of AIDS, was partying in the hospital, making a lot of noise with all his friends who were visiting. When I told him he could only have one or two friends in his room, he said, 'I'm dying. Cut me a break.'

"I had to be firm. I told him, 'Well, you're not dying tonight.'

"This really didn't hurt my relationship with Derek. He came to know I would be honest with him. He died a couple of months later."

•   •   •

In the best of situations, this process of setting limits is made easier by the cooperation of friends and family. When working as a team, they can understand the reality of the situation and the uselessness of antagonism or interfering adversarial relationships. Making sure boundaries are set is a necessary part of healing. Take time out for play and for relaxation. Everyone will benefit.

PRODUCTIVE DEPRESSION

Witnesses often feel depressed and may actually suffer from clinical depression. With the drama of life and death unfolding before them, it is no wonder that caregivers become sad, discouraged, and frustrated. Sleep disruptions and loss of appetite—compounded with a spiritual malaise—all encourage a feeling of depression. This depression can lead to further anxiety, shame, and fear about the witness's personal psychological and physical demise.

To most people, being depressed may seem to be a pathological state, something definitely abnormal, even sick. Depression can feel like being surrounded by a great blackness or being stuck in a gaping abyss. There is a loss of interest in the world and in the desire to do much of anything. Friends don't seem to help. Witnesses may feel cut off from creative energy and their sense of humor. Small tasks—like washing and dressing—seem like arduous chores. The witnesses' self-esteem is lowered, not measuring up to impossible standards set for themselves.

However, it may be a relief for witnesses to understand that depression can be normal and productive. According to Emmy Gut, depression is sometimes an ordinary, adaptive response in the process of working out a life event of magnitude, whether it be grief, loss, or simply a change in life-style or routine. Gut's theory is that depression is a signal that an important problem is not getting the attention it deserves; thus, depression is useful when it allows us time to grapple with change, to cope with failure, or to complete a physical or psychological effort.

The typical social withdrawal that accompanies depression enables adaptation, problem-solving, and personal development. This isolation, Gut suggests, serves "to facilitate and protect concentration on intensified conscious or unconscious scanning, exploration and integration of relevant experience in ways that can lead to a resolution of internal deadlock or to recognition that the situation cannot be changed, so that a fruitless effort to do so can be abandoned."

Gut suggests that it is wrong to judge whether the depression is productive or unproductive while in the midst of depression. She suggests that this effect should be measured only at depression's end. If, in the end, depression leads to insight, learning, growth, or the ability to understand and analyze the cause of the depression, it is, indeed, productive. Perhaps some behavior is changed or has become more effective, or perhaps plans and goals are realistically revised. On the other hand, depression becomes unproductive, she says, when no change occurs, and health deteriorates.

The advice, then, for depressed witnesses is to acknowledge depression and permit the process of depression to work. The decrease in energy is probably allowing time to process new solutions to problems that are too overwhelming for normal problem-solving techniques; sometimes the nature of the problem is still unknown. Some witnesses experience delayed depression, mysteriously occurring on the anniversaries of a patient's illness. Isolation may bring self-awareness, changed perceptions, and eventually renewed vigor.

The distinction between feeling depressed and clinical depression is difficult to self-diagnose. Thus, seeking a professional opinion or intervention is strongly advised if the symptoms of depression are severe, recurring, unending or result in feelings of suicide. Therapists may be able to accelerate the process of recovery from depression.

HEALTHY DISTRACTIONS
AND PLEASURES

. . . life without pleasure—without spontaneity and playfulness, sexuality and sensuality, esthetic experience, surprise, excitement, ecstasy—is a kind of death. People deprived of pleasure don't get kinder and gentler but meaner and nastier. . . . Guilt always backfires because it only aggravates the pleasure shortage.

– Ellen Willis

There is no such thing as inner peace. There is only nervousness or death. Any attempt to prove otherwise constitutes unacceptable behavior.

– Fran Lebowitz

Worried sick, burnt-out: both terms express the strong need for a respite. This is the time that witnesses need to identify what they need, and then find the time to get those needs met.

The idea of seeking pleasure while another suffers can be hard to accept. It can feel selfish or heartless. The witness may feel guilty about thinking about fun. Similarly, some caregivers experience *anhedonia*, the inability to find fun in activities that ordinarily provide pleasure. But, seeking pleasure and joy—for merely brief periods of time—is rejuvenating and affirms life.

There is always time for laughter and humor. A sense of humor often retreats when one is dealing with illness, but when it blossoms forth with just the right touch—when the joke really works, when the witticism has impeccable timing, or the unexpected one-liner is deliciously truthful and rebellious—laughter is a pleasurable emotional release. It can also serve to soften tension and entertain. In his quest to document and explore the benefits of humor, Norman Cousins found that laughter—what he called "internal jogging"—has significant biological and psychological effects. In addition to renewing physical and spiritual resources, he said laughter increases circulation, oxygen consumption, and creativity, provides physical exercise and perspective, bolsters the immune system, alleviates pain, helps to combat stress, and promotes the ability to appreciate the foibles of the human condition.

There are plenty of other simple pleasures: being in the company of others, taking a walk, swimming, going to the gym, appreciating the weather, taking a long, hot bath in candlelight, eating, getting a pizza delivery, touching, reading, listening to music, having sex, taking a small siesta, staying in bed all day, or experiencing a full night's sleep. Other forms of healthy distraction might include going out to the theater, watching a film, renting a video, watching television, playing games, or tending to a pet.

Though it may seem an unusual suggestion, even going to work can be a good distraction from the exhausting job of witnessing illness. Caregivers rarely realize the amount of work they are accomplishing. The stress of helplessness can accumulate. As a method to alleviate feelings of helplessness, the psychologist Martin Seligman suggests that outside work is essential. The persistent demands of a job and the actions of reading, writing, or solving problems might alleviate stress or fear by concentrating the mind on tasks that are possible to control. For many people, however, work is not always a pleasure, and caregivers should try to look elsewhere for relief from the rigors of witnessing illness.

OTHER WAYS TO REDUCE STRESS

The following is a suggested and partial list of general advice to help reduce stress and increase self-nurturance:

- perform regular self-examination of stressors, find the sources of the stress, and try to manage them;
- exercise, rest, eat balanced meals, monitor salt and sugar intake, reduce caffeine, and take vitamins;
- monitor personal health and visit a doctor when necessary;
- periodically rethink priorities and reassess goals;
- choose realistic options that reflect personal values and account for personal strengths and weaknesses;
- face the reality of situations that cannot be changed or tasks that cannot be accomplished;
- establish a reasonable routine: scheduling time for solitude and entertainment, and allowing time to cope with unexpected events;
- relate to others with sensitivity, humor, and politeness;
- ventilate emotions;
- take control by making decisions and organizing personal life for maximum comfort;
- recognize personal stress reducers and keep them handy—like books, toys, amulets, notepads, toiletries, or a favorite drink or snack.

CONCLUSION

Perhaps the last step in self-nurturance is self-acceptance: empowering ourselves with unconditional positive regard and quality care, dispensed with gentle kindness and compassion. For most people, self-acceptance is a process filled with occasional successes and failed attempts. Some fortunate few do accomplish the sweetness of total acceptance. But for the rest of humanity, this happens only on occasion. In striving for self-acceptance, we note our most basic frailties and imperfections. Some extraordinary few can accept their own imperfections: a love of self even with false starts, peculiar odors, inherent laziness, failed ambitions, and forsaken dreams. But more likely, our internal critic presses for more discipline, ambition, truth, exercise, patience, compassion, success, energy, wealth, beauty, integrity, and courage.

There is little humanity in the ideal, for inherent in the ideal is perfection, and the perfect excludes the rest of our moments of being all-too-human.

Witnessing illness can be a trap for compulsive helpers. On the other hand, there are people who feel that their most positive trait is caregiving, that being in the service of another is how they achieve self-esteem and how they matter to others. Again, perhaps balance is the key.

If witnesses don't take any time for themselves, they might suffer immediately after the crisis is over. They might feel depressed, or they might seem unable to shake the feeling that the patient is fine, but they are not. Something lingers that they cannot rationalize or define. This is the time when the whole experience finally sinks in, and the adrenaline is gone. Retrospection sets in with the pure exhaustion. The caregiver's own emotional or physical vulnerabilities may show themselves.

Adaptively attending to mind, body, and spirit in the face of assaultive change is crucial for survival. Witnesses will be of no help to others unless they pace themselves. As such, they should try to make sure to factor in personal needs as part of the pressing business of caregiving. Active witnessing does not mean being selfless; it is short-sighted to care for another at the expense of personal health and well-being.

7

THE PROCESS OF CHANGE
Anticipation, Loss, Letting Go, and Recovery

Hope, faith, love and a strong will to live offer no promise of immortality, only proof of our uniqueness as human beings and the opportunity to experience full growth even under the grimmest circumstances.
– Norman Cousins
Head First

Professionals talk too much about adjustment. I want to emphasize mourning as affirmation. To mourn what has passed, either through illness or death, affirms the life that has been led.
– Arthur Frank
At the Will of the Body

Any moment now, I could be wiped out like a word on a blackboard.
– Salman Rushdie
Haroun and the Sea of Stories

THE PROCESS OF CHANGE

For the witness, change begins with a suspicion that something is wrong and then progresses through a process of discovery. For most witnesses, the journey is continued with the patient through diagnosis and treatment. Throughout the journey, there is stress from acute events as well as the more mundane stress of chronic illness. For some, losing the patient and enduring the finality of dying becomes the next step in the process of witnessing. Yet, beyond grief stands the edifice of recovery.

ANTICIPATION

In exploring the minds of his patients, Freud observed that people have an almost universal fear of death. In some phases of life, particularly during youth, people believe and act as if they were immortal. He noticed that even in dreams, his patients woke up before they died. Some might call this a denial of death.

Denial is a well-documented phase in the literature of death and dying. When patients or witnesses hear the news of a terminal diagnosis or impending death, often the first spontaneous response is almost reflexive: "I can't believe it. This must be a mistake." Feelings may be inhibited, blocked, numbed, or avoided to mitigate their strength.

However, after this initial phase, witnesses may slip into *anticipatory grief*, an emotional response to the pain of separation, or change, before the actuality of loss. This period of advance grief when loss is perceived as inevitable is characterized by the stress of waiting, longing for relief, and confronting the fears of abandonment, loss of control, and pain.

• • •

The call came as a surprising interruption of my routine afternoon. In the midst of office hours I heard my mother choke out the words, "Your father collapsed at a pharmacy. The paramedics were working on him. You'll come, won't you?"

I'd been avoiding my grief—my dad had been ill with a weak heart and I'd known it, but the thoughts of the love left unsaid, and the intimate moments that had never matured beyond the realm of my imagination now consumed me.

At 35,000 feet above sea level, I calmed myself with alcohol. The gamut of emotions had run through me. I felt turned inside and out. I had both observed and experienced my emotions. I thought about options. But, options? There were none. I felt painfully limited. How long had I prepared myself for this loss? Hadn't I tried to make each day as full as I could? Alas, I was far from perfect in my efforts; shame and guilt competed with disappointment, grief, and sadness.

What will I find when I arrive at the hospital? How will I behave? I took comfort in knowing it was my father's wish not to go on with life if it was to be inactive, limited, without the meanings he had sought and attained. I could both respect and accept his wish, and I found solace in that knowledge. He'd never been a man of organized religion. His faith was in his values of honesty, integrity, and respect. In his way, it was his dignity. He could be stubborn and childish. He could be innocently hurt, as he'd been by the misadventure of the allergic reaction to the X-ray dye that had provoked the first of his heart attacks.

Perhaps it is my sense of guilt that shifted my thinking at that juncture—away from the line of who could be held accountable for his heart disease and dying, but not too far away. I wondered how well I really knew him. I did not expect him to survive. I believed that his will to live was diminishing. I was beginning to think of him in the past tense. I began to mourn his passage for me and for my mother, but I believed he would have his rest. I cried quietly, I think, unobserved by my fellow passengers.

In less than eight hours, I'd covered 2,000 miles and arrived at the hospital. As I entered the hospital, I reminded myself that I was alone. As on the plane, I could have sought out companionship. I could have tried to share my lonely passage. After all, everyone knows loss and grief and all are willing to share a few minutes to lessen a fellow traveler's pain, right?

My chest felt funny, my eyes were moist, my throat was tight—in the plane, at the car rental place, on the drive to the hospital, as I crossed the parking lot and entered the building on that humid Florida night. I did know the place. I had been there just a few months before on a similar journey, and even more than that, I'd spent more than 20 years working in such places. This trip felt peculiarly ominous. Now, I would find my way to yet another bedside, but this one was the most special ever. Soon, I would know if my father still breathed or if a machine was doing that for him. Though I am practiced in the arts of trying out thought in preparation for action, I felt leaden.

This part of witnessing is no fun. I knew I would endure. I would comfort my mother and reassure her with my presence. But the specter of soon being alone with her weighed heavily upon me. Though I often crave the pleasures of privacy, I did not envy her: this loss of the companion of her life. A marriage of some 45 years is a treasure

*not lightly surrendered. For the moment, the loneliness I imagined
she felt threatened to overwhelm me. Through the front door, into
the elevator, out to the ICU, and now down a short hallway...*

.   .   .

Though each witness story is different, there are common threads
of experience. In the process of anticipatory grief, there will be anxiety
and worry. There will be recollections of the past and projections of
future possibilities. There may also be the seemingly contradictory
wishes for dependence, wanting someone to lean on, and independence,
being solely heroic and strong in the face of adversity.

The patient faces the primary responsibility of whether to accept
life-sustaining high-tech treatment. Deciding can be a dilemma, since
treatments may or may not yield a higher quality of life. Witnesses
must follow the decisions of the patient, even though they may not
agree. They might think that the patient would not benefit from extreme life-support measures, or they might not want to let the patient
go, wishing for everything possible to be done to save the patient's life.

Very few witnesses go through an ideal dying and death scenario
with their loved ones. Such an ideal may include:

- the relative comfort of the dying patient;
- the patient in control, without pain and not incontinent;
- the patient unafraid of dying;
- the witness ready and capable of letting the patient go;
- the witness and patient being together at the time of death;
- leaving no unfinished business in the relationship: feeling resolved
  and at peace.

However, achieving this ideal is uncommon.

While anticipating death in loved ones with a life-threatening illness, there is usually a set of expectations about the process of dying.
There will be an obvious deterioration, perhaps a final hospitalization,
and an undeclared promise of closure, that final good-byes will be said
during this period. However, with the publication of Derek Humphry's
Final Exit and precise information about euthanasia comes an unexpected new problem for witnesses. There can be a sense of added
unpredictability.

• • •

Virginia, an educator in her early 40s, visited her father, Ben, who had been diagnosed with terminal lymphoma. He took her out to lunch alone.

They had just finished talking about Ben's near-death experience in a fire. He had been eating dinner at a friend's house when the house suddenly burst into flames. The lights went out, and he couldn't find an exit. He almost didn't escape, but luckily got out in time.

He then changed the subject. "I just went into the bookstore and bought a book," Ben started.

Virginia, a passionate reader, didn't think this was anything more than chit-chat. "Oh, what did you buy?"

"Final Exit," Ben said.

Virginia stared at him for a moment. "Are you giving me a message, Dad?"

"I'm telling you I'm going to take care of things. And I don't want you to tell anyone else."

"I just need you to call and say good-bye first," Virginia said.

"Is a fax okay? What if I get your answering machine?"

They joked around, but Virginia was left uneasy, thinking about the multiple conjugations of death. He could have died in the fire, he could die from cancer, he could die from the effects of chemotherapy, and now he could take his own life.

Yet, Virginia also felt freed. It was forcing her to take one day at a time. "I had become so disease-focused, I completely ignored that my father could die from other causes."

She aimed to keep her business with her father as complete as she could. And in a strange way, as a result of this life curveball, she let go of her thoughts of control, imagining and preparing for how her father would die.

• • •

Decision-making for witnesses (and physicians), however, becomes more complicated when patients want to die by assisted suicide or euthanasia. Though pain can be self-controlled by patients with intravenous narcotics, they might want to avoid a lengthy, agonizing, or undignified death. Because euthanasia is inconsistent with the Hip-pocratic oath and because it is not a legal option, most physicians will not assist either the witness or patient in suicide.

. . .

At age 58, Polly was diagnosed as having early Alzheimer's disease. As a wife and mother with a career in politics, she was devastated by the diagnosis. Second and third opinions confirmed her worst fears and left her feeling hopeless.

She told her husband, Alec, "I want a doctor who will help me to die."

They both went to Doug for a consultation.

As Doug listened to them, he felt Polly was depressed, a condi-tion that was treatable. Suicide and euthanasia are fatal. At this early phase of Alzheimer's, he knew of no way to predict how long she could continue being productive, nor how debilitating her ill-ness would become.

Instead, he wanted to help them both, but he also did not think she was in a terminal phase of her illness where he could have helped sedate her, narcotize her pain, and help "ease her way out."

He recommended antidepressants. They had a series of office consultations for psychotherapy of her depression, and he tried to increase her motivation to continue her productive life.

Some weeks passed. Her voice grew stronger, and her body strength visibly improved. She still spoke freely about her wish to be assisted with her suicide someday.

As doctor and witness, Doug faces the ethical dilemmas of suicide and euthanasia more frequently than he cares to admit. He tries to distinguish terminal days from feelings of depression when futility, helplessness, hopelessness, self-rage, and anger are paramount.

. . .

The controversy here is the fight between the inalienable right to life, liberty, and the pursuit of happiness (which perhaps includes the right to a planned death), and times when that inalienable right of decision-making is temporarily impaired by pathological depression.

During depression, death may be craved as an escape or relief from psychological pain, physical pain, and exhaustion.

Doctors and witnesses must try to assist patients to confront reality with conscience and accept the consequences of their actions. Both doctors and witnesses, empathically understanding the patient's fears of pain and desires for control, independence, and resolution, may easily wish to assist in suicide. They might imagine themselves in the patient's place someday and hope they might be assisted as well. However, since assisting suicide is not currently a comfortable option from both legal and ethical viewpoints, doctors and witnesses must think about protecting themselves as well as sparing the patient pain and an undignified decline. Fortunately, the hospice movement does provide help in offering inpatient services, home hospice services, respite services for caregivers, and nursing and pain management for patients who are dying. However, the hospice movement concentrates on giving care and relieving suffering; it does not offer help in assisting suicide or euthanasia.

Because euthanasia and assisted suicide are still a continuing debate, witnesses and patients can easily feel tortured by lack of information and assistance, especially when confronted with a terminally ill patient who is suffering and asking for help. *Final Exit* is providing witnesses and patients with specific information about how to die. To some this avenue may bring dignity, but assisting a suicide can be an extraordinarily difficult ordeal. Unless witnesses and those involved in the government and medical care system take an activist position to redefine the medical and lay ethics of euthanasia and assisted suicide, the current values and system will be perpetuated.

Though the book *Final Exit* increased society's awareness of the need for dignified death and provided needed information, many caregivers had already quietly faced the request of a family member's plea for an assisted suicide before its publication. There are times when witnesses are courageous enough to take whatever action is necessary to help a loved one, though they never would have anticipated doing so.

• • •

June and Michael knew it was their last journey in tending Michael's dying mother, Helen. She was in the last stages of colon cancer.

Helen had already been refusing food and intravenous feedings. She would take only ice cubes.

When they arrived, June sensed her mother-in-law was already withdrawing from people to prepare herself. She was no longer her demonstrative, outgoing self. Though she was not afraid to die, she was afraid of the process before it. She did not want to suffer the indignities of dying, nor did she want her family to be involved in a long and tedious bout of caregiving.

She asked June and Michael to help her die. Though they were willing to do anything to help, they had reservations. They were not concerned with any legal implications, because in their state, there were no laws concerning those who assisted a suicide. However, they felt the entire immediate family had to be informed and in agreement about the procedure. And since they were naturally in-experienced in helping someone die, they had to do research about how to do it. To their dismay, they found that assisted suicides were not always successful. They learned they could unintentionally put her in a coma or a worse state of suffering. When they talked to Helen about their research, she backed off.

Helen then steadily declined: her suffering increased and she was losing control and mobility. One night, she felt so wretched, she cried and begged that she wanted to go home.

That night, the family decided to help her. They had done more research and were fairly certain about what to do. They assembled, did what was necessary and then waited for the inevitable. After eight hours, Helen was still breathing. The worry and waiting were intolerable for the family. Helen asked them again to help her. After a while longer, they tried something else. Helen quietly died.

Relieved and yet grieving, the family nonetheless took comfort they had taken the right action and ended the suffering.

• • •

Being a witness to the process of death is not necessarily a terrible experience for all people. Some people experience a peaceful resolution to many years of conflict, and can enjoy watching their loved ones experience dynamic positive change in the face of death. Or, witnesses may feel grateful that they were able to help another in a time of deep distress. Here is a story of a distant witness, an account of a last conversation with a friend in a hospice, who had AIDS.

· · ·

Jim, a writer, received a call from his dying friend, Hal.

Hal asked him, "Am I dead?"

Jim assured him that he was not, but asked what was going on.

"I keep on doing stuff with my dead sister and my dead grandfather. When I first saw them, I was afraid and asked them what they were doing here."

Jim said that Hal should welcome them, that probably he was in a transitional state. Not dead, but dying, and that he would probably continue to do things with his family after he died. That he shouldn't be afraid.

"I knew I could talk to you about this," Hal said. "My lover thinks I am crazy, and just yells at me. I'm so glad you believe me."

Jim knew that Hal had never believed much in spiritual things or engaged in life-after-death theories, so he was impressed about Hal's near-death experiences. Jim realized this was his last conversation with his friend, but it was a talk he said he will always treasure. It gave him pleasure, because he was able to tell Hal what he needed to know, console him, and validate his experiences.

Jim heard that Hal died a few days later.

· · ·

Witnessing serious or life-threatening illness may be a series of final acts in a relationship. There may be discussions about medical directives, living wills, funeral wishes, or finishing emotional business. Sometimes, witnesses cannot bear to do this. It is not a matter of denial, necessarily. Instead, it can be an understandable awkwardness or reluctance about forcing the patient into a discussion about death. But because survivors must live with the memory of these times, witnesses may want to consider asking themselves certain questions, like: What will I regret most if this person died? What do I want to apologize for, recall with pleasure, explain or present in a truer light? What will I wish I had done or said? The answers might provide some perspective, help identify priorities, and set personal agendas. Some consideration of these issues may save witnesses from the kind of guilt and regret that interferes with mourning and remembrance.

LOSS

"I tell you, Doctor, I know that my wife is gone."
The elderly gentleman paused to choke back his grief. Then he continued, "I know that I have to accept her death. It's just that it's much easier to say it than to do it."

Death is the cessation of all the vital functions, and dying is the approach and the preparation. Grief is the emotional suffering caused by the loss. From the Latin source of the word *grief, gravis*, there is the additional metaphoric meaning of the weight of the sadness. Grief is felt when a person who is essential to our well-being or to our hopes for the future is lost.

Some distinguish grief from mourning. Grief is seen as the immediate physical, intellectual, and emotional state after an irretrievable loss; whereas mourning is considered the entire, lengthy, laborious process of bereavement. In its Anglo-Saxon origins, bereavement comes from the verb *berēafian*, to be robbed or plundered, and thus suggests being deprived of a loved one.

> *The process [of bereavement] is essentially private, because it is so much concerned with intimacies which were not, and could not be, shared with others. . . .The work of mourning is, by its very nature, something which takes place in the watches of the night and in the solitary recesses of the individual mind.*
>
> – Anthony Storr

Numerous studies conclude that grieving spouses—in conjugal bereavement—have increased risk of poor health and indeed death. The potential problems that widows face are daunting: isolation, financial loss, social change are only a few. In one study, Selby Jacobs and Adrian Ostfield conclude that men in the first six months after being widowed, women in their second year after being widowed, and younger widowed individuals have the highest risk of vulnerability to illness, suicide, and death. The authors speculate that depression may compromise the survivors' health; they may not care for themselves as well as they did with a partner, may neglect getting prompt medical care, or abuse drugs, medicine, or alcohol.

Some situations can complicate bereavement or increase the severity of grief reactions: high dependency on the deceased; pre-existing frustration or anxiety in relating to the deceased; unexpected or torturous deaths; a sense of alienation or antagonism to others; a history of multiple earlier or simultaneous losses that have not been integrated; and real or fantasized responsibility for the suffering or death itself. Grieving can even be complicated, because the memories associated with the person who has died are unpleasant. Getting through the grief process may mean acknowledging the good and bad parts of a relationship and feelings of anger, loss, guilt, and shame.

A healthy grieving process includes:

- confronting the reality and feelings associated with the death;
- layering the experience and memories within one's life, values, philosophies, and goals;
- trying to master thinking and emotions;
- building and maintaining mature relationships;
- attempting to make the unbearable into the describable;
- allowing patience for the process of grieving;
- conceiving the possibility and nurturing the capability of independence.

However, there is no easy way to take away the pain and suffering. The sadness is the unwelcome reward of a successful and treasured relationship that has reached its end. Grieving is the natural emotional aftereffect of a loss. The period of mourning is the extended adjustment of a lifetime in reconciling survival after the loss.

In its entirely individual rhythm, mourning is a process that may entail experiencing and releasing sadness, and reviewing the inventory of memories of the person who is lost. There may be yearning, anger, preoccupation, crying, forgetfulness, and anxiety. During the process of bereavement, some caregivers contemplate mortality. Carol Staudacher, in her book *Beyond Grief*, lists seven common philosophies about death:

- Death is being in heaven with God.

- Death is an invisible force of destiny that comes when one's time is up.
- Death is a time of judgment when life is evaluated.
- Death is an existential experience of nothingness.
- Death is a transformation to another form of nonmaterial life that is peaceful and without pain.
- Death is a rebirth.
- Death is a state of being before another lifetime, as in reincarnation.

Many have struggled to try to make death a fulfillment and consummation rather than an empty and meaningless end. Because the gay population has been among the first to be hit severely with the AIDS epidemic, they are in the forefront in organizing caregiving efforts, medical activism, and in dealing with dying, death, and bereavement. With AIDS, more people are witnessing "untimely" deaths, experiencing more grieving than is usual. Instead of watching an older generation die, many are watching their own generation die and those who are younger yet. Many are in multiple stages of grief, being unable to complete grieving before another loved one dies. In some cases, entire friendship networks die, one by one. Yet, some communities have faced this challenge by creatively transforming not only caregiving, but memorial rituals as well.

. . .

Sarah, the Unitarian minister who works with people with AIDS, sat with her friend Mitch in a restaurant by the sea on a beautiful day.

Mitch was declining badly, but they weren't talking about it. Sarah purposely avoided mentioning his illness, because the day felt so perfect. She felt she couldn't bear the sadness, but Mitch suddenly asked Sarah what she would say about him at his funeral.

Sarah said, "Why don't you show up and find out?"

With his friends, Sarah then organized a huge service for him— and for his friends and loved ones—before he died. They had his favorite foods—nachos and chicken wings—and they decorated the place with balloons. They had dancing music and many speakers testifying about Mitch's importance in their life. They taped the event.

The next night, friends gathered in Mitch's house. They packed his room with the balloons from the night before. Mitch was in critical condition. They gave him morphine to ease the pain, and they played the tape from the night before.

Though Mitch was semiconscious with his eyes rolled up or closed, whenever he heard a particularly complimentary comment like, "Never has a friend meant more to me," Mitch would suddenly perk up, grin and ask, "Could you rewind the tape and play that again?"

Life pressed into that room where he was dying. He died later that night.

．　　　．　　　．

Whether or not witnesses can find meaning in observing death and dying, there is no doubt that grieving can be a long and difficult process. For parents who suffer the tragic death of a child, bereavement is particularly brutal. In one study, it was found that 50 to 70 percent of parents experienced marital discord or divorce after their child died of cancer. Mourning is also a formidable process for spouses and lovers who will need to master loneliness. Often a sense of security and connection is lost, leaving an emptiness that defies description.

．　　　．　　　．

"You know, doctor, a few days ago, when they brought Ben into the ICU after his heart attack, there was an 18-year-old man in there so sick, I realized that Ben wasn't the only one who was suffering. I prayed that—whatever life Ben had—God would take it and give it to that young man. Today, when I went by to thank the nurses for what they did for Ben, that same young man was sitting up in a chair. Maybe he'll make it."

After about an hour, as Rose was discussing the dying of her husband, Ben, she became more frustrated and angry. She was feeling powerless and bitter about her impending loss and abandonment.

"He said that he's sorry they brought him back to life. I just feel I can't let him go. I want him to get well enough to take him home. Then I'll buy a gun, shoot him, and then I'll shoot myself."

Exhausted and afraid, Rose was coming to the end of her husband's lengthy and progressively crippling bout with heart disease. In confronting her ultimate loss, she was angry and in shock, unable to see any other alternative to her future life other than taking control—committing murder and then suicide.

A few days later, Rose called me to tell me her husband had died quietly with his family in attendance at the hospital. She was calmer, and there was no talk of suicide. Her husband's process of dying was mercifully brief. His level of consciousness declined quickly. Within several days, he moved from being animated and coherent to confusion, delirium, narcotized sleep, and death.

"An old nurse like me knows. When the urine flow slowed down, I knew the end was near." Choking back her tears, Rose told me it was hard to see Ben go. "He was always there for me. I couldn't let him down. I just hope that now my faith will sustain me and see me through."

I told Rose that her husband was concerned about her and that he asked that I continue to see her to take care of her. Thus, for a year after Ben died, I saw Rose once a month.

A year after Ben's death, when Rose came back from a trip to Montana to see her daughter, she sounded animated. Though she looked relaxed, I could see the sadness and grief around her eyes. She confided that she still spoke with her husband each night as she sat on the edge of her bed. It was part of her ritual for preparing herself for sleep. And no doubt, part of her grieving process.

Rose also used continuing therapy to help her during her period of bereavement. She benefited by being in a "safe haven," having a listener validate her emotions as she struggled with putting her feelings into words. Periods of intense unhappiness at her aloneness continued. So, too, did periods of intense anger and emptiness.

·   ·   ·

Sigmund Freud wrote that mourning is often characterized by a painful frame of mind, a loss of interest in the outside world, a loss of the capacity to adopt new objectives, a turning away from activity that is not connected to thoughts of the person lost: an expression of exclusive devotion to mourning that leaves little left over for other purposes or interests. Yet, some caregivers have a mystical or spiritual experience after their loved ones die, which soothes their process of grieving.

．　．　．

"The night before my mother's death, the doctor and the nurses all told me she wouldn't last for more than a few hours. My two children were there, and my brother and my husband.

"They had to change her every hour, but she wouldn't go. One time, the nurses put her in the death position with her arms folded on her chest, but she didn't appear to be comfortable. I moved her back onto her side.

"I realized she was in pain, so I chased everyone away. I had spent six months teaching her to relax when she hurt. I would hold her, rock her, talk softly, tell her to listen to my voice, relax and let the pain go away. It took a lot of time, but we had learned how to do it.

"I climbed right in bed with her. I wanted to tell her she wasn't alone. I gave her a teddy bear, and I held her. I told her to feel the fur of the teddy, and she'd stroke it a little.

"She was very ill and losing blood quickly. It was as if the cancer inside her had turned to liquid. I don't know how she stayed alive so long.

"I wanted to stay with her until the end. As I held her, she got colder and colder. She lost color. In voices so low that my mother wouldn't hear, the nurses whispered that she wouldn't make it through the night.

"I must have fallen asleep beside her. It was 5:38 when I woke up. For some reason, my mother was warm, even hot. Not like she had been.

"I put my hand on her neck, I felt no more pulse, and I heard no more breathing. I had the strangest sensation of feeling her leaving.

"Right after my father died, I had felt I had a visit from him during the night as I slept. My husband and I woke up as the lights in my bedroom were mysteriously turned on, and I felt his presence. It was 5:38. I remember.

211

"My mother's death turned into a mystical and special experience for me. It was a little spooky, but I felt a calm reassurance that my father was there to greet my mother and make it all right for her. Her pain was over."

. . .

In another case, a nineteen-year-old college student experienced what could be called a witness life-after-death experience soon after the death of her grandfather with whom she had always had a very special bond. The following is an excerpt from Lee's journal.

. . .

March 1, 1991: It has been one month and six days since Grandpa died. It still hurts. I think it always will. I've tried to convince myself that he's better off, because he's not suffering anymore. It is just that I can't believe he's really gone. He was such a big part of my life. He still is. I think now he's in my heart more than ever.

I don't want to let go. It's hard, because my memories are vivid and alive. My mother told me that it's important to keep the memories strong. She said we don't have to forget to ease the pain. I find it hard to believe, but people say that the initial pain should lessen with time.

Before my grandfather got sick, he seemed so immortal. He was always there for me, always full of compliments. I wish I had some kind of proof that he can still see me. I wish I knew for sure that he is watching over me.... I would give anything just to hug him again.

March 2, 1991: I had an incredible dream last night. At least I think it was a dream. Grandpa came to visit me. He looked healthy again.

I was asleep when I felt someone stroking my hair. I assumed it was my mother, not remembering that I was at school. Then I heard his voice.

"Hello, dolly," he said. I opened my eyes and just stared at him without saying anything. He was sitting beside me in my bed. I

reached and slowly brushed my hand against his cheek. As soon as I felt the coolness of his skin, I sat up and hugged him. He wrapped his arms around me. I didn't bother to wipe the tears away as they flowed down my face. After a few minutes, he slowly released his embrace and took my hands in his.

"Are you okay?" he asked as he began to wipe away my tears.

"I miss you so much."

"I miss you too, more than anything. But Lee, please understand that I'm better off now. I promise that one day we'll all be together again."

"Are you sure?"

"Positive."

"Grandpa, can I ask you a silly question?" He nodded with a smile. "Grandpa, can you see me from heaven?"

"Sometimes. I hear you when you talk to me. Each and every time I'm in your thoughts I can feel it in my heart. Thank you for speaking at my funeral. I can't tell you how much that meant to me."

"What about Grandma? Did you visit her?"

"I've been watching over her as much as possible. I know she can feel my presence. Somehow I think it's giving her strength."

"So she hasn't seen you?"

"I don't think she's quite ready for that. I don't think she could handle that."

"Why me, then?"

"Because I've been watching you. I felt that we needed to talk. You needed my reassurance."

"Have you seen your parents?"

"They were there right at the beginning." He smiled. "My sister Betty was there, too, and your Grandpa Nat."

"How is Grandpa Nat? Did you tell him about me?"

"Actually I started to, but he knew everything already. Lee, he's just as proud as I am."

"Oh Grandpa, when you were sick, my biggest fear was that you were frightened. I wanted so badly to reassure you, but I didn't know how."

"I was a little frightened. Now I realize I had absolutely nothing to fear."

"I'm glad. Grandpa, what's heaven like?"

"All I can say is that it's a wonderful place, because no one is sick, and no one is in pain. Years from now, when your time comes, you have absolutely nothing to fear. Lee, for now all you have to worry about is living your life to its fullest. You'll always make me proud, and I still love you very much."

"Oh Grandpa, I love you so much! Will I see you again?"

"Probably not for a while, but yes, we will definitely meet again."
I hugged him as tightly as I could.

"I'll never stop loving you."

"I know, sweetheart, I know." He stroked my hair. "I wish I could stay longer. Unfortunately, I must be getting back. I just wanted you to know that I'm doing fine. I love you, dolly."

"Will you wait until I fall asleep?"

"If you like." His smile gave me an incredible sense of security. Slowly I pulled away and rested my head upon my pillow. I slept peacefully for the rest of the night.

•   •   •

The acceptance of death as a natural portion of living is a lesson gradually learned, but which also requires much practice to achieve proficiency. In many cultures and religions, there is a presumption about the amount of time to be spent mourning, usually one to two years being the outside limit of normal bereavement. Yet, as with all emotions, grief rarely follows a timetable. There may be no end of the process, but a vaguer transition to a course that needs to find its completion. Every experience with death will be different.

By remembering the lessons that life teaches, we can achieve a tempered wisdom called acceptance. Perhaps this is the essence of that which we call letting go.

LETTING GO

There are at least two kinds of letting go. First, there is the immediate release of the patient who is near death and in the process of dying. In some cases, people talk of letting the dying person go while the process of dying is occurring: when a witness actually sits at bedside and gives the dying person permission to surrender to death. Doing this requires the acceptance of another's finiteness and mortality. Then, over the longer haul, there is the letting go of companionship and physical presence. This is a more spiritual matter. It is the ending or later portion of the grieving process, when a choice is being made to accept and acknowledge the loss and layer the experience into one's life.

. . .

For Jeremy, the psychotherapist whose lover died of AIDS, "letting go" would ultimately require a long-term process.

At first, at the time of Stephen's death, there were nine photographs of Stephen on his walls at home. "I didn't take them down. I was making a public statement that Stephen was still important to me."

When Jeremy started a new relationship, he reduced the number to five. And now, one picture of Stephen remains: a photograph that is joyous and playful.

"It's about integrating Stephen's presence in my life. The impact of his life and my experience with him is still there every day. I don't want to lose his memory or let go in terms of forgetting. But I also do not want to stop living."

. . .

Letting go is the conscious choice of remembrance, honoring the memory *and* moving forward day to day, choosing to focus on life: participating in social activities and planning new goals. Letting go is not a single gesture, a final wave of the hand, but in fact, a complex process, a series of many ongoing internal and external changes.

. . .

I was 35 when my grandmother died. She was my last living grandparent. She was tolerant and concerned, and I always felt like a special grandson to her.

I still become inarticulate when I think about my grandmother and her death. I get a little choked up, and feel sad, frustrated, and angry when I recall my grandmother's words, "Doug, I'm tired. I'm tired of living with stomach cancer. I'm tired of transfusions, I'm tired of going to the hospital. I don't want to go on. I want to die."

I told her, "I'm not ready to let go of you."

She told me she understood my grieving. Yet, it was her choice. I would have to respect it and put up with it.

I cried.

The images, the words constrict my throat and moisten my eyes. My sensitivity and ability to tolerate loss have grown as I have studied the works of scholars and absorbed the teachings of my patients and the support of my friends.

My grandmother showed me the importance of permitting her to pass away. My memories of her and my loss of her continue to educate me. I thank her for this gift.

. . .

Just how the complicated psychology of adjustment takes place remains a mystery. Letting go is a highly personal enterprise of the psyche.

. . .

When I was told by a spiritual counselor—some 15 years after my mother's death—to let her go, I was not only perplexed, I was enraged.

What did she mean by this? And how could I accomplish this even if I trusted her advice? She did not explain. She told me only that I would discover its meaning and be healed when the work was over.

I spent a long time contemplating the meaning of her words. Does letting go mean letting go of memories? Does this mean forgetting my mother, ignoring her lessons in values? Do I disconnect the ever-present connection in our genetic makeup? Do I pretend not to see the similarities in our bodies and dispositions? Do I give away her photographs? Do I force myself not to speak her name or think of her on Mother's Day or on her birthday or mine? What do I do with the sounds I hear or the images that evoke her?

I knew the counselor was talking about grieving, and I thought she might mean that I discontinue my grief about my mother's absence. But I felt that was as impossible as forgetting my own name. How could I excise her by will when my love and thoughts about her continued despite her death?

There were no other memories I was told to delete from my mind. No one has told me to forget my childhood, how to draw, how to add or multiply, yet I am told to selectively let go of my mother.

Surely, this was not what the counselor meant either.

A letting go of her relationship to me was perhaps closer to the counselor's intent, I thought. But that, too, was impossible. I could still remember and benefit from my mother's words, which still function to strengthen my courage, buoy my spirits, and buy that expensive new dress.

So what did letting go mean? Learning to live and cope without her presence? Substituting her role as mother by finding another to serve her function or by replacing her nurturing voice with my own to adapt to the loss?

This letting-go advice—or perhaps it's pure semantics—still does not work completely for me. I live instead with periods of sadness and with loving memories. I live with a longing for her style of love, her hug, and I accept these gestures from others, appreciating them, loving them, and knowing they are not the same and never will be.

Is letting go acceptance of reality? Maybe.

•   •   •

It is not necessary or even desirable to forget in order to achieve healing from a loss. Remembering the experience and remembering the person who was lost are crucial tools in restructuring an effective present and future. Many experience the healing as an ongoing process: not hoping for an end point, but a time when the sadness no longer dominates, when the experience is integrated into daily life. The analogy of scar tissue is a good one. After a time, a loss becomes like an old wound or scar. Skin may cover over the rupture, but the capacity for pain—and fear of it—still remains.

Some aftereffects can last a lifetime. Some witnesses complain about symptoms similar to those of post-traumatic stress syndrome:

nightmares, evocative dreams, sleep disturbances, flashbacks, and fear of repeating the same witness scenario. Many witnesses, after experiencing the death of their friend or loved one, may have recurrent, intrusive recollections of the lost relationship, the events of illness and death, triggered by sight, smell, sound, taste, word, action, or other stimuli. The witness might recall life before the illness, scenes from the sickroom, contacts with medical personnel, smells of the hospital, the rituals of the burial. It is as if the mind demands that until the experience be reworked and digested as a tolerable memory, the continuing reverberation and reliving of the experience must be endured. Memories might cause witnesses to grieve once more, relive the past, or suffer more intensely with renewed anxiety, depression, guilt, and decreased ability to function. Though it is unclear exactly why or how this phenomenon is physiologically true, if a witness feels guilt or shame about the event, memories become exacerbated and even more deeply etched: particularly vivid and intense.

Some witnesses may experience occasional emotional numbing and desires for social withdrawal. In psychiatric literature about psychological trauma, victims of trauma are said to perceive life through a *trauma lens*, or they construct a defensive *trauma membrane*. In looking through a trauma lens, a person subsequently distorts all events; in creating a trauma membrane, a person develops a protective boundary to avoid being traumatized again (Freud called this a *stimulus barrier*). In a logical extension of what we have observed, in a witness context, the death of a loved one, especially when it is the first death experience, may cause witnesses to significantly alter their philosophical life view, because they have faced their own and another's mortality. Similarly, because of pain, witnesses, too, may set up a barrier to try to suffer less pain; maybe they might become more reluctant to commit to relationships or perhaps, they don't become as attached to others as much as they might.

Getting stuck is the opposite of letting go. It is difficult to gauge what normal is, but if witnesses experience an extreme of these symptoms, or if they feel the death of a loved one has been traumatic, it may be a good idea for them to seek out a therapist to help process the grief. Trauma may kindle depression, and depression may compromise physical health and well-being. Not enough is known about this phenomenon to treat it successfully or make it disappear, but apparently, it is common and natural for strong, emotionally charged memories not only to remain etched in our minds, but to be triggered by similar but distinctly different cues. Unfortunately, this is yet another form of suffering that witnesses endure.

Joseph Campbell has said the benefit of suffering is that it evokes compassion, and it reminds us of the pain of being truly alive. He said that to escape suffering, one must be in a psychological position of being untouched by desire or fear. Few of us can attain this nirvana. Similarly, Carol Staudacher has said the only way to live without grief is to exist without love. Few of us want to.

It may be impossible just to observe and make judgments about who has successfully "completed" the grieving process. For some people, the grieving process will be ongoing throughout life. Some attachments are so strong and precious that it may be unfair to try to limit grieving time or label its length or severity as pathological.

After the death and dying experience, witnesses might discover what more they could have done. They might learn about a better doctor, a different treatment, or they might even learn something about themselves that might have made them more thoughtful caregivers. Memories might be replayed with the benefit of more wisdom and experience. Hindsight might blend with memory to create guilt.

· · ·

Joan Borysenko, in the last chapter of her book Guilt Is the Teacher; Love Is the Lesson, *describes sitting vigil with her dying mother. It is a most moving passage: a parting with grace that Borysenko describes as the finest hour of her life.*

As a reader, I found that a detail punctured my heart. She said she placed a yellow rose beside her mother on her pillow the night she died.

This triggered the memories of the last days of my mother's dying at home in a bedroom connecting to mine. She had lost her beauty by then. Her cheeks were sunken, her stomach swollen. The whites of her eyes yellowed, as did her delicate and long willowy fingers. She lost her mobility, her speech, her calligraphic handwriting, even the sheen of her jet-black hair. Then came the incontinence. The bloody bowels. The loss of consciousness. The loss of breath.

And suddenly, I realized I didn't remember whether I placed flowers in my mother's room while she was sick. Roses were her favorite flower. I could have done that. Why didn't I think of it? She would have loved it.

I started to grieve once more—for my mother and lost opportunities, for knowledge and wisdom and grace I did not have then, 20 years ago.

Some people would say this kind of thinking is foolish, a waste of time and tears. That hindsight is easy.

I found myself apologizing to my mother for the oversight. I bought a red rose as a ritual of remembrance, and then I forgave myself. I make mistakes.

.   .   .

We have found that many people have regrets and much hindsight, especially concerning completing their business and good-byes. Many have said that mistakes are an opportunity for growth. Most people, however, don't feel that way at the time; instead they get angry at themselves or feel guilty. However, hindsight is an analytical tool necessary to the learning process: examining what could have been done and determining what could be done differently the next time. Memory both enriches and depletes us. Such is our mental economy.

.   .   .

Tony, a free-lance researcher, had a long history of being unable to say good-bye to the people he loved.

When he was a young teenager, Tony had a close relationship to his grandmother who practically raised him. They were always honest with each other.

When his grandmother became ill, her doctor and his parents conspired not to be forthright with her about the seriousness of her illness. They forbade Tony to tell her the truth. As a result, he was unable to say good-bye to her. He thus made a vow never to make the same mistake again.

That vow, however, became difficult to fulfill. While Tony was in his 20s, three close friends of his were diagnosed with AIDS and died within 5-6 years. He was unable to complete his relationship with them and say good-bye as well, though every circumstance was different.

Tony's friend Mark started getting sick with hepatitis. He couldn't shake it. It was early in the history of AIDS, so Tony didn't have a clue about the real nature of Mark's illness, even though he noticed that Mark also had skin lesions: what he would later learn to be Kaposi's sarcoma. After Mark moved home to his parents' house, the relationship continued by correspondence. Mark preferred the privacy of letters. After the letters stopped coming, Tony called. Mark's parents tersely told him Mark had been dead for months.

Tony's friend Jay moved to San Francisco before he, too, became sick with AIDS. In phone calls with Tony, Jay was always upbeat and fun. Even when he turned HIV-positive, Jay continued to work. After a while, Jay moved to New York to live with his parents, and Jay promised to invite Tony to visit as soon as he settled in. Soon after, Tony got a call from Jay's parents to hurry and come visit. Despite poor weather conditions, Tony hopped in his car and drove through the night until state troopers told him he could go on no farther in the snowstorm. He checked into a hotel room and called Jay's parents the next day. Jay was dead.

With a third friend, Paul, who was also diagnosed with AIDS, Tony was able to participate more in the caregiving and was more of a presence. He visited the hospital, made videotapes and music tapes, and spent time caring for Paul at home. However, a subsequent home caregiver was strict and possessive, and he didn't notify Tony until it was too late to say good-bye.

Because of these missed chances, Tony now regularly helps AIDS patients in his church congregation. He listens, cooks, cleans, shops, and tends to their needs until they die. Many he wouldn't have chosen to be his intimate friends, but he is able to do what he couldn't have done with his own friends. "If I can help," Tony says, "I now find I cannot turn away."

His work is not entirely altruistic. He continues to learn. Peter, one of the AIDS patients Tony cared for, went blind. Instead of giving up, Peter called on a teacher and started to learn braille. From Peter, Tony said he learned about the will to live and the depths *of courage. He has also seen that every ending of life is unique, "Everyone dies differently—physically and psychologically. I have learned finally how to say my good-byes."*

. . .

In a related illustration about saying good-bye, it took a couple of missed opportunities to learn that a lesson was in progress.

. . .

Simon, a professor of acting and a theater director in his mid-40s, first encountered AIDS when his student confided in him about his illness.

Simon saw the student a few times after that, but the student died a year and a half later. "I went into denial. I didn't make much effort to complete my relationship with him. I guess I figured if he wasn't around, it wasn't happening."

Simon's second encounter with AIDS was with the student's lover. Simon talked to him, but again he didn't rush to spend any time with this student, though Simon said he was more available.

"While it was happening, I was busy. I had appropriate, clear, rational reasons not to be involved. It was not that I was homophobic, nor that I had any particular aversion to the disease. Of course, I don't like being around anything that seems like the Black Death.

"However, when I looked back on my behavior, I thought it was revealing. I didn't want to go to the memorial services. It wasn't dramatic. I didn't get to the door and turn back. It was more unconscious. Yet I felt guilty. I should have been a better friend and teacher."

A colleague became his third encounter with AIDS, and this time, Simon chose to behave differently. He talked to his colleague regularly, wrote to him, and when his colleague died, he went to his memorial service. "I was able to tell my colleague what his presence meant to me in my life, and the memorial service put my friend in a larger context where I was able to celebrate his entire life. I laughed, and I cried. His service made me understand that the ritual was about living, and it made the whole experience with him complete.

"I took a look at what was humane, and I decided I wanted to be with my friends all the way. It took a choice to be more conscious of my avoidance in the past. I know that my feelings will often persuade me into boorish neglect and evasion. But now, I am committed to act appropriately according to the relationship, and not to my feelings about death.

"I am less frightened. I see death as less alien, the way life turns out. I've learned that to engage in all aspects of life is to be free."

．　　．　　．

Such examples not only speak about the power of defense mechanisms like denial, but the length of time sometimes needed to digest, learn, and act on a lesson; also that apparent "failures" are really steps in the process of acquiring wisdom.

There are many ways to let go. Only the bereaved can take the inner steps to heal the self and open the way to growth, recovery, and new attachments.

RECOVERY

The moral lesson illness teaches is that there are undesired and undeserved pains that must be lived through. . . . Change, caprice, and chaos, experienced in the body, challenge what order we are led to believe—need to believe—exists. Disability and death force us to reconsider our lives and our world.

– Arthur Kleinman

Having assimilated the "inevitable transformation of presence into absence," witnesses will certainly be changed. How this change influences each witness will be different, but no doubt behavior will no longer be the same. What happens will depend on background, intellect, resilience, the ability to assimilate the experience, and the capacity to use or transform experience for personal or societal growth. Some people will be more angry, cynical, and disillusioned; others more sensitive and empathic. Some people will remain stuck in the past; others might restructure their focus and future goals.

For some, the aftereffects of witnessing illness bring the realization that life is booby-trapped. This is especially true for people experiencing the trauma of their first encounter with illness or death. Life doesn't seem to be the smooth course previously envisioned; it feels out of control and fragile.

What may also be true is that witnesses become gifted with an increased perception and sensitivity, especially toward others who are ill and fellow witnesses. Some find a way to use this gift.

·   ·   ·

When Julia lost her father, she was thoroughly devastated. He was 45 when he died of lung cancer. They had been very close. It was her first experience of deep loss.

Julia had grown up in a farm in the rural Midwest. Her family was poor. They didn't have much, not even indoor plumbing, but they were rich in generosity. Her mother always volunteered, as she still does at age 87. They took in families to live with them who were even poorer and had nowhere to live.

Julia decided to take the pain and sorrow of her father's death and turn it into something positive. As a personal challenge, she works four hours a week with children diagnosed with cancer at a children's hospital. Once a year, she works for a week at a camp for families with children who have life-threatening illnesses.

Julia was drawn to the children because she felt they taught her strength, courage, perspective, and hope. "They taught me that whatever life has dealt you, you don't give up."

She says she feels privileged to be in the company of these special children and feels honored to share their lives. She speaks of the special moments.

"There was the time in camp when it was night and I was in a pitch-dark tent with a blind girl who was reading poetry to me from her braille book.

"There was Jessica, one of my favorite patients, who was extremely ill, but insisted on helping me do my job. With her I.V. in tow, she would help me wheel other patients to get their radiation treatments. She planned her own funeral.

"There was John, who wrote this on a piece of paper for his room, 'Help me to remember, Lord...That nothing is gonna happen today that you and me can't handle together.'

"There was the 5-year-old boy who was dying of leukemia who walked down the hall to give his balloons to another sick boy. He told the boy, 'I'm leaving. I don't need the balloons anymore.' He died the next day."

The job is not easy. Often, Julia becomes broken-hearted, especially after a patient dies. "I have to leave occasionally to regroup if I need to cry. But then, I quickly pull myself together, because there is always someone else who needs me. The children know who has died on the floor, and they need to talk about it, too, sometimes.

Rather than feeling burdened by the time she gives each week, Julia says she has been enriched by the children and their parents. She feels she gets more than she receives, and that she is much calmer.

"This experience has been a leveler for me. I don't get upset as easily, though I have less tolerance for trivial complaints. I can be in a snarled traffic jam and just think about the children who will never get a chance to drive.

"I'm not doing this work for the reward, yet it is rewarding. I hate it when someone tells me it's wonderful that I volunteer. The wonder is in the children."

•   •   •

REWARDS OF WITNESSING

Perhaps one of the strangest paradoxes in witnessing illness is that it is an experience filled with not only suffering, but the beauty of giving. Though unexpected, witnessing an illness can produce moments of what Mihaly Csikszentmihalyi calls *optimal experience*, a deeply felt sense of joy "when a person's body or mind is stretched to its limits in a voluntary effort to accomplish something difficult and worthwhile." Though the experiences may be painful, in the long run, he says, they add up to "a sense of mastery...or participation in determining the content of life that comes close to what is usually meant by happiness."

If lucky, rewards can come in a continued relationship. Not all serious illnesses result in death and dying.

. . .

It is a rainy Sunday morning, too miserable to go out. I sit in front of our living room fireplace and snuggle with David. I purr like a happy kitten in his arms.

"If anyone had a camera and recorded us today, they'd guess we were pretty damn happy."

David agrees, but says, "We still do have our quibbles."

I nod and tell him when he lets food crust on unwashed dishes, life gets difficult. He tells me he hates it when my plucked eyebrow hairs cling to the bathroom sink.

I protest it's an unwitting failure on my part. I don't see them if I don't have my contact lenses in. But then, I admit I don't seek them out either. I tell him it's a problem I'll have to work on.

"You know," he says, "maybe in the next 20 years, we'll work the problems out."

As I turn and watch the warm fire glow, I tell him, "I hope so."

. . .

8

THE FUTURE ROLE
OF THE WITNESS

It's easy to be heroic in times of crisis. What's difficult is to behave even moderately well at ordinary times.

– Aldous Huxley
from the screenplay *A Woman's Vengeance*,
based on his story "The Gioconda Smile"

What lies ahead in the twenty-first century?

Some issues and emotions that witnesses confront are timeless. There will always be illness. There will always be another epidemic. Witnesses will always need to choose close or distant involvement and to balance the satisfactions of caring with the necessity of taking care of themselves. They, no doubt, will always feel anxiety, relief, sadness, and loss. They will always face the basic fears of loss of control, pain, abandonment, and death.

It also seems certain that the need for witnesses as caregivers will remain an unchanging phenomenon. Witnesses will continue to be in demand in the near future as increased medical costs practically guarantee shortened hospital stays, more outpatient surgery, more chronic mental patients in shelters for the homeless, and more limits on nursing home care.

Though some aspects of witnessing remain constant, other aspects are more changeable. Continuing advances in technology raise medical costs and spark debates on care rationing. There is also an ongoing flow of legislation about medical insurance, ethics, procedures, and issues. As patients' rights and support for the caregiver struggle for priority, the future role of witnesses may include confrontation with medical controversies and medical activism.

CONTINUING MEDICAL CONTROVERSIES AND DEBATES

Present Changes in the Medical Care System

An example of legislation shaping the future of the witness and patient relationship is the Patient Self-Determination Act (PSDA). Passed in 1990, the act requires every hospital, long-term care facility, hospice, and a variety of other medical institutions or agencies, including health maintenance organizations (HMOs) participating in Medicaid or Medicare, to maintain written policies and procedures on advance directives for "all adult individuals receiving medical care by or through the provider organization." The act also mandates community education.

In essence, staff members must ask all admitted patients whether they have advance medical directives—either a living will or a durable power of attorney. If the patient has directives, the hospital or medical facility must document them in the patient's medical chart. Patients are then advised of the right to refuse or to select treatments under pertinent state laws, and the staff must inform patients of the institution's policies for implementing these laws. Patients may decline to have such directives, and that choice is documented in the patients' records.

The central idea of this act is to require capable patients to make choices about medical care should they become unconscious or otherwise incapacitated. This act also represents an effort to confront problems such as loss of control and fear of pain, abandonment, and death rather than to avoid or deny these issues.

Because making advanced responsible choices is now a United States government mandate, witnesses and patients may have fewer conflicts about openly discussing these issues. Witnesses can ask for a doctor's help in discussing medical directives with patients, or they can choose to wait for a patient admission where a third party may help. Primary witnesses are the most likely candidates to be involved in a supervisory role in such advance directives as the durable power of attorney, instructing medical personnel about the patient's wishes concerning types of medical care when the patient is unable to handle the responsibility. If witnesses do not feel comfortable being given the durable power of attorney, they should decline and offer to help the patient choose someone more suitable.

In any event, it is prudent that all people think about what health care directives they would like *before* an emergency arises. If patients are not capable of offering their informed consent to accept or decline medical procedures, surely they would want someone responsible making that decision for them. For this reason, we have included in the appendix examples of both a living will and a durable power of attorney for health care.

Access to Medical Care

At the time of this writing, an estimated 38 million U.S. citizens are uninsured, thereby suffering limited access to health-care delivery systems unless uncompensated or charitable care can be obtained. Those who have access to medical care pay a great deal for it. Few estimates are available for those who are underinsured, and fewer still for those who struggle with the frustrations of the cost-conscious, HMO-style insurance programs, where physician assistants may see patients before the doctor, who, in turn, is pressured by time-management consultants to practice parsimoniously.

The goals of expanding access to medical care and reducing or controlling costs at the same time make this problem difficult to solve. Physicians have been challenged to meet their professional and societal responsibilities by providing health care to all, but physicians can afford to give only a limited amount of uncompensated care. Many already give 10 to 20 percent of their time to charitable cases. The possibility of a tax break may make this option more attractive to the private practitioner, but such a tax incentive does not yet exist. With high malpractice insurance and current plans for reshaping Medicare reimbursements, physicians who worry about their future economic health find the prospect of giving more free medical care distasteful.

Health-care rationing is a proposed system to address fair access to medical care. Attempting to offer balance, rationing aims to capture the benefits of high-tech life extension and lifesaving without neglecting the quality of life and its maintenance. This means offering both lifesaving acute care and follow-up care. However, setting priorities is necessary and often becomes a tricky matter.

In Oregon, where an experiment of health-care rationing is being considered, the state government, the medical establishment, and advocacy groups have formulated some basic principles and goals:

- universal access for all citizens to basic health care;
- public debate over policy and periodic reassessment;
- incentive to providers and users to define effective treatment and use those methods;
- disincentive to overutilization and/or overtreatment;
- economic stability with explicit and predictable funding.

There are still problems that the doctor, patient, or the witness may confront in such a system. For the doctor, there are the problems of time management, patient confidentiality, and potential confusion and frustration in getting effective treatment for all diagnoses.

In a hypothetical example, a doctor has a patient with a lung infection, which explains the symptoms of cough, fever, and malaise. Since the cough produces sputum, a simple, inexpensive rapid laboratory test can be performed to determine what "bug" is causing the infection. The next day, the lab reports that the infection is caused by bug XYZ, which is killed by the inexpensive antibiotic A, B, or C. This answer is no problem, because of the inexpensive, effective treatment in the low-cost setting of office and home. However, if the lab reports that bug Q (which is not killed by any inexpensive drug) is present and that the infection has spread from the lung to the blood stream, the doctor may face a problem. The appropriate treatment for bug Q requires life-support technology while highly toxic and very expensive experimental drugs are used to try to enable the body of the patient to overcome the invader and recover. The patient needs to be admitted to the high-cost hospital setting. The treatment may extend life, but its efficacy is neither assured nor proven. Should the doctor treat the patient with the bug XYZ, but not the patient with bug Q? The fear is that a rationing system may not allow treatment of bug Q if the dollars are not there. This type of problem is a major dilemma of medical ethics and cost containment and has far-reaching social and emotional consequences.

The witness has a political, economic, and moral voice to exercise in encouraging an accessible, accountable, and affordable health-care system. A universal health-care plan provided by federal or state governments would insure medical access. But until one exists, witnesses and patients alike will surely expect to pay higher health insurance premiums, more deductibles, and more co-payments. For that money, we must be careful not to purchase less health care and an expanding administrative bureaucracy.

Managed Health Care

Many witnesses have discovered that the pathways of our health-care system are complex and often tortuous. Cost, most often measured in terms of dollars, must also be measured in time spent. As a method to contain the spiraling cost of medical care, managed health care has been invented. In managed care health plans, the health-care provider— like a doctor or other designee—must precertify to insurance companies or negotiate the need for hospital medical care for all nonemergency cases. Some 80 percent of group medical insurance policies now contain such provisions for managed health care.

In a positive vein, such a strategy rightfully requires doctor and patient to use precious resources thoughtfully and to consider less costly and less restrictive options than expensive full-scale hospitalization. It also encourages, even forces, the doctor to promptly study and reassess the diagnosis and the treatment plan.

On the other hand, the constraints of cost control reduce the freedom of treatment choice for the doctor and patient. Many physicians get angry when their judgment is challenged about what disorders require necessary medical treatment. Doctors must become negotiators when the disembodied voice from the insurance company on the phone suggests that hospitalization is "not medically necessary" for a particular patient. In this case, if the doctor and patient do go ahead with the proposed admission, the insurance company will likely not accept responsibility for the bill. Doing this does save money for the insurance company, but it is another example of how the burden of health-care is being returned to the family. Unfortunately, this type of consultation between the insurance company and health-care provider additionally infringes on the sanctity of the doctor-patient relationship, disrupting privacy and confidentiality.

Doctors are also spending more unpaid time on the phone and on committees, and preparing reports that they feel compromise the time they could be spending on healing and communicating with patients. For example, admission procedures—with their complex justifications and record keeping—can take twice the amount of time spent in the past.

Current practices of utilization review and quality assurance also affect the doctor-patient relationship. Like managed health care instituted by private insurance carriers, the federal government's Medicare program has established a Peer Review Organization (PRO) to assess the necessity of expenditures for health care. In this case also, witnesses might hear doctors explaining that the PRO reviewers do not agree with their choice of treatment and that its costs will not be reimbursed.

The doctor, patient, and witness must cope with review boards, which sometimes are generous and life-giving, and sometimes mean-spirited and condemning. This means that all parties must be tolerant, humble, and industrious in struggling to obtain access to quality health care.

Educating the New Generation of Medical Personnel

Patients have complained bitterly about "detached" physicians who are primarily technicians. Though patients appreciate the technical expertise, many long for physicians who are also trained to support the patient emotionally. The psychiatrist Arthur Kleinman suggests that a different approach to medical care is crucial to obtain proper treatment. He believes that physicians must try to perceive the social, cultural, and psychological subtleties of a patient's illness, because the personal details of a patient's life are inseparable from disease and thus crucial to treatment. Norman Cousins made a similar point in his book *Head First*, encouraging a more enlightened physician style: increased compassion; willingness to listen to the patient's needs and views; sensitivity to the patient's life in addition to the illness; and enhanced communication skills, especially during a crisis. He also suggested educating physicians about the efficacy of recognizing and using witnesses as part of the healing team. Doing this might require additional training for physicians or new courses added in medical school about patients' physical *and* psychological suffering within their healing environment.

There will always be debate among medical educators over the balance in the curriculum. Many will advocate teaching the basic details of science. Fewer will insist on teaching the skills of humane communication, unless there is continuing pressure from health-care consumers.

New Technology

In the realm of new technologies, a combination of genetic research and miniaturization is generating great interest among futurists. Working machines on a scale of micrometers (millionths of a meter) or nanometers (billionths of a meter) are conceivable. Such devices could operate within cells and engineer changes in DNA and in protein synthesis within the cell. This possibility leads to revolutionary consequences. Tiny machines will be able to operate as microscopic surgeons to clear arteriosclerotic plaque as it forms on the lining of arteries. Cancer cells might be shut off at the genetic level. Viral and bacterial infections could be immobilized. By genetic engineering, inherited disorders could be rectified by restructuring the DNA to normalcy. These processes seem to promise less grossly invasive medical techniques of treatment, prolonged life, and perhaps even cures for diseases that continue to confound medical professionals.

Eventually, people might even find out more information about their health than they might need or want to know. This possibility will be a continuing source of debate. With the Human Genome Project of the National Institutes of Health and the Department of Energy, researchers are currently mapping the human genome (our genetic structure). This will enable us to learn the truth of our genetic jeopardy. Yet, we might not want to know the facts of our genetic destiny, particularly when there may be nothing we can do about it. This foreseeable technological breakthrough also raises bioethical questions of privacy: for instance, the individual's right to protect this genetic information from employers and insurance companies who might want to know the details of their risks.

New problems can emerge for witnesses as sometimes high-tech treatments can both enhance and *compromise* a patient's quality of life. For instance, in the case of kidney failure where hemodialysis and kidney transplants can prolong a patient's life, patients and witnesses suffer some tough problems. Sustained by artificial means, patients often become resentful about their chronic fatigue, moderation of life activities, and dependence on machines. Witnesses and health-care professionals alike may feel this resentment, and sometimes watch patients struggle with their will to continue their life ordeal.

·   ·   ·

With a history of juvenile diabetes, Jennifer, 35, suffered kidney failure and underwent treatment. At her family meeting, which Doug was requested to conduct, Jennifer announced she could not see the point of going on anymore. She had been through enough in the past year.

She, indeed, had a very rough year and was depressed. She had a kidney and pancreas transplant, but within a few months, both failed. She was hospitalized with many complications for almost five months. When she was released from the hospital, she returned to work, but soon after, she was fired. Her boyfriend then moved to another state.

Medical complications continued. She needed more surgery when the shunt in her arm between an artery and vein—the access for the dialysis machine—clotted and shut down. Another transplant was arranged, this one a donation from her uncle—a perfect match.

Within weeks, the perfect match was rejected by her body. Jennifer felt that she failed her uncle. When her sister offered her kidney, she refused. Jennifer didn't want her sister to take the risk since her sister had children.

With the family refusing to let her go, Jennifer chose to go back to ambulatory dialysis, though her life is being sustained with great pain and suffering. The family was nonetheless relieved by her decision to go on.

·   ·   ·

There are other instances when technology can unintentionally cause much suffering. Those who are dying may curse those who have brought them back, living with machines that control their life.

.   .   .

Esther, an 82-year-old retired widow living alone in Florida, was in the intensive care unit in the hospital. Her daughters all flew down to see her, because they were told she was about to die. She had just had a serious heart attack.

The physician then discovered her kidneys had shut down, and told one of the daughters that he might be able to "jump start" her kidneys by hooking her up to a dialysis machine. The daughter agreed to the procedure. For the first four times, it didn't work. The daughter pushed for another try, and the fifth time, the procedure was successful. However, Esther now became dependent on a dialysis machine. She was not independently mobile, the daughters all lived out of state, and they now had to plan to find a dialysis unit and move their mother.

Neither Esther nor the daughters were happy about this. Home after being discharged from the hospital, Esther could barely talk or bathe herself. A couple of days later, she died of another heart attack.

.   .   .

Technology does not always bring easy solutions. Witnesses and patients alike will have to investigate carefully and choose new technological options, contemplating the issue of quality of life.

ADDITIONAL CONTINUING MEDICAL CONTROVERSIES AND CONCERNS

There are many other medical issues that are currently being debated that we cannot describe at length. For instance:

- problems and concerns about the inequalities of medical testing done more extensively on male than female patients, which leads to lack of data on how such drugs affect women;
- medical negligence in hospitals;
- the impact of malpractice suits on physicians and patients: tort reform regarding malpractice law; physicians' leaving their practices, because of the high risk of their specialties (for example, obstetrics and neurosurgery) and the high expense of malpractice insurance; patients being overtested to avoid malpractice suits, etc.;
- the slow access to experimental drugs by the Food and Drug Administration, which has especially been difficult for AIDS patients;
- creating ways to increase the donor organ pool;
- the regulation of *orphan drugs*, drugs that are effective, but don't have a big enough population of sales to be economically rewarding for drug manufacturers to produce or distribute; alleged suppression of the existence of such orphan drugs;
- alleged price gouging by some profit hospitals and pharmaceutical manufacturers;
- finding a long-term solution to the nursing shortage;
- current medical testing procedures and some types of surgery that are being challenged for their overuse, for example, hysterectomies, radical mastectomies, D & C's, and prostate surgery;
- the increasing incidence of "granny dumping," elder Americans who are being abandoned on hospital emergency doorsteps by friends and family members who are exhausted from the pressures of caregiving, a practice that is perhaps a symptom of the inadequacies of long-term care policies. Medicare does not pay for custodial nursing-home care or at-home long care. Hospitals do not offer custodial care, because Medicare will not reimburse them.

This list goes on. What is clear is that the health-care industry will be investigated, scrutinized, and regulated more carefully by the private sector, the insurance industry, and government. Continued pressure won't hurt.

WHAT WITNESSES CAN DO: MEDICAL ACTIVISM

In the course of witnessing, some caregivers will encounter problems in the medical system that relate to them specifically and capture their sympathy or conscience. Witnesses may encounter diseases for which there are no cures and research is underfunded. They might find they are caught in an insurance dilemma where the patient is not covered or is denied access. They might find out that there are not enough community services to support their needs. This discovery usually leads to a time when witnesses might become motivated to get involved to solve a current problem or make changes in government or the medical system that will make life easier for future patients and witnesses. When motivated, witnesses can use some of the following strategies:

- **Conduct research:** Find out more about the topic: read and interview experts in the field. Accumulate the facts so informed action can be taken.
- **Educate the public:** Talk to community organizations, news media, local educators about the issue.
- **Form a support group or organization:** Help each other.
- **Apply political pressure:** Writing letters to legislators can be remarkably effective. For every letter written, government officials calculate there are 500 additional people who feel the same way, but are too busy to write.
- **Raise money for medical research and public awareness.**

Members of the gay community have been steadfast in their energetic commitment to medical activism and creating innovative support programs. In response to the need for help and community for AIDS patients, Dan Bailey, Roger MacFarlane, and Mitchell Cutler started the Gay Men's Health Crisis Buddy Program in 1982. Cutler said, "These buddies...could provide a myriad of services for *people with AIDS* [PWAs] and their families: running errands, making hospital visits, translating for parents and doctors, cleaning homes, and offering general support by using common sense and compassion to enable PWAs to proceed with their lives in a dignified and more independent manner."

In a democratic society, the witness will face complex political and social forces. The state and federal governments—and the politicians elected within the governments—will continue to affect major healthcare delivery systems by regulation and by law and executive order. The private sector will protect itself and pursue profit, with the occasional exception of organizations or companies demonstrating social conscience and grace. Thus, both the government and the private sector may act against the best interests of the patient. Witnesses, then, need to protect the interests of the patient and themselves as caregivers from the constraints of government and industry.

Activism is not for everyone. Witnesses, during or after their ordeal, may feel too exhausted to take the serious and time-consuming steps needed to see a problem through to its solution. However, activism can often be achieved in subtle ways. Being kind to one person, expressing care to a fellow witness, voicing an opinion, taking time to make a phone call or write a letter can make an enormous impact. The witness possesses an extraordinary capacity to influence change.

CONCLUSION

With medical staff in busy hospitals, patients can have trouble being recognized beyond their disease—the AIDS case, the girl with leukemia, the old woman on dialysis. Witnesses, too, have trouble being recognized. The caregivers' experience is underappreciated by many. Not only may caregivers be slighted or ignored by medical staff, their own friends might equally ignore them while they focus on the sick person. Though witnesses rarely use the expression "we're ill," they are going through the experience of illness, though in a different fashion.

Unlike patients, witnesses wear no visible scars or experience physical regeneration to announce something major has happened to them: something lost, gained, learned. There are no medals, or recognition of a task well done. We hope this situation will continue to change: support groups, volunteerism, and activism are alive and growing.

Like patients, witnesses not only suffer, but some gain wisdom, improved relationships, and a keener appreciation of health along with a desire not to waste time or energy in trivial pursuits or arguments.

·   ·   ·

When I asked Nick about how AIDS has affected his life, at first, he joked, "It certainly has shrunk my Christmas card list."

He then turned serious, "When I watched all my friends die, I thought I couldn't survive it. I had so much sadness that I even gave up counting how many friends of mine died. But somehow I knew I would survive. My work had purpose, and I slowly learned to live for the moment. I now laugh at myself when I'm late for a meeting or don't get my own way.

"I hate to say something positive about AIDS. I don't like giving this view much support, but I see the plague of AIDS as a good thing as much as it is horrible.

"I've seen the way people have changed. All kinds of people get AIDS. I've seen prejudice and fear being substituted by compassion. I've seen elementary school children selling doughnuts every morning to contribute to AIDS research. I've seen elderly men work on the AIDS quilt. I've seen a 75-year-old Catholic nun become part of the Buddy Program.

"It has done so much for dealing with death. Before, death was like an obscenity. We are no longer isolating people who are dying. That much has changed. We are learning that nothing can be more intimate than witnessing the death of another.

"I also watch how my circle of friends treat each other. I see them treasure each other more, making more of an effort. It certainly has made me more alive, a better person.

"Somehow, I feel we'll get through this. And along the way, we'll all learn lessons about supportive and loving relationships.

"I hate to sound 'Californian,' but it almost feels as if the planet is maturing under the weight of tragedy. It's an evolution of all different facets in humanity. It's time to educate children about sex and intimacy. It's time to learn about spiritual nourishment to replace self-destructive alternatives.

"In a larger perspective, if we are deeply honest, we remember that there is not much difference between being healthy and being sick. All of us can imagine ourselves having a short future. It doesn't have to be devastating. It can make the present rich and lighthearted. Hope breathes magic into the present."

•   •   •

This recognition changes our quality of life—not just for those who witness AIDS, but those who witness all types of illnesses. While this internal, psychological gain is rather profound, we would still like to see the role of witnesses recognized and the work of witnesses validated.

Witnessing is a complex series of events over time. Though ideals can be described, perfect coping and perfect resolution remain elusive goals. This book is a first step in recognizing the role of the witnesses as caregivers and their importance as members in the healing team. We hope that medical professionals, patients, and witnesses will all benefit from a clearer perspective of the caregivers. We especially hope that the witnesses will feel strengthened, empowered, and enriched.

Chapter Notes

Introduction

Page 3: **Currently there are approximately 20-25 million Americans suffering from chronic illness:** U.S. Bipartisan Commission on Comprehensive Health Care, 1990, also known as the U.S. Pepper Commission Report.

Chapter 1

Page 8: **According to the U.S. Pepper Commission Report, there are 38 million adults:** U.S. Bipartisan Commission on Comprehensive Health Care.

— **Three-quarters of all home care is provided without financial compensation:** U.S. Bipartisan Commission on Comprehensive Health Care.

Page 9: **Only 15 years ago, this same operation usually required about a week's stay in the hospital:** Similarly, in the 1970s, patients who suffered heart attacks typically stayed in the hospital for six weeks. In the early 1990s, they are most often discharged within two weeks.

— **. . . decisions for patient release dates are strongly influenced by medical care statistics which serve the financial interests of the government and the insurance companies:** Instituted by Medicare in the 1980s, the Diagnostic Related Groupings (known as the DRGs) are a statistically based, financial cost-containment tool; insurers compute their own reimbursement scale for different kinds of illnesses.

Page 10: **Bernie Siegel,** *Love, Medicine & Miracles* (New York: Harper and Row, 1986). Siegel defines exceptional patients as those who refuse to be victims, those who educate themselves about their illnesses and treatments—all the while demanding control and dignity. Refer to his book for a fuller explanation.

— **Herbert Benson,** *Your Maximum Mind* (New York: Times Books, 1987).

— **Sociologists contend that patients with a supportive community:** James S. House, Karl R. Landis, Debra Umberson, "Social Relationships and Health," *Science Magazine,* July 29, 1988, 241:540–545.

— **There are also more support groups of patients for specific illnesses:** The National Self-Help Clearinghouse, 33 W. 42nd Street, New York, N.Y. 10036, (212) 642-2944, is a resource for finding local support groups. In a *Newsweek* article, "Unite and Conquer," Feb. 5, 1991, Charles Leerhsen et al. estimated that 15 million Americans are now taking advantage of 500,000 support groups for different problems, some of which were for people with physical and mental illnesses and their families.

Page 11: **Most experts agree that our health care system is strained and in disorder:** The issue of *JAMA, Caring for the Uninsured and Underinsured,* May 15, 1991, discusses issues concerning access to medical care, and reform in the economics of caregiving in organized medicine.

— **14.5 million Americans infected with AIDS by the year 2002:** Dr. Myron Allukian, Jr., president of American Public Health Association; deputy commissioner, Boston Department of Health and Hospitals, "Looking to the Millenium," *Boston Globe,* Jan. 1, 1990, p. 51.

Page 15: **Thus, all witnesses can further be divided into two categories: active and passive:** Throughout the book, witnesses are assumed to be in ages ranging from young adulthood to maturity. Obviously, a child witness or one who is elderly will involve special considerations, such as maturity and capability.

Page 18: **The traditional definition of** *healing* **is to make whole; to restore health, make sound, well or healthy again:** Healing has different meanings in diverse cultures. For example, Kleinman points out that in traditional Chinese medicine, the character for healing, *chih,* means good government, management, and control; in other societies, illness is disorder, and healing transforms this chaos into order. Arthur M. Kleinman, M.D., "Some Issues for a Comparative Study of Medical Healing," *International Journal of Social Psychiatry,* Autumn/Winter, 1973, V: 19 (3 + 4):159–165. For Native Americans, healing may mean a realignment with their relationship to the rhythms of nature, the currents of life. Through right action, thankfulness and prayer, they can make "peace with the sun and moon in [their] hearts." Dhyani Ywahoo, *Voices of our Ancestors: Cherokee Teachings From the Wisdom Fire* (Boston & London: Shambhala, 1987), p. 134.

— **Ted Kaptchuk and Michael Croucher,** *The Healing Arts: Exploring the Medical Ways of the World* (New York: Summit Books, 1987), p. 97.

Page 19: **Healing also has multiple perspectives, different for the patient, the family, the health practitioner, and the researcher:** A. Kleinman and L. H. Sung, "Why Do Indigenous Practitioners Heal?" *Social Sciences and Medicine,* 13B (1979), p. 21.

— **Kleinman . . . defines the subtle distinction between disease and illness:** Kleinman and Sung, pp. 7-26.

— **Because of the high cost of health care and the resulting time management practices, professionals may neglect the humanity of healing:** As the psychologist Kenneth R. Pelletier asserts, rarely will a single therapeutic factor—nutrition, self-knowledge, stress reduction, meditation, finding God, sex, health foods—lead to a state of health. More often, it is a combination of efforts. "[A single-factored] approach to health and healing is too narrow and is unlikely to be any more effective than approaches focusing on a single cause of disease." Kenneth R. Pelletier, *Mind as Slayer, Mind as Healer* (New York: Delta, 1977), p. 317.

Page 21: **. . . suffering that comes not just from the disease itself, but from fears of:** This idea has been expanded from Kaptchuk and Croucher's thoughts on illness and suffering, *The Healing Arts,* p. 117.

— **. . . witnesses can help heal the patient by relieving or alleviating the suffering just by empathic partnership:** Quite naturally, while talking about ways the witness can be a healer, the focus of attention is on patients, but it is also necessary to take a moment to focus on witnesses who are primary caregivers. They might need help as well, particularly in times of crisis or during a patient's acute episodes. They may need their own witness—a witness to the witness, so to speak: support from the family or social network. Most primary caregivers are reluctant to ask for attention, because they might appear to be selfish or insensitive, in relation to the needs of the patient. However, to focus adequately on the needs of the patient, primary caregivers will need time to regroup their emotions and regenerate energy. This is such an important point, Chapter 6 will be devoted to the wisdom of self-nurturance. Primary caregivers will not be able to help the patient if they are sick, too.

Page 22: **One recent study found that the lack of social relationships constitutes a more serious health risk factor:** James House, Karl R. Landis, Debra Umberson, "Social Relationships and Health," *Science Magazine,* July 29, 1988, 241:540–544.

Page 24: **Ram Dass, Paul Gorman,** *How Can I Help?* (New York: Alfred A. Knopf, 1985), pp. 7, 9, 10, 14, 24.

Page 25: **When she finally did share her concerns with me . . . :** As a stylistic note, Karen is the one who is using the first person, "I" and "me."

Page 26: **Witnesses may also endanger their health, because they don't have time to take care of their own needs or because of loss or grief:** In 1944, Erich Lindemann presented the hypothesis that acute grief is a definite syndrome. E. Lindemann, "Symptomatology and Management of Acute Grief," *American Journal of Psychiatry,* 101:141, 1944. In 1964, Parkes presented evidence that recent bereavement adversely affects the health of a surviving spouse. C. M. Parkes, "Effects of Bereavement on Physical and Mental Health: A Study of Medical Records of Widows," *British Medical Journal* 2:274, 1964. John Bowlby explored the importance of separation and attachment, loss, and grief in *Attachment and Loss*, vol. 1 (New York: Basic Books, 1969), vol. 3 (New York: Basic Books, 1980).

Page 28: **Gabriel García Márquez,** *Love in the Time of Cholera* (New York: Alfred A. Knopf, 1988), p. 345.

Chapter 2

Page 30: . . . **if the initial doctor does not take the problem seriously:** In Rebeccah's initial search for a diagnosis, she went to four doctors before she found out she had Hodgkin's disease. It is also true that not all diagnoses are obvious at the time of the initial complaint, and Hodgkin's disease is sometimes quite difficult to diagnose.

Page 34: **Though this is hard to prove (or remember), Freud has suggested:** Sigmund Freud, *Introductory Lectures on Psycho-Analysis*, Standard Edition, XVI (London: The Hogarth Press, 1963), pp. 396-397.

— **Judith Viorst,** *Necessary Losses* (New York: Simon & Schuster, 1986), p. 22.

— . . . **anxiety** . . . **"disturbs the mind and keeps it in a state of *painful uneasiness"*:** *Webster's Unabridged Dictionary, second edition* (New York: Simon & Schuster, 1979), p. 83.

— **Joseph Campbell,** *The Hero with a Thousand Faces* (Princeton, NJ: Princeton University Press, 1949), p. 81.

Page 35: . . . **delayed by a terrible catastrophe:** There is another interpretation of why we might feel this. We may be angry at the person who is late and, not being able to deal with the anger, harm them in our imagination.

Page 36: **Joan Borysenko,** *Minding the Body, Mending the Mind* (Reading, MA: Addison-Wesley, 1987), p. 20. She says that the term *awfulizing* was first used by Albert Ellis.

— . . . *physical and psychological symptoms of anxiety:* This is quoted from Karen Horney in Alfred M. Freedman, M.D., Harold I. Kaplan, M.D., Benjamin J. Sadock, M.D., *Modern Synopsis of Psychiatry II*, 2nd ed. (Baltimore: Williams and Wilkins, 1976), pp. 1283–1285. Some of the symptoms apply better to panic disorder. We have not altered the list for witness situations.

Page 37: **Dr. David Stutz**, Dr. Bernard Feder, and the Editors of Consumer Reports Books, *The Savvy Patient: How to be an Active Participant in Your Medical Care* (Mt. Vernon, N.Y.: Consumers Union, 1990), p. 86.

Page 39: **Find out the doctor's style of handling good or bad news:** A note from Karen: Our family doctor routinely sends us a letter detailing all test results after every visit. If a particular test result is troublesome, our doctor—when she is available—will speak to us on the phone to discuss any action necessary. An admirable policy, we know what to expect. We have also accumulated a personal medical file. David's oncologist previously sent personal letters detailing test results, and he would personally call if a test needed to be repeated. However, his secretary seemed to be in a perpetual backlog, delaying the good news. Now, his doctor has a form letter for test results which we receive as soon as the tests are finished.

Page 44: **Patients and witnesses might have to budget time with their doctors:** This issue is discussed more fully in Chapter 4.

Page 46: **Annie Dillard,** "The Writing Life," *Tikkun,* vol. 3, no. 6, p. 24.

Chapter 3

Page 49: **E. Fuller Torrey,** *Witchdoctors and Psychiatrists* (New York: Perennial Library, Harper & Row, 1986), p. 18. We have expanded his principle to include diagnosis of all physical and psychological problems, not just in the naming of problems in psychotherapy, as he explained in his book.

Page 50: **Jeanne Achterberg,** *Imagery in Healing: Shamanism and Modern Medicine* (Boston: New Science Library, Shambhala, 1985), p. 156.

— **Emmy Gut,** *Productive and Unproductive Depression* (New York: Basic Books, 1989), pp. 32-33.

Page 54: **. . . they may also be losing their financial support:** Barbara Sourkes, Ph.D., *The Deepening Shade: Psychological Aspects of Life-Threatening Illness* (Pittsburgh: University of Pittsburgh Press, 1982), pp. 25-27.

— **the witness's own support group may be inattentive or less patient with the grieving process:** Refer to Chapter 7 for a fuller discussion on grief. Also George L. Engel, "Is Grief a Disease?" *Psychosomatic Medicine* 23:18, 1961. C. M. Parkes, "Effects of Bereavement on Physical and Mental Health," p. 274. M. B. Young and C. Wellis, "The Mentality of Widowers," *Lancet* 2:454, 1963.

— **parents cope during a child's illness:** P. Chodoff, S. Friedman, D. Hamburg, "Stress, Defenses, and Coping Behavior: Observations in Parents of Children with Malignant Disease," *American Journal of Psychiatry,* 120:743, 1964.

— **D. Kaplan,** R. Grobstein, A. Smith, "Predicting the Impact of Severe Illness in Families," *Health and Social Work* (1976), 1:71–82.

— **"it could have easily been me":** Sourkes, p. 26.

Page 59: **Joseph Campbell,** *The Hero with a Thousand Faces,* pp. 32-33.

Page 60: **"powerful need to make sense of the incomprehensible":** Sourkes, *The Deepening Shade,* p. 47.

— **danger of answers that may create guilt or a fantasy of omnipotence:** Borysenko, *Guilt is the Teacher,* p. 153.

— **There are other philosophical styles used**: This list was partially inspired and adapted from the book that outlines six styles of meeting death: M. C. McCoy, *To Die with Style!* (Nashville: Abington Press, 1974).

Page 62: **Susan Sontag**, *Illness as Metaphor; AIDS and Its Metaphors* (New York: Anchor Books, Doubleday, 1977, 1978, 1988, 1989), p. 3.

Page 63: **As the secondary witness, I had an easier time:** A general piece of advice is that primary witnesses might find that during a crisis it is helpful to have another witness present to help.

Page 66: **Witnesses who may be particularly resilient are those who:** This list was partially compiled from Doug's clinical observations and our discussions, and inspired by results from resiliency research done with Hawaiian children by Emmy E. Werner of the University of California, and Ruth S. Smith.

Page 67: **Iatrogenic illness is unwittingly precipitated, aggravated or induced:** *The American Psychiatric Association's Psychiatric Glossary* (Washington, D.C.: American Psychiatric Press, Inc., 1984).

Page 68: **Gut,** *Productive and Unproductive Depression,* p. 18.

— **John Bradshaw**, *Healing the Shame That Binds You* (Deerfield Beach, FL: Health Communications Publishing Co., 1988), p. 52.

— **"basic human nightmare of being entirely helpless in the hands of malignant persecutors"**: Anthony Storr, *Solitude: A Return to the Self* (New York: Free Press, Macmillan, Inc., 1988), p. 46.

Page 72: **David's apparent anaphylactic shock**: With hindsight, I have learned that the diagnosis of anaphylactic shock was probably incorrect. When using Compazine, doctors have since learned that severe muscle spasms are a recognized side effect from this antinausea medication.

Page 74: **I tried psychic healing twice**: We want to make it clear that we believe in using all known resources for healing. We do not advocate psychic healing instead of traditional medical treatment. We think a holistic approach—trying to use spiritual, psychological and physical resources—is the best strategy to maximize healing.

Page 76: **Amy Wallace, Bill Henkin**, *The Psychic Healing Book* (Berkeley: Wingbow Press, 1978).

Page 80: **Many researchers are now examining the toll of so-called negative emotions**: Norman Cousins, *Head First: The Biology of Hope* (New York: E.P. Dutton, 1989), p. 2. We highly recommend this book for further understanding of the field of psychoneuroimmunology, and to read about the many studies that discuss the impact of emotions on health.

Page 82: **disaster syndrome . . . as soon as the crisis point diminishes, they crumble physically and emotionally, sometimes becoming "nearly stuporous"**: Martin E. P. Seligman, *Helplessness: On Depression, Development and Death* (San Francisco: W.H. Freeman & Co., 1975), p. 40.

Page 83: **Martin Seligman defines helplessness**: Seligman, pp. 9, 10.

— **Seligman's thesis about helplessness . . . may interest witnesses who have repeated traumas**: For those who have had only one trauma or relatively minor traumas, Seligman discusses that time can mend feelings of helplessness.

— **. . . helplessness distorts a future perception of control**: Seligman, pp. 22, 23.

Page 84: . . . **they will not be able to nurture or relieve suffering**: Seligman, p. 93.

Chapter 4

Page 89: . . . *premature cognitive commitment*: Labeled by Ellen Langer, *Mindfulness* (Reading, MA: Addison-Wesley, 1989), p. 25. See also B. Chanowitz and E. Langer, "Premature Cognitive Commitment," *Journal of Personality and Social Psychology* (1981), 41:1051-1063. This term is also similar to cognitive dissonance.

Page 91: **Norman Cousins**, *Head First*, p. 268. He argues further—citing evidence from the S. Levy, R. Herberman, M. Lippman, T. d'Angelo study, "Correlation of Stress Factors with Sustained Depression of Natural Killer Cell Activity and Predicted Prognosis in Patients with Breast Cancer," *Journal of Clinical Oncology* (1987), 5:348–353—how depressed behavior is associated with accelerated tumor spread.

Page 97: **Bernie S. Siegel**, M.D., *Love, Medicine & Miracles* (New York: Harper & Row, 1986). We are paraphrasing Siegel's definition of the term, "exceptional patient." In his book, he writes about exceptional patients in his practice who have cured their illnesses with a varied combination of traditional medicine, relaxation techniques, therapy, and a positive attitude.

Page 102: **For senior citizens, . . . :** Other resources include: The Children of Aging Parents, Woodbourne Office Campus, Levittown, PA 19057; American Association of Retired Persons, 601 E Street, N.W., Washington, D.C. 20049.

— **. . . review available health books and references**: Jeffrey R. M. Kunz, M.D. and Asher J. Finkel, M.D., eds., *The American Medical Association Family Medical Guide* (New York: Random House, 1987) is a useful home reference book containing information about anatomy, diseases, drugs, symptoms, etc.

— **Check out all the alternative therapies that are available**: Jean Carper, *Health Care U.S.A.* (Englewood Cliffs, NJ: Prentice-Hall, 1987), lists where to get the best standard and alternative treatment for some 120 illnesses.

Why seek out alternative healing systems? No one really can say definitively how healings occur, or why certain types of medicine work differently on people with the same ailment. Therefore, why not investigate or use, within reason, several healing modalities? Though currently in the United States there is considerable prejudice against non-Western healing traditions, in the future, many will discover the wisdom of using a more holistic approach to medical care.

— ... **outline of information a patient is likely to need**: David R. Stutz, M.D., Bernard Feder, Ph.D., and the Editors of Consumer Reports Books, *The Savvy Patient*. The research categories were partly inspired by suggested questions that patients should raise during their illness. This book is a handy resource for the patient and advocate alike, with its detailed approach to being a wise health-care consumer and participant.

Page 107: **physicians should be well-trained, competent, accessible, organized**: For patients and witnesses making a choice about a physician, ask about the doctor's office policy: rules of the practice; emergency communications; method of informing patients of test results; office visit cost; insurance policy compatibility; nature of delays in office hours; hospital affiliation.

— **The editors also suggest** . . . : Jeffrey R. M. Kunz, M.D., and Asher J. Finkel, M.D., eds., *The American Medical Association Family Medical Guide*, p. 745.

Page 108: **Doctors should provide "responsible reassurance"**: Cousins, *Head First*, pp. 269–270.

Page 111: **A second opinion can be sought through the primary physician**: In a hospital, a primary physician is often called the attending physician, the professional who is in charge of directing and communicating with all the other consulting physicians and medical personnel dealing with the patient. Most often, primary physicians are the family doctor, pediatrician, or internist. When a specialist is the principal physician, he or she will function as the attending physician, notifying the family doctor when to resume primary responsibility.

— **A second opinion by an unassociated doctor may be more advantageous**: Second opinion panels help patients with choosing physicians. Some second opinion panels include: Northwestern University, Chicago, (312) 908-5284; Montefiore Medical Center, New York, (212) 920-4826; St. Vincent Cancer Center, Little Rock, Arkansas, (501) 660-3900; University of Texas Cancer Center, Galveston, (409) 761-2981; University of California at San Diego, (619) 543-6178. This list was compiled by Gina Kolata, "Body and Mind: Vital Opinions," *Sunday New York Times*, April 16, 1989, pp. 46, 47.

Witnesses can also call 1(800) 4-CANCER for a computerized database called P.D.Q. (Physician's Data Query) which contains state-of-the-art treatments for different types of cancer. So far, this kind of hotline is only available for cancer. It should be available for all kinds of illnesses, and until it is, the burden of research will be on the patient and witnesses.

Page 113: **the option of getting a durable power of attorney**: Consult an attorney, social worker, or The Society for the Right to Die, 250 W. 57th Street, New York, NY 10107, for more information and forms.

Page 116: **To achieve a better doctor-patient-witness relationship to facilitate cooperation, communication, and negotiation**: For a more detailed discussion on negotiation, we recommend reading Roger Fisher and William Ury's *Getting to Yes* (New York: Penguin Books, 1981).

— **James E. Groves, M.D.**, "Taking Care of the Hateful Patient," *New England Journal of Medicine*, vol. 298, no. 16, April 16, 1978, pp. 883–887.

Chapter 5

Page 123: **its etymology:** *Third Barnhardt Dictionary of New English*, 1990.

— **the definition of caregiver has expanded:** *The Random House Dictionary of the English Language, 2nd edition unabridged.*

Page 125: **To make the distinction clearer, empathy is an "insightful awareness,":** The American Psychiatric Association's *Psychiatric Glossary* (Washington, D.C.: American Psychiatric Press, Inc., 1984).

— **Eric Cassell**, "Recognizing Suffering," *Hastings Center Report*, vol. 21, no. 3, May-June 1991, p. 24.

Page 126: **The psychologist Sandra Levy, at the Pittsburgh Cancer Institute:** This study was reported in an article by David Gelman with Mary Hager, "Body and Soul," *Newsweek*, Nov. 7, 1988, pp. 91, 92. S. M. Levy, R. B. Herberman, et al., "Prognostic Risk Assessment in Primary Breast Cancer by Behavioral and Immunological Parameters," *Health & Psychology* (1985), 4:99-113.

— **Dr. Herbert Benson has proven the patient can contribute to the process of healing by using the relaxation response:** For more information about the relaxation response and his many studies, consult Herbert Benson's books: *The Relaxation Response, The Mind/Body Effect, Beyond the Relaxation Response,* and *Your Maximum Mind.*

Page 127: **if the witness can genuinely feel "unconditional positive regard" for the patient:** Carl R. Rogers, "The Necessary and Sufficient Conditions of Therapeutic Personality Change," *Journal of Consulting Psychology*, vol. 21, no. 2, 1957, p. 98. Rogers notes that unconditional positive regard is an ideal concept; in reality, most people will feel this only sometimes, with conditional positive regard far more common.

Page 129: **Anatole Broyard**, "Good Books about Being Sick," *New York Times Book Review*, April 1, 1990, p. 29.

Page 131: **Michael Franz Basch**, *Understanding Psychotherapy: The Science Behind the Art* (New York: Basic Books, Inc., 1988), p. 19.

— **Precisely defining psychotherapy is more complicated:** Jerrold S. Maxmen, M.D., *The New Psychiatry* (New York: New American Library, 1985), p. 116. In briefly explaining psychotherapy and presenting an overview of the psychotherapeutic process, we acknowledge the complexity of the topic and the breadth of the field. We understand this attempt will be an incomplete explanation, but, nonetheless, worthwhile for our purposes.

— **Psychiatrists, psychotherapists or psychologists**: We will be using the term *therapist*, throughout the chapter. A *psychiatrist* is a licensed physician who specializes in the diagnosis, treatment, and prevention of mental and emotional disorders. Additional training is necessary for psychoanalysis. A *licensed psychologist* generally holds a doctoral degree from an accredited graduate program in psychology and has had two years of supervised work experience. These definitions are from the American Psychiatric Association, *A Psychiatric Glossary*, 5th ed. (Boston: Little, Brown, 1980), pp. 111, 112. **Basch**, pp. 14, 19.

Page 132: **Basch**, p. 48.

Page 134: . . . **the therapist tries to release or reduce the client's anxiety**: Samuel G. Trull, "Strategies of Effective Interviewing," *Effective Communication* (Harvard Business Review Reprint series, No. 21073), pp. 39–44. The article first appeared in the *Harvard Business Review*, Jan.-Feb. 1964.

Page 135: **Broyard**, p. 29.

Page 136: **Ralph G. Nichols and Leonard A. Stevens**, "Listening to People," *Effective Communication* (Harvard Business Review Reprint series, No. 21073), pp. 31–34. The article first appeared in the *Harvard Business Review*, Sept.-Oct. 1957.

— **Researcher Samuel Trull offers additional interviewing tips**: Trull, pp. 39–44.

Page 139: **empathic partners can help patients sort out and validate their feelings and find meaning in the experience**: Arthur Kleinman, M.D., *The Illness Narratives: Suffering, Healing, and the Human Condition* (New York: Basic Books, 1988), pp. xxii, 17, 26. This book is a noteworthy resource for caregivers and empathic partners who are dealing with the chronically ill.

— **Kleinman**, p. 44.

Page 140: **Patients must be able to express their feelings—without editing or censorship**: In the extreme, if patients become unbearable, empathic partners should leave, or try to remove themselves mentally from the situation. It is possible that witnesses will be not be able to handle the patient's responses. If necessary, consider persuading the patient to consult with a professional therapist.

— **Losses can be staggering**: Sourkes, p. 31.

Page 142: **On occasion, empathic partners will want to coach patients when their spirits are deflated**: In his book *Head First*, Norman Cousins used the phrase, "Don't deny, defy the verdict," to encourage patients, p. 83. However, to get patients to transform depression into a fighting spirit, he taught them biofeedback techniques to demonstrate the power patients can have over their bodies. In Chapter 6, biofeedback will be discussed as a lay healing technique.

Page 143: **Words can also . . . disturb**: Wendell Johnson, *Your Most Enchanted Listener* (New York: Harper & Brothers, 1956), p. 185.

Page 146: **Arthur Frank . . . contends that patients who deny:** Frank, p. 67.

Page 148: **. . . denial is considered to be a "defense mechanism. . . ":** The American Psychiatric Association's *Psychiatric Glossary* (Washington, D.C.: American Psychiatric Press, Inc., 1984).

— **Dialogue helps to expose and identify problems:** In cognitive therapy, there is great importance placed on clients' storytelling and the words they use. The focus is on the patients' present "script" and changing or editing their words, the theory essentially being: you are what you think you are. You are your thoughts. Basch puts it another way, "*. . .* one's picture of oneself tends to shape one's experience of the world, literally determining what one sees and hears and what information signifies," p. 21.

Page 149: **In psychotherapeutic terms, clarification "aims at placing the psychic phenomenon being analyzed in sharp focus:** Ralph R. Greenson, *The Technique and Practice of Psychoanalysis*, vol. 1 (New York: International Universities Press, Inc., 1967), p. 38.

Page 151: **Nikki had read Louise Hay's book:** Louise Hay, *You Can Heal Your Life* (Santa Monica, CA.: Hay House, 1984).

Page 152: **Sigmund Freud,** "Construction in Analysis," Standard Edition, XXIII (London, The Hogarth Press, 1963), pp. 255–269.

Page 153: **. . . steps to optimize and facilitate problem-solving:** We are modifying and using Betty Edwards' stages of creativity, as first suggested by the physicist Herman Helmholtz and then refined by the psychologist Jacob Getzels. Betty Edwards, *Drawing on the Artist Within* (New York: Simon & Schuster, 1986), p. 26.

— **George Prince** developed the concept of creating an internal experimental self where these traits enhance the creative process. Prince is chairman and cofounder of Synectics, Inc., a training and consulting firm in Cambridge, Massachusetts, devoted to innovation and creative problem-solving.

Page 154: **Preconceived solutions or fixed thinking can blind ourselves to innovative discoveries and block creativity:** Edwards, p. 26.

Page 155: **Working through refers to the "repetitive, progressive, and elaborate explorations:** Greenson, p. 42.

Page 157: **Empathic partners should take care . . . :** In getting a patient to look at issues that are blocking healing, the empathic partner should not attempt to make *judgments* about the causes of thoughts, feelings, or patterns of behavior that carry the burden of blame. Making patients feel guilty about their illness or behavior is *not* healing.

— **Insight is self-understanding:** American Psychiatric Association, *A Psychiatric Glossary*, 5th ed. (1980), p. 52.

Page 158: **Gayle A. Dakof, Shelley E. Taylor,** "Victims' Perceptions of Social Support: What Is Helpful from Whom?" *Journal of Personality and Social Psychology*, 1990, no. 1, pp. 80–89.

Page 159: **. . . researchers found that regular volunteer work correlated with increased life expectancy:** Study reported in "Compassion: The

Power of Caring," *Dimensions Magazine* published by the Grey Nuns of Youville Hospital of Cambridge, Massachusetts.

— **Terrence Des Pres**, *The Survivor: An Anatomy of Life in the Death Camps* (New York: Oxford University Press, 1976), pp. 37, 38.

Chapter 6

Page 162: . . . **the particular stressful life event of witnessing illness often threatens a caregiver's equilibrium by**: Mardi Jon Horowitz, M.D., *Stress Response Syndromes*, 2nd ed. (Northvale, NJ: Jason Aronson, 1986), p. 93.

Page 163: **Caregivers should not be a work force of "co-dependents"**: In the context of drug and alcohol addictions, *co-dependency* is a modern term describing unhealthy, entangled relationships where co-dependents are said to "enable" the addict to remain sick or addicted. In a witness context, in some circumstances, witnesses may "enable" a sick person to stay sick. On the other hand, witnesses can "enable" a sick person to work at the job of healing by removing burdens that would prevent or slow the act of healing.

Anyone who has been sick knows how wonderful it can be to be served chicken soup and made comfortable: to have the luxury of being able to count on another for help. It is also true that some people deplore being dependent and reject care that is offered, because it emphasizes their incapacitation which, in turn, makes them angry.

Witnesses will have to judge for themselves whether taking an active role in caregiving is helping or hindering recovery. The test may be whether they are helping at the expense of the sick person—and themselves.

— **Mihaly Csikszentmihalyi**, *Flow: The Psychology of Optimal Experience* (New York: Harper & Row, 1990).

Page 164: **Long-term stress can lead to increased blood pressure**: Jon Kabat-Zinn, Ph.D., *Full Catastrophe Living: Using the Wisdom of Your Body and Mind to Face Stress, Pain and Illness* (New York: Delacorte Press, 1980), p. 256. Additions to the list are from Andrew E. Slaby, M.D., Ph.D., M.P.H., "Sixty Ways to Make Stress Work for You," *Fair Oaks Hospital Psychiatry Newsletter*, vol. V, issue 9–10 (October-November, 1987), p. 52.

Page 165: **Stress can even increase susceptibility to flu viruses and build tooth plaque**: Intense stress reactions may produce adrenaline and other stress hormones, which in turn, suppress white blood cell count, and thus the immune system response. The same adrenaline reaction causes dry mouth, which stimulates salivation, which, then, causes increased plaque buildup.

— . . . **list of stress symptoms**: Slaby, p. 52.

— **This has been called mental toughness, learned optimism, or mindfulness**: Martin Seligman, *Learned Optimism* (New York: Knopf, 1990). Ellen J. Langer, *Mindfulness* (Reading, MA: Addison-Wesley, 1989).

Page 166: **meditation . . . a "formal exercise in turning off the negative ego's voice and quieting the critical, judgmental mind.":** Rob Krakovitz, M.D., *High Energy: How to Overcome Fatigue and Maintain Your Peak Vitality* (New York: Ballantine Books, 1986), p. 205.

— **. . . [meditation] "takes the mind out of its boundaries":** Deepak Chopra, M.D., *Quantum Healing: Exploring the Frontiers of Mind/Body Medicine* (New York: Bantam Books, 1989), p. 236.

— **Meditation can preserve physical and mental health:** Maharishi Mahesh Yogi, *Transcendental Meditation* (New York: Signet Book, New American Library, 1963), p. 318.

— **. . . more specifically, [relaxation techniques] can help relieve tension headaches . . . :** Benson, pp. 80–82.

— **It has even been reported that meditation slows the aging process:** Chopra, p. 230. Chopra bases this claim on a study of TM meditators done by Robert Keith Wallace, ending around 1978, measuring aging by the variables of: blood pressure, acuteness of hearing, and near-point vision. He also reports a Blue Cross/Blue Shield study in Iowa of 2,000 meditators that showed they were healthier in 17 major areas of physical and mental disease. For example, the meditators were hospitalized 87 percent less often than nonmeditators.

— **J. K. Kiecolt-Glaser and R. Glaser, and others:** "Psychosocial Enhancement in a Geriatric Population," *Health Psychology* (1985), 4:24–41.

— **quiet sitting, body-scan meditations, walking meditations:** Kabat-Zinn, pp. 50–58.

— **concentration or mindfulness meditation:** Benson, pp. 88–90.

— **. . . meditations for self-healing, centering, aura cleansing, and to dissolve self-limitations:** Barbara Ann Brennan, *Hands of Light* (New York: Bantam Books, 1988).

Page 167: **meditations using crystals as concentration objects or for specific healing rituals:** Katrina Raphael, *Crystal Enlightenment: The Transforming Properties of Crystals and Healing Stones*, vol. 1 (New York: Aurora Press, 1985).

— **Another method to achieve relaxation is yoga:** *Richard Hittleman's Yoga 28 Day Exercise Plan* (New York: Workman Publishing Company, 1969), p. 27.

— **Benson,** p. 22.

— **you can try using a "focus word," also known in some meditation traditions as a mantra:** In the past, some students of meditation paid to get the proper personal mantra, and unfortunately, some people stayed away from the practice of meditation, because of the cost. Any word or combination of words—the simpler the better—will work. If the words are privately meaningful or have personal religious or spiritual relevance, that is also helpful.

— **Step 5: Focus on breathing slowly and naturally, taking time to breathe in and out fully:** Brennan suggests another way to focus this step. During the "in" breath, she says to breathe in the future and all its possibilities and what you want to create. On the "out" breath, breathe out the past and all that went with it, and all the false limitations. Brennan, p. 265.

— **Physiologically, the body experiences a slower heartbeat and breathing**: Chopra, p. 189.

Page 168: **Ann bought a simple biofeedback machine that looked like a small transistor radio**: Though helpful especially for those people who need proof that they are successful in relaxing, biofeedback machines are not always necessary to achieve the relaxation response.

Page 172: **Achterberg**, p. 156.

— **Randolph C. Byrd, M.D.**, "Positive Therapeutic Effects of Intercessory Prayer in a Coronary Care Unit Population," *Southern Medical Journal*, vol. 81, no. 7, July 1988, pp. 826–829.

Page 173: **Woody Allen** and Marshall Brickman, *Annie Hall*, published in *Four Films of Woody Allen* (New York: Random House, 1977 film copyright, 1982 book copyright).

Page 174: **Ellen J. Langer**, *Mindfulness*. Langer also uses the term *premature cognitive commitments* to describe a person's mindset, a decision already made in the past that sticks in all future situations. This type of thinking, for example, is at the root of all types of prejudice.

— **Kabat-Zinn**, pp. 32–40.

Page 175: **Frank**, p. 90.

— **Harriet G. Lerner**, *The Dance of Anger: A Woman's Guide to Changing the Patterns of Intimate Relationships* (New York: Perennial Library, Harper and Row, 1985). This book is an excellent resource about how to cope with and process anger. Another resource is Carol Tavris, *Anger: The Misunderstood Emotion* (New York: Simon & Schuster, 1982). Transforming and processing anger is complex. Discussing the subtleties of handling different types of anger using different strategies is beyond the scope of this book. The suggested books will be worthwhile not only in a witness context, but in other life situations.

— **Lerner**, p. 7.

Page 176: **Emmy Gut contends that anger speeds up thought and action**: Emmy Gut, *Productive and Unproductive Depression*, p. 22.

— **Lerner postulates that, "anger is neither legitimate or illegitimate"**: Lerner, p. 4.

— **Assertiveness is an adaptive way to channel anger**: Joel Yager, M.D., "Clinical Manifestations of Psychiatric Disorders," in Harold I. Kaplan, M.D., Benjamin J. Sadock, M.D., *Comprehensive Textbook of Psychiatry/V*, vol. 1, 5th Ed., (Baltimore: Williams & Wilkins, 1989), p. 575.

Page 177: **Lerner suggests that simply venting anger is often not enough**: Lerner, p. 4.

— **Almost any creative act . . . can alleviate helplessness**: Storr, p. 129.

Page 179: **Carolyn G. Heilbrun**, *Writing a Woman's Life* (New York: Ballantine Books, 1988), p. 15.

— **James W. Pennebaker and Sandra Klihr Beall**, "Confronting a Traumatic Event: Toward an Understanding of Inhibition and Disease, *Journal of Abnormal Psychology*, 1986, vol. 95, no. 3, pp. 274–281.

Page 180: **Sandra G. Shuman**, *Source Imagery: Releasing the Power of Your Creativity* (New York: Doubleday, 1989).

Page 181: **It can also be an extraordinary opportunity—granted a mixed blessing—for intimacy**: A recommended book about intimacy—Harriet Goldhor Lerner, Ph.D., *The Dance of Intimacy: A Woman's Guide to Courageous Acts of Change in Key Relationships* (New York: Perennial Library, Harper & Row, 1989).

— **J. K. Kiecolt-Glaser**, et al., "Chronic stress and immunity on family caregivers of Alzheimer's disease victims," *Psychosomatic Medicine* 49 (1987), pp. 523–535.

Page 183: **Ruth Gordon**, *The Actress*, MGM, 1953.

— **In a study exploring the effects of living with a depressed person . . .** : James C. Coyne, Ronald C. Kessler, et al.,"Living with a Depressed Person," *Journal of Consulting and Clinical Psychology*, vol. 55, no. 3, 1987, pp. 347–352.

Page 188: **Primary caregivers are especially prone to illness**: J. K. Kiecolt-Glaser, R. Glaser, et al. "Chronic Stress and Immunity in Family Caregivers of Alzheimer's Disease Victims," *Psychosomatic Medicine* 48 (1987): 523–535.

Page 191: **Witnesses often feel depressed and may actually suffer from clinical depression**: "Feeling depressed" is often used as a colloquial expression to describe a mood when a person feels despair, sadness, hurt, confusion, fatigue, and listlessness. This is a normal feeling state. Clinical depression can be more severe. It can be a symptom in mental or physical disorders or a syndrome that may also include symptoms of slowed thinking, decreased physical activity, guilt, hopelessness, and eating and sleeping disorders. Definition partly from American Psychiatric Assocation, *Psychiatric Glossary*, 1984 ed.

Page 192: **According to Emmy Gut, depression is an ordinary response**: Gut, *Productive and Unproductive Depression*.

— **This isolation, Gut suggests, serves "to facilitate and protect concentration"**: Gut, p. 1.

— **. . .it is wrong to judge whether the depression**: Gut, p. 12.

Page 193: **Ellen Willis**, "The Neo-Guilt Trip," *Mirabella*, May 1990, p. 48.

— **Fran Lebowitz**, *Metropolitan Life* (New York: Fawcett Press, Ballantine Books, 1977).

Page 194: **Cousins,** *Head First: The Biology of Hope* (New York: E. P. Dutton, 1989), p. 133.

— **Martin Seligman**, *Helplessness*, p. 103.

— **The following is a list of general advice to help reduce stress and increase self-nurturance**: The list of suggestions, though altered, was inspired by Slaby, pp. 50-63.

Chapter 7

Page 198: **anticipatory grief, an emotional response to the pain of separa-tion, or change, before the actuality of loss**: Sourkes, p. 67.

Page 200: **Derek Humphry**, *Final Exit: The Practicalities of Self-Deliverance and Assisted Suicide for the Dying* (Hemlock Society, 1991). Mention of this text does not mean we advocate its contents.

Page 206: **Grief is felt when a person who is essential to our well-being**: Gut, p. 21.

— **Some distinguish grief from mourning**: John Graves, M.D., "Differen-tiating Grief, Mourning and Bereavement" (a letter to the editor), *American Journal of Psychiatry*, vol. 135, no. 7, (July 1978), pp. 874–875.

— **Anthony Storr**, *Solitude: A Return to the Self* (New York: The Free Press, A Division of Macmillan, 1988), p. 32.

— **The potential problems that widows face**: Milton Greenblatt, M.D., "The Grieving Spouse," *American Journal of Psychiatry*, vol. 135, no. 1, (January 1978), pp. 43–47.

— **Selby Jacobs and Adrian Ostfield**, "An Epidemiological Review of the Mortality of Bereavement," *Psychosomatic Medicine*, vol. 39, no. 5, (Sept.-Oct. 1977), pp. 344–357.

Page 207: **Some situations . . . increase the severity of grief reactions**: Horowitz, *Stress Response Syndromes*, 2nd ed., p. 42.

— **Carol Staudacher**, *Beyond Grief: A Guide for Recovering from the Death of a Loved One* (Oakland, CA: New Harbinger Publications, 1987), p. 44.

Page 208: **Many have struggled to try to make death a fulfillment and consummation**: Herman Feiful, editor, *The Meaning of Death* (New York: McGraw-Hill, 1959). Judith Viorst, *Necessary Losses* (New York: Simon & Schuster, 1986), Ernest Becker, *The Denial of Death* (New York: The Free Press, a division of Macmillan, 1973). Elisabeth Kübler-Ross, *On Death and Dying* (New York: Macmillan, 1969).

Page 209: **In one study, it was found that 50 to 70 percent of parents experienced marital discord or divorce**: D. Kaplan, R. Grobstein, A. Smith, "Predicting the Impact of Severe Illness in Families," *Health and Social Work*, 1:71-82.

Page 210: **Sigmund Freud**, "Mourning and Melancholia," 1917, p. 5.

Page 214: **There may be no end of the process, but a vaguer transition to a course that needs to find its completion**: Freud, "Mourning and Melancholia."

Page 218: **It is as if the mind demands that until the experience be re-worked and digested as a tolerable memory, the continuing rever-beration and reliving of the experience must be endured**: Phenomena such as kindling and reverberation were discussed by Bessel van der Kolk, M.D., at the Cape Cod Summer Symposium for Mental Health Professionals, July 29–August 2, 1991. Recent work in the fields of neuroanatomic and neurochemical research suggest the role of the limbic system and the hippocampus are central in the production and control of emotions.

— **In psychological literature, victims of trauma are said to see life through a *trauma lens* or they construct a *trauma membrane*:** The study of post-traumatic shock disorder has prompted research about how memory works in the human brain. Though the following references are technical and written for students of neuroscience and/or psychotherapy, readers who want to read more about the vision of life through the "trauma lens" and to explore beneath the "trauma membrane" might want to consult these resources. Gerald Edelman, *Neural Darwinism* (New York: Basic Books, 1987). Bessel van der Kolk, Onno van der Hart, "Pierre Janet and the Breakdown of Adaptation in Psychological Trauma," *American Journal of Psychiatry*, vol. 146, no. 12, (Dec. 1989), pp. 1530–1540. Henry Krystal, "Trauma and Affects," *Psychoanalytic Study of the Child*, 33, 81-116, 1978. Bessel van der Kolk, "The Compulsion to Repeat Trauma," *Psychiatric Clinics of North America*, vol. 12, no. 2, (June 1989), pp. 389–411.

Page 219: **Joseph Campbell with Bill Moyers**, *The Power of Myth* (New York: Doubleday, 1988), pp. 165–183.

— **Staudacher**, p. 4.

— **Borysenko**, *Guilt is the Teacher, Love is the Lesson*, p. 214.

Page 223: **Kleinman**, *Illness Narratives*, p. 55.

— **"inevitable transformation of presence into absence"**: Sourkes, p. 37.

Page 225: **Mihaly Csikszentmihalyi**, *Flow: The Psychology of Optimal Experience* (New York: Harper & Row, 1990), p. 4.

Chapter 8

Page 228: . . . **advance directives:** A copy of an advance medical directive including a form for the durable power of attorney for health care and a living will is included in the appendix. The information was supplied by the New Hampshire Hospital Association, Concord, N. H.

Page 230: **In Oregon, where an experiment of health care rationing is being considered,** they have formulated some basic principles and goals: Oregon State Senator John Kitzhaber wrote these principles, though not all of his goals are listed here. See *The Center Report, The Center for Public Policy and Contemporary Issues*, vol. 2, no. 1, University of Denver, Winter/Spring 1990. Additional information was obtained from Richard C. Lippincott, M.D., Department of Psychiatry, Oregon Health Sciences University, Salem, Oregon. At the time we go to press, the federal government is refusing to give Oregon permission to proceed with this experiment. It is thought that rationing could infringe upon the federal mandates in the Americans with Disabilities Act of 1992.

Page 231: **Some 80 percent of group medical insurance policies now contain such provisions:** This statistic was reported by John Docherty, M.D., at the New Hampshire Psychiatric Society in October 1991. This information was gathered for the American Psychiatric Society.

Page 232: **Arthur Kleinman,** M.D., *The Illness Narratives: Suffering, Healing and the Human Condition* (New York: Basic Books, 1988).

— **Cousins,** *Head First,* p. 32.

Page 236: **the increasing incidence of "granny dumping":** Robert P. Hey, Elliot Carlson, "'Granny Dumping:' New Pain for U.S. Elders," *AARP Bulletin,* vol. 32, no. 8, (September 1991), pp. 1, 16.

Page 237: **Cutler said, "These buddies . . . could provide a myriad of services:** Sasha Alyson, editor, *You Can Do Something about AIDS* (Boston: The Stop AIDS Project, 1988), pp. 104–105.

Recommended Reading

Achterberg, Jeanne. *Imagery in Healing: Shamanism and Modern Medicine*. Boston: New Science Library, 1985.

Alyson, Sasha, editor. *You Can Do Something about AIDS*. Boston: The Stop AIDS Project, 1988.

Basch, Michael Franz. *Understanding Psychotherapy: The Science behind the Art*. New York: Basic Books, 1988.

Becker, Ernest. *The Denial of Death*. New York: The Free Press, Macmillan Publishing Co., 1973.

Benson, Herbert, M.D., with William Proctor. *Your Maximum Mind*. New York: Times Books, 1987.

_____. *The Relaxation Response*. New York: William Morrow, 1975.

_____. *The Mind/Body Effect*. New York: Simon & Schuster, 1979.

_____. *Beyond the Relaxation Response*. New York: Times Books, 1984.

Borysenko, Joan, Ph.D., with Larry Rothstein. *Minding the Body, Mending the Mind*. Reading, MA: Addison-Wesley Publishing Co., 1987.

_____. *Guilt is the Teacher, Love is the Lesson*. New York: Warner Books, 1990.

Brennan, Barbara Ann. *Hands of Light*. New York: Bantam Books, 1988.

Broyard, Anatole. "Good Books about Being Sick," *New York Times Book Review*. April 1, 1990, p. 29.

Burns, David B., M.D., *Feeling Good: The New Mood Therapy*. New York: New American Library, 1980.

Campbell, Joseph. *The Hero with a Thousand Faces*. Bollingen Series. Princeton, NJ: Princeton University Press, 1949.

Carper, Jean. *Health Care U.S.A.* Englewood Cliffs, NJ: Prentice-Hall, 1987.

Cassileth, Barrie, Ph.D., editor. *Caring for the Patient with Cancer at Home: A Guide for Patients and Families*. American Cancer Society, 1988.

Chopra, Deepak, M.D., *Quantum Healing: Exploring the Frontiers of Mind/Body Medicine*. New York: Bantam Books, 1989.

Cousins, Norman. *Anatomy of an Illness as Perceived by the Patient*. New York: Norton, 1979.

_____. *Head First: The Biology of Hope*. New York: E.P. Dutton, 1989.

Csikszentmihalyi, Mihaly. *Flow: The Psychology of Optimal Experience*. New York: Harper & Row, 1990.

Dass, Ram, and Paul Gorman. *How Can I Help?* New York: Alfred A. Knopf, 1985.

Eidson, Ted, editor. *The AIDS Caregiver's Handbook*. New York: St. Martin's Press, 1988.

Feiful, Herman, editor. *The Meaning of Death*. New York: McGraw-Hill, 1959.

Feinstein, David, Ph.D., and Stanley Krippner, Ph.D. *Personal Mythology: The Psychology of Your Evolving Self*. Los Angeles: Jeremy P. Tarcher, Inc., 1988.

Frank, Arthur. *At the Will of the Body*. Boston: Houghton Mifflin Co., 1991.

Gut, Emmy. *Productive and Unproductive Depression*. New York: Basic Books, 1989.

Horowitz, Mardi J., M.D. *Stress Response Syndromes*, second edition. Northvale, NJ: Jason Aronson, Inc., 1986.

Humphry, Derek. *Final Exit: The Practicalities of Self-Deliverance and Assisted Suicide for the Dying*. Hemlock Society, 1991.

Iyengar, B.K.S. *Light on Yoga*, revised edition. New York: Schocken Books, 1977.

Kabat-Zinn, Jon, Ph.D. *Full Catastrophe Living: Using the Wisdom of Your Body and Mind to Face Stress, Pain and Illness*. New York: Delacorte Press, 1980.

Kalish, Richard A. *Death, Grief, and Caring Relationships*. Monterey, CA: Brooks/Cole Publishing Co., 1981.

Kaptchuk, Ted, and Michael Croucher. *The Healing Arts: Exploring The Medical Ways of the World*. New York: Summit Books, 1987.

Kleinman, Arthur, M.D. *The Illness Narratives: Suffering, Healing, and the Human Condition*. New York: Basic Books, 1988.

Krakovitz, Rob, M.D. *High Energy: How to Overcome Fatigue and Maintain Your Peak Vitality*. New York: Ballantine Books, 1986.

Kübler-Ross, Elisabeth. *On Death and Dying*. New York: Macmillan, 1969.

Kunz, Jeffrey R. M., M.D., and Asher J. Finkel, M.D., eds. *The American Medical Association Family Medical Guide*. New York: Random House, 1987.

Langer, Ellen J. *Mindfulness*. Reading, MA: Addison-Wesley, 1989.

Lerner, Harriet G. *The Dance of Anger: A Woman's Guide to Changing the Patterns of Intimate Relationships*. New York: Perennial Library, Harper & Row, 1985.

_____. *The Dance of Intimacy: A Woman's Guide to Courageous Acts of Change in Key Relationships*. New York: Perennial Library, Harper & Row, 1989.

Levine, Stephen. *A Gradual Awakening*. New York: Anchor Books, 1979.

_____. *Healing into Life and Death*. Garden City, NY: Anchor Press/Doubleday, 1987.

Locke, Steven, and Douglas Colligan. *The Healer Within*. New York: Dutton, 1986.

Ornstein, Robert, Ph.D., and David Sobel, M.D. *Healthy Pleasures*. Reading, MA: Addison-Wesley, 1989.

Pelletier, Kenneth R. *Mind as Slayer, Mind as Healer*. New York: Delta, 1977.

Progoff, Ira. *At a Journal Workshop: The Basic Text and Guide for Using the Intensive Journal*. New York: Dialogue House Library, 1975.

Ring, Kenneth. *Heading toward Omega: In Search of the Meaning of the Near-Death Experience*. New York: William Morrow and Co., Inc., 1984.

Seligman, Martin E. P. *Helplessness: On Depression, Development and Death*. San Francisco: W.H. Freeman & Co., 1975.

_____. *Learned Optimism*. New York: Knopf, 1990.

Shuman, Sandra, Ph.D. *Source Imagery: Releasing the Power of Your Creativity*. New York: Doubleday, 1989.

Siegel, Bernie S., M.D. *Love, Medicine & Miracles*. New York: Harper & Row, 1986.

_____. *Peace, Love, & Healing*. New York: Harper & Row, 1989.

Simonton, O. Carl, Stephanie Matthews-Simonton, and James Creighton. *Getting Well Again*. Los Angeles: Jeremy P. Tarcher, 1978.

Smolan, Rick, Phillip Moffit, and Matthew Naythons. *The Power to Heal: Ancient Arts and Modern Sciences*. New York: Prentice Hall Press, 1990.

Sontag, Susan. *Illness as Metaphor: AIDS and Its Metaphors*. New York: Anchor Books, Doubleday, 1977, 1978, 1988, 1989.

Sourkes, Barbara, Ph.D. *The Deepening Shade: Psychological Aspects of Life-Threatening Illness*. Pittsburgh: University of Pittsburgh Press, 1982.

Staudacher, Carol. *Beyond Grief: A Guide for Recovering from the Death of a Loved One*. Oakland, CA: New Harbinger Publications, Inc., 1987.

Storr, Anthony. *Solitude: A Return to the Self*. New York: Free Press, Macmillan, Inc., 1988.

Strong, Maggie. *Mainstay: For the Well Spouse of the Chronically Ill*. Boston: Little, Brown, 1988.

Stutz, David R., M.D., Bernard Feder, Ph.D., and the Editors of Consumer Reports Books. *The Savvy Patient: How to be an Active Participant in Your Medical Care*. Mt. Vernon, NY: Consumers Union, 1990.

Tavris, Carol. *Anger: The Misunderstood Emotion*. New York: Simon & Schuster, 1982.

Viorst, Judith. *Necessary Losses*. New York: Simon & Schuster, 1986.

Wallace, Amy, and Bill Henkin. *The Psychic Healing Book*, Berkeley, CA: Wingbow Press, 1978.

APPENDIXES

Durable Power of Attorney for Health Care

Living Will

DISCLOSURE STATEMENT FOR THE DURABLE POWER OF ATTORNEY FOR HEALTH CARE

THIS IS AN IMPORTANT LEGAL DOCUMENT. BEFORE SIGNING THIS DOCUMENT YOU SHOULD KNOW THESE IMPORTANT FACTS:

Except to the extent you state otherwise, this document gives the person you name as your agent the authority to make any and all health care decisions for you when you are no longer capable of making them yourself. "Health care" means any treatment, service or procedure to maintain, diagnose or treat your physical or mental condition. Your agent, therefore, can have the power to make a broad range of health care decisions for you. Your agent may consent, refuse to consent, or withdraw consent to medical treatment and may make decisions about withdrawing or withholding life-sustaining treatment. Your agent cannot consent or direct any of the following:

- commitment to a state institution
- sterilization
- or termination of treatment if you are pregnant and if the withdrawal of that treatment is deemed likely to terminate the pregnancy unless the failure to withhold the treatment will be physically harmful to you or prolong severe pain which cannot be alleviated by medication.

You may state in this document any treatment you do not desire, except as stated above, or treatment you want to be sure you receive. Your agent's authority will begin when your doctor certifies that you lack the capacity to make health care decisions. If for moral or religious reasons you do not wish to be treated by a doctor or examined by a doctor for the certification that you lack capacity, you must say so in the document and name a person to be able to certify your lack of capacity. That person may not be your agent or alternate agent or any person ineligible to be your agent. You may attach additional pages if you need more space to complete your statement.

If you want to give your agent authority to withhold or withdraw the artificial providing of nutrition and fluids, your document must say so. Otherwise, your agent will not be able to direct that. Under no conditions will your agent be able to direct the withholding of food and drink for you to eat and drink normally.

Your agent will be obligated to follow your instructions when making decisions on your behalf. Unless you state otherwise, your agent will have the same authority to make decisions about your health care as you would have had if made consistent with state law.

It is important that you discuss this document with your physician or other health care providers before you sign it to make sure that you understand the nature and range of decisions which may be made on your behalf. If you do not have a physician, you should talk with someone else who is knowledgeable about these issues and can answer your questions. You do not need a lawyer's assistance to complete this document, but if there is anything in this document that you do not understand, you should ask a lawyer to explain it to you.

The person you appoint as agent should be someone you know and trust and must be at least 18 years old. If you appoint your health or residential care provider (e.g. your physician, or an employee of a home health agency, hospital, nursing home, or residential care home, other than a relative), that person will have to choose between acting as your agent or as your health or residential care provider; the law does not permit a person to do both at the same time.

You should inform the person you appoint that you want him or her to be your health care agent. You should discuss this document with your agent and your physician and give each a signed copy. You should indicate on the document itself the people and institutions who will have signed copies. Your agent will not be liable for health care decisions made in good faith on your behalf.

Even after you have signed this document, you have the right to make health care decisions for yourself as long as you are able to do so, and treatment cannot be given to you or stopped over your objection. You have the right to revoke the authority granted to your agent by informing him or her or your health care provider orally or in writing.

This document may not be changed or modified. If you want to make changes in the document you must make an entirely new one.

You should consider designating an alternate agent in the event that your agent is unwilling, unable, unavailable, or ineligible to act as your agent. Any alternate agent you designate will have the same authority to make health care decisions for you.

This power of attorney will not be valid unless it is signed in the presence of two (2) or more qualified witnesses who must both be present when you sign and acknowledge your signature. The following persons may not act as witnesses:

- **the person you have designated as your agent**
- **your spouse**
- **your lawful heirs or beneficiaries named in your will or a deed**

Only one of the two witnesses may be your health or residential care provider or one of their employees.

New Hampshire RSA 137-J

DURABLE POWER OF ATTORNEY
FOR HEALTH CARE

I, _____ , hereby appoint _____ of _____
(Name)   (Name of Agent)   (Agent's address and phone #)

as my agent to make any and all health care decisions for me, except to the extent I state otherwise in this document or as prohibited by law. This durable power of attorney for health care shall take effect in the event I become unable to make my own health care decisions.

Statement of Desires, Special Provisions, and Limitations Regarding Health Care Decisions.

For your convenience in expressing your wishes, some general statements concerning the withholding or removal of life-sustaining treatment are set forth below. (Life-sustaining treatment is defined as procedures without which a person would die, such as but not limited to the following: cardiopulmonary resuscitation, mechanical respiration, kidney dialysis or the use of other external mechanical and technological devices, drugs to maintain blood pressure, blood transfusions, and antibiotics). There is also a section which allows you to set forth specific directions for these or other matters. If you wish you may indicate your agreement or disagreement with any of the following statements and give your agent power to act in those specific circumstances.

1. If I become permanently incompetent to make health care decisions, and if I am also suffering from a terminal illness, I authorize my agent to direct that life-sustaining treatment be discontinued.

    _____ YES NO (Circle your choice and initial beside it.)
    (Initials)

2. Whether terminally ill or not, if I become permanently unconscious I authorize my agent to direct that life-sustaining treatment be discontinued.

    _____ YES NO (Circle your choice and initial beside it.)
    (Initials)

3. I realize that situations could arise in which the only way to allow me to die would be to discontinue artificial feeding (artificial nutrition and hydration). In carrying out any instructions I have given above in #1 or #2 or any instructions I may write in #4 below, I authorize my agent to direct that (circle your choice of (a) or (b) and initial beside it):

    _____ (a) artificial nutrition and hydration *not* to be started or, if started,
    (Initials)   be discontinued, or

    _____ (b) although all other forms of life-sustaining treatment be
    (Initials)   withdrawn, artificial nutrition and hydration *continue* to be
    given to me.

    If you fail to complete item 3, your agent will not have the power to direct the withdrawal of artificial nutrition and hydration.

4. Here you may include any specific desires or limitations you deem appropriate, such as when or what life-sustaining treatment you would want used or withheld, or instructions about refusing any specific types of treatment that are inconsistent with your religious beliefs or unacceptable to you for any other reason. You may leave this question blank if you desire. (attach additional pages as necessary) _____

    _____

    _____

In the event the person I appoint above is unable, unwilling or unavailable, or ineligible to act as my health care agent, I hereby appoint _____
(Name of alternate agent)

of _____ as alternate agent.
(Address and phone # of alternate agent)

I hereby acknowledge that I have been provided with a disclosure statement explaining the effect of this document. I have read and understand the information contained in the disclosure statement.

The original of this document will be kept at _____
(Address)

and the following persons and institutions will have signed copies: _____

_____

In witness whereof, I have hereunto signed my name this ___ day of _____ , 19___
(Day)   (Month)   (Year)

_____
Your Signature

I declare that the principal appears to be of sound mind and free from duress at the time the durable power of attorney for health care is signed and that the principal has affirmed that he or she is aware of the nature of the document and is signing it freely and voluntarily.

Witness: _____ Address: _____

Witness: _____ Address: _____

To be completed by notary.
STATE OF _____ COUNTY OF _____

The foregoing instrument was acknowledged before me this _____ day of _____ ,
(Day)   (Month)

19___, by _____

Notary Public/Justice of the Peace _____

My Commission Expires: _____

New Hampshire RSA 137-J

LIVING WILL

Declaration made this _____ day of _____ , I, _____ ,
                                                (Month, year)   (Name)

being of sound mind, willfully and voluntarily make known my desire that my dying shall not be artificially prolonged under the circumstances set forth below, do hereby declare:

If at any time I should have an incurable injury, disease, or illness certified to be a terminal condition or a permanently unconscious condition by 2 physicians who have personally examined me, one of whom shall be my attending physician, and the physicians have determined that my death will occur whether or not life-sustaining procedures are utilized or that I will remain in a permanently unconscious condition and where the application of life-sustaining procedures would serve only to artificially prolong the dying process, I direct that such procedures be withheld or withdrawn, and that I be permitted to die naturally, with only the administration of medication, sustenance, or the performance of any medical procedure deemed necessary to provide me with comfort care.

I realize that situations could arise in which the only way to allow me to die would be to discontinue artificial nutrition and hydration. In carrying out any instruction I have given under this section, I authorize that artificial nutrition and hydration not be started or, if started, be discontinued.

> YES NO (Circle your choice and initial beneath it.
> **If you do not choose "yes," artificial nutrition and**
> _____ **hydration will be provided and will not be removed.**)
> (Initials)

In the absence of my ability to give directions regarding the use of such life-sustaining procedures, it is my intention that this declaration shall be honored by my family and physicians as the final expression of my right to refuse medical or surgical treatment and accept the consequences of such refusal.

I understand the full import of this declaration, and I am emotionally and mentally competent to make this declaration.

Signed _____
                          (Your name)

State of _____   _____ County

We, the following witnesses, being duly sworn each declare to the notary public or justice of the peace or other official signing below as follows:

1. The declarant signed the instrument as a free and voluntary act for the purposes expressed, or expressly directed another to sign for him.
2. Each witness signed at the request of the declarant, in his presence, and in the presence of the other witness.
3. To the best of my knowledge, at the time of the signing the declarant was at least 18 years of age, and was of sane mind and under no constraint or undue influence.

_____ Witness

_____ Witness

The Affidavit shall be made before a notary public or justice of the peace or other official authorized to administer oaths in the place of execution, who shall not also serve as a witness, and who shall complete and sign a certificate in content and form substantially as follows:

To be completed by notary.

Sworn to and signed before me by _____ , declarant

_____ and _____ , witnesses

on _____
        (date)

Signature _____

Official Capacity _____

New Hampshire RSA 137-H

Index